# THE FOREIGN LANGUAGE LEARNER:

## A Guide for Teachers

by

### Mary Finocchiaro, Ph.D.

*Professor-Emeritus of Education*
*Hunter College of the City University of New York*

*Specialist, Languages and Linguistics*
*U. S. Department of State*

and

### Michael Bonomo, M.S. in Ed.

*Lecturer in Education and Language Teaching*
*Hunter College and Queensborough Community College*
*of the City University of New York*

*Instructor, Foreign Languages*
*New York City Schools*

REGENTS PUBLISHING COMPANY, INC.

*To*
DR. CIPRIANA SCELBA
Director of the Fulbright Program in Italy
*whose inspiration, enthusiasm, and interest*
*made the writing of this book possible*

*Published by*
*Regents Publishing Company, Inc.*
*Two Park Avenue*
*New York, N.Y. 10016*

*Printed in the United States of America*

# CONTENTS

# Introduction

The inclusion of foreign languages in school programs is no longer a controversial topic in the majority of countries around the world. Political leaders, educators, and lay people have all become acutely aware that in this period of history international cooperation assumes a greater importance than ever before and that this need cannot help but grow in the immediately foreseeable future. Thanks to the efforts of scientists and writers in many fields, these same people know that effective cooperation must be based on an intimate knowledge and understanding — by as many citizens as possible — of the language and culture of the persons with whom they are seeking to establish desirable working relationships.

This knowledge and understanding can be brought about only by teachers who possess personal qualities of understanding, enthusiasm, dedication, and the ability to identify with others, but who, in addition, have been prepared to transmit to others the knowledge, skills, and attitudes needed to create an enlightened citizenry capable of communication with speakers of other languages.

Preparation for this crucial role should include three major dimensions. First, teachers must be given a firm theoretical foundation so that they can make intelligent decisions throughout their professional careers — decisions based on a sound knowledge of the results of scientific research in many related fields. Second, they must be helped to develop intellectual curiosity and inquiring minds so that they will continue not only to study throughout their lives but also to question the results of hasty, unscientific experimentation. Third, they must be provided with a systematic, practical knowledge of the factors and processes involved in teaching so that they can develop confidence in themselves as they perform their day-by-day tasks. Only thus will their creative energies be released. Only thus will they allow their intuitive feelings about the desirability of using certain procedures — whether or not they have read about them — to hold sway.

Teachers we have had the good fortune to work with in many parts of the world are keenly conscious of the need for such preparation. Neither one of us has ever met any teacher-in-service (and many of these were already truly superb teachers) or any prospective teacher who did not want to become more effective. This textbook is dedicated to all of them.

While establishing theoretical foundations for making judgments, this Guide provides the teacher or the prospective teacher with the step-by-step procedures useful in developing communication skills and cultural insights in learners. Most essential, it pleads throughout for a flexible and "judicious" approach to teaching — scientific, of course, but subject always to the revisions demanded by the individual differences among learners, by the local situation, and by the considered judgment of the dedicated, conscientious teacher.

Although written for teachers, this is a student-oriented textbook. In the following pages, it reiterates in numerous ways that the student — his needs, his aspirations, his attitude, his abilities — must always remain at the very core of the educational process.

An exhaustive treatment of many of the themes we have included would have required a much thicker volume. Where we know that there are excellent books on the subject (e.g., psychological theories, visual aids, laboratories), we have limited our discussion but hope we have whetted your appetite. Readers are urged to examine the texts in the "Additional Reading" sections at the end of the chapters and those in Appendix III for additional guidance or differing viewpoints.

Moreover, some ideas where pertinent have been restated in several chapters. This was purposely done since we know that a supervisor, a curriculum writer, or a lab assistant, for example, might wish to turn to chapters related to his immediate area of concern before reading the entire text.

And now, a special word of gratitude must be said to several persons: to Prof. Titone, Dr. Ambroso, and Dr. Francesconi of the University of Rome; to Eugene Hall; to our editor, Harold S. Pollock, for his painstaking reading of the manuscript and excellent suggestions; and to Dr. Santo Finocchiaro, without whose patience in serving as the "sounding board" for the inclusion or rejection of ideas, this book could never have been written.

MARY FINOCCHIARO
MICHAEL BONOMO

# I

# Teaching and Learning
# a Foreign Language

## WHAT IS LANGUAGE?

If our goal is to help other persons learn to communicate in a second or third language, we should begin by asking ourselves what we really know about language. While all of us have been speaking our native tongues since we were about two, we have done so with little or no conscious thought. Many of us might find it difficult or even impossible to explain our behavior (what we do when we speak our language) or to give a definition of language.

Fortunately, the last several decades have witnessed a tremendous upsurge of activity by scientists who have sought answers to these very questions. Psychologists and linguists (as language scientists are called) do not yet have all the solutions to questions about language, but thanks to the fact that they are scientists, they check and recheck the data they have collected and they continue asking other more probing questions. New theories or refinements of older ones are constantly evolving. There is consensus, however, on several basic generalizations about the nature of language which point to new directions in learning and teaching and which determine the methods and techniques teachers should use to help their students learn another language.

### Some Basic Premises

What are some of the results of the research of linguists which have been shared with other scientists and educators in some excellent books on the subject? Let us state them briefly:

— Language is a social as well as an individual phenomenon. As such, it has a place both among the humanities and among the social sciences. It permits human beings in a community who know the language of the community — the code — to communicate orally and/or in writing. At the same time, it mirrors the culture of the society of speakers who use it. While each individual speaker may use the language to express himself differently from his neighbor, the individual

1

expression is always within the "code" shared by all community members. If this were not so, little or no understanding would be possible among the speakers of the language.

— Language is not only a component of culture — indeed the central feature of a culture — but it is also the primary system through which all other components of the culture of a society are expressed.

— Language, the exclusive possession of all human beings, is culturally acquired. While man is born with the physiological and neurological capacity to speak, he learns to do so only as he hears language around him in his home and in his community; that is, in the culture in which he lives.

— Spoken language is universal. It is available to all members of the human race. All normal people in the world can speak. No group of people without a spoken language has ever been discovered.

— All human beings in a community understand and speak well enough to carry out the basic activities of life. (Many of these same people cannot read and write, however.)

— There are no "primitive" languages. Every language in the world is rich enough and sufficiently complete for its speakers. People who do not need iceboxes probably will have no word for icebox. When the need arises, new words or expressions can be borrowed from another language or can be coined from elements of the existing language. The sounds and patterns of the new words will generally be those of the "borrowing" society rather than those of the society from which the words were taken.

— Language is one of the most rigidly constructed of all human activities. As we shall see later, only certain sound sequences or word arrangements are permitted in any particular language.

— Every language speaker can produce an infinite number of sentences but all of these are derived from a relatively small number of sentence types (pattern sentences). The native speaker has the *competence* to recognize all the sentences of the language. His production of them, his *performance*, will depend, however, on his exposure to them and on his aptitude, as well as on such temporary factors as fatigue or illness.

In speaking our native language, we employ a system of "rules" which we have unconsciously internalized through numerous language experiences with other speakers of the language.

— While we tend to think of language in use as involving a speaker, a hearer, and a situation, it may also be stimulus-free. Our inner thoughts are expressed with language. Any object or event in the environment may elicit speech without a listener necessarily being present.

— All languages are different. Although the basic needs and drives

2

of all human beings are the same, each society expresses its interaction with its own environment in different ways.

— <u>All languages change across time and space.</u> Most languages of the world as spoken today bear little resemblance to the languages spoken centuries ago in the same milieu.

Changes because of geographical distance also produce *dialects* of the same mother tongue. Some dialects are vastly different from the mother tongue in sounds, grammar, and vocabulary.

— The language understood, spoken, and shared by all members of a society of speakers is generally called the code — *la langue* — to use the term of De Saussure. The individual's use of the code is his idiolect or his *parole* — a term also used by De Saussure to distinguish between the social and individual aspects of language.

— Each language is a unique system which can be described only in terms of itself and not in terms of any other language.

— The system is extremely complex and consists of several sub-systems which are interrelated. All of the sub-systems come into play in any speech act. These sub-systems will be explained more fully below.

— Writing is considered a secondary system derived from speech and incomplete in several ways.

The writing system, for example, does not indicate the melody and pitch of the voice, the rhythm of speech, or the gestures which generally accompany speech.

— The meaning of any utterance or stretch of speech depends not on the meaning of individual words, but on the total perception by the listener or reader of its sounds, intonation, grammar, and situational and cultural content.

## A Definition of Language

What is language, then? Let us examine a more formal, generally agreed-upon definition:

Language is a *system of arbitrary vocal symbols* which permits all people in a given culture, or other people who have learned the system of that culture, to communicate or to interact.

Let us expand the definition. What is meant by *system, arbitrary,* etc.? Every language operates within its own *system;* that is, within recurring patterns or arrangements which are meaningful to speakers. The sounds used to form the words which are used in speech utter-ances* are always arranged in particular ways or designs to convey the

---

* An utterance unit is a stretch of speech by one person before which there was silence on his part and after which there is silence on his part. (Fries, C., *The Structure of English*, p. 23.)

same meaning to all speakers of the language. Let us examine some examples.

When, in English, we say the words "the man," you know we are speaking of one man and of a man previously mentioned. "The men," on the other hand, conveys the meaning of more than one man. The difference was made by the [ε]* sound used in the second example. The sound [t] at the end of "walked" gives an immediate clue that we are referring to an occurrence that took place in the past. (There are, of course, other devices in language to signal plurality, time, aspect, etc.)

When a Frenchman says "l'homme," his hearers will know that he is talking of one man previously mentioned or of the general term "man." "Les hommes" will convey the meaning of more than one man. The difference was produced by the sounds [εz] which preceded "homme." Note also how the two languages differ: in English, "the" remained the same for singular and plural, but "man" changed to "men." In French, the singular and plural nouns contained the same sounds, but the determiner (the definite article) indicated plurality.

The sounds [aba] attached to the root of certain verbs in Spanish indicate that an action took place in the past either repeatedly or when another action was occurring.

To continue with our definition of language, word order is generally an important feature of the grammatical system of a language. Although a speaker of English would know the meaning of each word, "spoke his brother to" would not make any sense nor would "parlé son a il frère à" to a Frenchman.

Examining still another feature of the system, we find that in English adjectives do not agree with the gender and number of nouns. We say, "The girls are tall," "the tall girls"; "The boys are tall," "the tall boys." In other languages, the system may require agreement as well as a different word order. Note, in Italian, "Le ragazze sono alte," "le ragazze alte"; "I ragazzi sono alti," "i ragazzi alti."

Furthermore, any listener would know that in English, "The boy is ill," with the voice dropping at the end, is a statement while a rising intonation indicates a question. Languages have other devices, too, for signaling a question. In English, we would say, "Is the boy ill?"; in French, we could say either "Est-ce que le garçon est malade?" or "Le garçon, est-il malade?" or "Le garçon est malade?" with rising intonation.

A basic feature of a language system is, as we noted above, that it contains few kernel (basic) sentences. These kernel sentences can be transformed in several ways, however, to produce the infinite number of sentences that we are capable of understanding or saying. Basic

---

* See pp. 43-44 for the phonetic symbols used here and throughout.

sentences may be added, combined, or contracted, but the resulting sentences will all be related to the basic kernel.
Note:

| English | French |
|---|---|
| It's a house. | C'est une maison. |
| It's a pretty white house. | C'est une jolie maison blanche. |
| Who lives in that pretty white house? | Qui demeure dans cette jolie maison blanche? |
| The house I live in is pretty. | La maison dans laquelle je demeure est jolie. |

In some languages, the surface structure (the arrangement of sounds and words we actually hear or say) may come from different basic sentences. It is important that we, as teachers, be aware of this so that we will present and give practice in the concept we actually wish to practice. In English, for example, "John is eager to please" and "John is easy to please," to use the well-known examples, are similar on the surface, but their underlying meaning is completely different because they are derived from two different sets of kernel sentences: the first from "John pleases. He is eager"; the second from "They please John. It is easy."

On the other hand, in French, while the surface structure of the examples cited above would be substantially different from that of English ("Jean est anxieux de plaire" and "Il est facile de plaire à Jean"), it is obvious that they are also transformations of two different sets of kernel sentences.

To take another well-known example, "The growing of flowers" and "The growling of lions" have the same surface structure. Their deep structures — the kernels from which they have been derived — are: "People (they) grow flowers" and "Lions growl."

Let us continue with our definition. *Vocal* means that we make sounds in our mouths using the *tongue,* the *teeth,* and the *lips.* (We use other organs such as the vocal cords and the lungs to produce or make the sounds of the language.)

Every language has its own arbitrary symbols or words to express the meaning of an object or an idea. Stated in another way, the symbols — either sound or letter — and their referents have no inherent relationship. Why does "bread" mean what it does in English? Why is "horse" the name for the animal it represents? No one knows why words convey certain meanings, but *all* speakers of a language do know and can use the general terms associated with the common objects or concepts in their environment or world. Some specialized words, related to a particular trade or profession, may be known only by those

5

who practice that trade or profession, but the sounds and sound arrangements within the words or the position of the words in utterances would be familiar to all speakers.

The words "communicate" and "interact," as used in the definition, signify to *understand* and to *speak;* to be able to *hear* and to *respond* or *react* (by carrying out directions, for example) to the spoken words. They imply, too, the ability to talk about something that happened in the past, that is happening at the present time, or that may happen at some time in the future.

Communication through the use of the spoken language means understanding and reacting to what someone says. The response or reaction may be to make a statement; to ask a question; to agree or to disagree; to carry out a direction; to answer a question in the affirmative or in the negative with a long answer or with a short answer (e.g., "Are you going to the movies tomorrow?" "Yes" or "Yes, I am") ; or to use what we call a "formula," that is, a fixed expression in the language (e.g., the response to "Thank you" might be "You're welcome" or "Don't mention it" in English, but "Il n'y a pas de quoi" or "De rien" in French and "Prego" in Italian).

In communities whose members read and write, communication would also include understanding and conveying messages through the printed word.

Writing, as we have said, is considered a *secondary system* derived from the spoken language. We write *symbols* (in English, the letters of the alphabet and punctuation marks) to convey the words and ideas which are themselves symbols of objects or ideas. For example:

| *referent* | *sound* | *written word* |
|---|---|---|
| | [hɔrs] | horse |
| | [baʊ] | bough |

In some languages, the sounds and the graphemes (the written symbols) have a one to one correspondence. In Spanish, for example, where "the fit" is considered good, the written letter "a" usually represents the sound [a]. In English, the letter "a" can be pronounced [ɔ], [æ], [a], or [ə] — depending on its environment (the surrounding letters).

Since language is the medium through which people express their experiences and their ideas of the world in which they live, it carries within it cultural meaning. Native speakers who have been brought

6

up in a particular culture or who have shared experiences in the culture are aware of differences or shades in meaning which gestures, words, or expressions convey. The various ways of expressing *you* in many languages are bound to the culture of the speakers of that language. To take another example, although the total expression "I'm having breakfast" has an equivalent in all languages, the sentence may evoke different thoughts or images in speakers of different native languages depending upon the timé they usually eat, what they eat, where they eat, etc.

It is obvious, therefore, that utterances can be completely understood only when the sound patterns, the structural items, the vocabulary items, and the cultural meanings are shared by both speakers and hearers or, in their written manifestation, by writers and readers.

Three summaries of statements by scholars in the field about the nature of language would seem particularly appropriate for your further consideration. The American linguist, Robert Hall,[1] has stated that languages have the following properties: 1) duality (They contain units of sound and units of form.)[2]; 2) productivity (It is possible to create new utterances.) ; 3) arbitrariness (There is no inherent relationship between a symbol [a spoken word] and its referent.) ; 4) interchangeability (Human beings can receive and send messages; they can take the role of hearer or speaker.) ; 5) specialization (All languages have their own system.) ; 6) displacement (People can talk about the present, the past, or the future. They can talk of concrete things as well as of abstract thoughts.) ; 7) cultural transmission (Language is learned; it is not a physical inheritance.).

Charles Hockett's list will also give us further insight into the nature of language.[3] Briefly condensed, he states that language 1) gives *freedom* to coin new messages; 2) has the ability to *refer to things remote* in time and space; 3) is *available* to all members of the species; 4) provides complete *feedback* to the speaker; 5) displays *arbitrary relationship* between sounds and referents; 6) exhibits *duality* in phonological and grammatical patterning; 7) is *passed down by teaching and learning*; 8) possesses *interchangeability:* speakers transmit and receive linguistic signals.

And finally, let us look at a list formulated by the Modern Language Association of America. The twelfth fact has been omitted because it concerns methodology, an important topic we will examine later.

---

[1] Hall, R., *Introduction to Linguistics.*

[2] Comments in parentheses added.

[3] In Greenberg, J. (ed.), *Universals of Language,* pp. 1-22.

7

# A Dozen Facts about Language

(These are revisions of some ideas first formulated at an MLA Conference on Linguistics and Language Learning in May 1963.)

1. Speech is one or more sounds made by human beings for purpose of communication. The communication is language.

2. Languages are different, not just in having different words for different things, but in arranging words in different ways to express different reactions to reality.

3. A language is more than just a string of words; people also communicate by such means as structure, stress, pitch, and pauses.

4. Changes in language depend on time, place, social level, stylistic level. These changes are not corruptions but normal features of all languages.

5. Speech and writing are different, though related, language systems. In all languages, speech precedes writing. Most of the world's languages still have no written systems.

6. Language has nothing to do with race. Primitive peoples do not speak "primitive" languages. The languages of simple cultures ("primitive peoples") are not necessarily simpler than the languages of highly complex cultures.

7. English sounds just as strange to a foreigner who doesn't know English as the foreigner's language sounds to monolingual speakers of English.

8. Different languages have different taboos. In English, *Good Lord!* is milder than *Good God!*, although they mean the same thing. In ancient Hebrew, the word for God, IHVH (Yahweh), was unmentionable; another word was always substituted for it.

9. Words for "the same thing" in two languages are not "equal to each other" unless both basic meanings and connotations correspond, and they hardly ever do.

10. Lexical meaning, expressed by selection of words (tall man, short man), must be distinguished from grammatical meaning, expressed by their inflection (speak, spoke) or arrangement (house dog, doghouse).

11. No language is inherently difficult. If it were, the people who speak it would soon simplify it. Any normal child has a firm control of his own language by the time he goes to school.

## LANGUAGE LEARNING

In addition to formulating assumptions on the nature of language, psychologists and linguists have also done extensive research on native language learning.

What are some of their findings, which are related to language learning and have implications for us as teachers?

## Learning a Native Language

— Language is learned behavior. All normal children are born with the ability to make sounds, but the sounds take shape and become meaningful only through the constant hearing and repetition of those sounds *which produce responses*. Although all normal persons are born with the capacity to understand and to speak, the baby probably learns to say the word "water" because he is given water every time he produces sounds that are close to the sounds in "water." He also hears the word "water" used many times each day for several years, generally in association with water.

— Native speakers of a language are not conscious of each sound or word they say or of the sequence of the sounds or words. They are conscious primarily of the thoughts they are trying to convey. The stringing together of sounds in certain positions is generally unconscious. It is a habit which is usually automatic by the time children are six or seven years old. After that, they may, perhaps, sharpen their knowledge of the grammar, increase their stock of vocabulary, and develop one or more styles of speaking, depending on the situation, but the basic knowledge of the sound system and the meaningful arrangement of the sounds into words and utterances have already been acquired.

— Native adult speakers, even those who are illiterate, have linguistic competence. They can generally recognize all the well-formed (grammatical) utterances in the language although they may not be able to produce them. They have internalized in their own way — through association of utterances and experiences, analogy, or trial and error — the "rules" which govern verbal behavior in their tongue.

The quality and degree of their general performance in the language will be determined, of course, by the performance of other native speakers by whom they have been surrounded at age levels when such influences are most effective, by opportunities they have had to speak and read, by formal teaching, and by their innate aptitude and ability.

## Learning a Second Language

While there is some consensus among scientists about the acquisition of one's native language, to date there is no such agreement on second language learning.

No one really knows with absolute certainty how a second language is acquired. Psychologists have formulated two major theories

9

of language learning. Numerous assumptions about how any learning or behavior is brought about in the human organism also exist. In addition, the research of scientists into the description of languages and into language behavior has contributed to our knowledge of what should be given priority in bringing about language learning and what may interfere with the learning process.

Since people may learn in different ways and at different rates, it is important that the teacher know about and use information from linguistics, psychology, and other related sciences for guidance in selecting, grading, and presenting the elements of language to be learned and in developing the skills to be acquired. Subscribing to any one scientific theory exclusively may neglect "the learning style" of some of our students.

It may be desirable to start by examining what is generally meant by language learning at the secondary school level. The ultimate goal, of course, is that the student develop the competence and performance of a native speaker of the same age level. He should understand any message spoken by a native speaker and should eventually be able to create the utterances that will allow him to respond appropriately to the messages as well as to express his wants, needs, or desires spontaneously; that is, without the continuous stimulus of the teacher. He should be able to create these utterances using the sound, grammar, and vocabulary systems in the cultural situations in which they are normally used by native speakers.

This is no simple task. Let us take a hard look at the factors involved in the listening skill. From hearing a series of undifferentiated noises, the learner should progress to the stage where he can distinguish features of the sound system, of the basic grammatical elements, and of the lexicon (the vocabulary). He should gradually learn to perceive the features of the language which are redundant, the multiple clues that exist in most languages to indicate grammatical relationships (e.g., English: The *two* boys *are going*. . . .; Spanish: *Los dos* hombre*s* van. . . .). He should learn to listen for the "information" in the message, the bits or features of the message (the words, forms, or sequences) which narrow the choice or alternatives he will have in decoding the message. For example, in English, the word ending -*s* of "walks" in the verb slot will narrow the listener's choice to *he, she, it,* or *who* and to the concept of the simple present tense.

In listening for the answer to the question, "Who's Mr. X?," he would have learned to expect "He's the . . .," but he would have to listen carefully to the following word — butcher, lawyer, or any one of a dozen other alternative words which could fit into that slot and which are therefore considered high in information.

He should learn, therefore, to expect redundant features and to interpret the information contained in the total message he will have to decode. Moreover, he has to develop the memory span sufficient to hold the individual sound units in his mind until he hears all of them, thus enabling him to put them together in a meaningful whole so that the total message becomes clear to him and he can *decode* it.

The speaking skill is even more complex since the learner will have to 1) decide what he wants to say; 2) choose the pattern he is going to use; 3) select the words that fit into the pattern and convey his meaning; 4) use the correct arrangement of sounds, voice pitch, and forms; 5) make sure that what he wants to say is appropriate in the situation; 6) place his tongue and lips in certain positions to produce the sounds. *All of this must be done simultaneously.*

Second language learning involves the acquisition of 1) a definite set of habits — for example, the habit of articulating sounds in certain ways or of adding certain endings to words based on "rules" which have also been acquired and internalized; 2) a store of linguistic and cultural items; and 3) the ability to understand and create authentic utterances and connected discourse in the social and cultural situations in which they are appropriate.

It sounds formidable, doesn't it? But foreign languages are learned by millions of people, and fortunately the learner brings certain innate abilities to the task. There is, moreover, in most circumstances, the teacher who can facilitate the language-learning process in numerous ways.

What role does the learner play? As he hears the different "noises" again and again, he unconsciously forms theories related to the sounds and their meanings. He groups the sounds, restructures them in his own way, and attempts to discover their relationships not only within the target (foreign) language but also between his native tongue and the foreign language. The new material he learns is added to and interacts with familiar material — either in his native tongue or in the foreign language — until he perceives the entire configuration, pattern, or "gestalt" into which it fits.

### Two Theories of Learning

The learner's active participation in the learning process is a fundamental premise of the two currently favored learning theories. Stated simply, one — the cognitive code theory — underscores the fact that the learner brings to the task of learning an innate mental capacity. He brings his perception of relationships and his unconscious formulation of the "rules" resulting from his discovery of the structure and organization of new material and from his perception of its relationship with known material. Closely tied in to this theory of the impor-

11

tance of the individual's mental organization of learned material is research which seems to indicate that the nervous system stores up images and memories which can then be evoked without a preceding stimulus.

The other theory — the association or operant conditioning theory — is based on experimentation indicating that bonds can be forged between a stimulus and a response and that responses are shaped and strengthened or extinguished by the reinforcements or rewards which should always follow the learner's response to a stimulus. Such continuous association between stimulus and response, followed immediately by confirmation of the learner's correct response by a teacher, a tape, a record, a programmed text, etc., leads to the formation of the habits needed for placing sounds and words in appropriate arrangements.

## What the Linguists Tell Us

Linguistic scientists, while not directly concerned with skill development and learning theories, have formulated some assumptions and principles related to language acquisition which warrant serious consideration. Those which have immediate application for teachers are:

— The ingrained habits of one's native language (of making certain sounds or of placing sounds in certain positions) often cause serious conflict or interference with the learning of a new language. Although similar sounds may exist in one's native tongue, they may be found in different sequences and different positions in the second language. Other elements of the sound system may operate in different ways. For example, English uses stress or accent (e.g., convért/cónvert; the Whíte House/the white hóuse) to convey meaning. Other languages may not.

The same is true of the structure or grammar of the language. The forms of words (morphology) and the order or sequence of words (the syntax) are important. In English, for example, a "race horse" is not the same as a "horse race." They may have no importance or they may mean something quite different in another language.

— The contrasting features in the target language, including contrasting sounds or intonation patterns and contrasting word forms (e.g., *boy* versus *boys; boys* versus *books; walks* versus *walked* or *is walking*) signal meaning to listeners and speakers and thus should be given priority.

— There are few kernel sentences but an infinite number of sentences derived from them. With skillful guidance, students should be taught the relationships between kernels and their transforms.

— Every utterance can be said to be a frame composed of various slots. For example, the *subject* slot may be filled by a nominal, the *verb* slot by a verbal. Learners should recognize the slots in the sentences and the class of words which may fill the slots. In the question, "Did he go to the store this morning?," *she* can be used instead of *he; ride* instead of *go; office* instead of *store;* etc.

There are other research findings in the fields of linguistics, psychology, psycholinguistics, and sociology which must be taken into account in considering the learning process. A few of these are listed here briefly, but further reading is highly recommended.

— The attitude of the learner toward the persons whose language he is learning is significant in learning. A positive attitude, in which the learner seeks to identify with the foreign speakers, termed "integrative orientation" by the sociologists who have studied this phenomenon, outweighs many other factors within the learners.[1]

— At the same time, however, the learner must be helped to retain pride in his own language and culture as he moves gradually toward the acceptance of the foreign language and culture. A traumatic feeling of "anomie" — of belonging to neither the native nor the foreign community — may develop unless the teacher fosters this pride.

— The learner's aptitude and general intelligence are important. These may be considered inherent characteristics, but central, too, are the learner's motivation, his opportunities for hearing and speaking the language, and the quality of instruction as, for example, the clarity of presentation. In some recent research reported at a conference, the renowned psychologist, John Carroll, underscored the importance of these factors[2] and also focused on the aspect of "time." Is the student given adequate time to perform a learning task? Is the time in harmony with his particular aptitude, motivation, and attitude? You will note that in the last three factors mentioned, the teacher and the materials of instruction assume great importance. (More will be said of these factors later in this book.)

— There is a difference between learning one's native language and learning a second language, particularly after childhood. The child learning his native language normally listens to it most of the day over a period of five or six years. This is usually not possible after early childhood. Moreover, a second language is often learned in an environment in which it is not heard outside of the classroom.

While it is generally agreed that the optimum age for many persons to learn to pronounce a language is before the age of ten or eleven, the

---

[1] See Peal, E. and W. Lambert, "The Relation of Bilingualism to Intelligence," in *Foreign Language Teaching*, J. Michel (ed.), and Gardner, R. and W. Lambert, "Motivational Variables in Second Language Acquisition," in *Canadian Journal of Psychology*, 1959, p. 13.

[2] We are indebted for this information to Prof. Mario Ferencich, Director of the UNESCO Testing Program for Italy.

older person learning a second language has several advantages: he can observe, analyze, and make generalizations, and he can be given the rationale for his difficulties or for doing things in a certain way. Although, for example, he may no longer be able to hear or produce a sound by imitation only, he can be told the reason for his difficulties and be given specific instructions for improving its production. If after hearing and saying several examples of the form of a word or of the sequence of words in a sentence he is encouraged to describe what he has heard and said, he will generally be able to put this description to use in producing other similar words or utterances.

Moreover, not all children learning a second language imitate sounds and produce speech automatically. In an experiment conducted several years ago with children of five and six, it was obvious not only that certain children had a greater aptitude for learning, but also that learning took place in a classroom setting only when the teacher engaged the children in numerous experiences in which the language items to be learned were heard and said repeatedly over long periods of time.

— The learner is and must be an active agent in the learning process. No one can control what the learner does mentally with the material presented to him.

— The interference mentioned above may come not only from the contrasts between the hearer's native language and the foreign (target) language but also from the contrasting incompletely or poorly learned forms within the foreign language.

— The more and different kinds of association the learner has with any material, the more likely he is to learn it.

## What Psychology Tells Us

From the *psychological sciences,* there is some evidence, for example, that: 1) Learning takes place when it is related to the needs, experiences, and aspirations of the learner. 2) The learner must be convinced that the knowledge he will acquire is worth knowing; that it will be valuable in his life in the future as well as at the present time. 3) The student's perception of the structure and organization of the items and skills being taught is essential. 4) Material will be more easily learned if it progresses in small steps from the known to the unknown and from the simple to the more difficult. 5) Many repetitions are needed to develop habits. The learning of any skill takes place in proportion to practice in that skill.* 6) Repetitions of material through its reentry in

_____

* Many experiments seeking to prove the superiority of one method over another have verified what good teachers have always known: students learn to speak when emphasis has been placed on speaking; they learn to read when they have practiced reading.

14

later lessons should be spaced at increasingly longer intervals. 7) Knowledge that a response is correct leads to the learning of that response. Knowledge that it is incorrect leads to the "extinguishing" of the response. 8) Learning is favored when meaningful association is established between sounds and concepts, and between concepts and cultural or social situations. 9) Understanding of the roles which separate elements play in the listening, speaking, reading, or writing abilities promotes learning. Learners need insight into the place and function of individual language items and subsidiary skills in authentic communication activities. 10) The transfer of learning is not generally automatic. The learner will not transfer individual language elements learned in one context to other contexts unless he is helped to understand the general principles underlying the use of the elements and he is given practice in making the transfer of identical elements to numerous appropriate contexts. 11) Successful performance and a sense of achievement are powerful motivating forces in learning.

Much more will be said about each of these assumptions as we discuss the teacher's role in the selection, grading, and presentation of material.

## PRINCIPLES OF LANGUAGE TEACHING

Our knowledge of the nature of language, our greater insight into learning theory, and our observation of the conflicts caused by the habits of one's native language have given rise to some generally accepted principles of language teaching. These are stated here briefly under the four basic sub-systems of a language: sound, grammar, vocabulary, and culture. They will be expanded where pertinent in the chapters which follow.

1. Since spoken language is primary, the sounds of the language should take precedence in our teaching. The sounds may be taught one at a time with priority given to those impeding comprehension and/or by contrasting them in what is called "minimal pairs." For example, "pit/ pet" is a minimal pair in English because one sound alone makes the difference in the meaning of the words. "Père/mère" is a minimal pair in French. The learner should be enabled to identify any sound as similar to the others he will hear or as different from them.

— It is imperative, however, that a sound which may have been practiced in isolation be inserted immediately in words, phrases, utterances, or sentences which have, in addition, the stress, rhythm, pauses (or junctures), and intonation — the "suprasegmentals" — which are characteristic of the language being learned.

2. In addition to the sound system, learners must be taught the grammar system of the language. Through numerous examples in sit-

15

uations which clarify and reinforce their meaning, learners must be given insight into word order, inflection, and the other meaningful features of the language (e.g., "The boy *is* going . . .," "The *boys are* going. . . ."; "I wash every morning," "I wash*ed* yesterday," etc. Note the Italian for the same sentences: "Il ragazzo *va* . . .," "*I* ragazzi *vanno*. . . ."; "Mi lavo ogni mattina," "Mi sono lavato [*lavata* for the feminine] stamane.").

— Insight is not enough, however. Students have to learn the forms and the basic patterns thoroughly in order to be able to understand them, to respond to them, and to create similar ones in other communication situations in which they may find themselves.

— Learners must be taught which other words within word classes (nouns, verbs, etc.) can be used in the place (the slot) of each of the words in an utterance. In the French, "A-t-il écrit à sa mère?," for example, *elle* can be used instead of *il; parlé* instead of *écrit; soeur* instead of *mère*.

— In addition, through numerous examples and practice activities, students must be made aware of the lexical combinations required, the words which must co-occur, or those permitted by the language. For example, in English, we must say: "I enjoy *walking*," but we may say either: "I like to *walk*" or "I like *walking*." In Italian, we must use the auxiliary "essere" (to be) in verb phrases containing verbs of motion; e.g., "Io sono andata." But we may use either the auxiliary "avere" (have) or "essere" (be) with the verb "piovere" (to rain).

— The limitations or restrictions imposed by the system must be taught along with the language features being presented. Not all the limitations or exceptions will be taught at once, of course, but priority should be given to those which may cause students to make false analogies. For example, in English we would have to teach concurrently with the "-ing" present the fact that *want, need,* and *like* (very common verbs generally taught at the beginning level) are never used in the "-ing" present.

— Pupils have to be given such thorough control of the sounds and structures of the new language through a variety of practice activities that they will be able to understand, speak, and later read and write without having to stop and think about the position of each word in the sentence or the form of each word (e.g., In English, when do we use: s*i*ng, s*a*ng, s*u*ng; boy, boy*'s*; child, child*ren*?).

— Second language teaching implies helping learners acquire new habits or ways of using the speech organs, and learning the forms and the arrangements of forms required by the system.

— It means, with older learners especially, giving them — but preferably guiding their discovery of — the principles or rules underlying the recurring patterns of the second language through the study (listen-

16

ing, repeating, practicing) of many examples. Any reference to the recurring pattern should be made after the study of several examples. The reference, moreover, should be a description of what actually happens in speech. We will have more to say about this later.

If they are ever to be able to produce new utterances in new situations, they must have a grasp of the underlying principles related to the sounds, forms, arrangements, and functions of the language. It is the principle or "rule" which they must learn to transfer to the new situation; it is the principle or rule which they must be helped to internalize.

— The sounds, forms, or word sequences must be taught and practiced systematically in a progression and order which will permit learners to associate and integrate each small segment of newly acquired language with every other segment they have already acquired.

— Students should be helped to perceive the relationship between the basic (kernel) sentences of the language and their transforms. This too is brought about systematically in short, sequentially logical steps.

— It is preferable that students be encouraged to "discover" the meaningful linguistic signals and the transformational relationships by themselves through questioning by the teacher, visual cues, or other devices.

— Language activities in the classroom and laboratory (where one exists) should give learners practice in asking and answering questions, in making statements, and in producing the normal, authentic utterances used by native speakers. For example, when someone asks, "Where did you go last night?," a possible normal response is "To the library." It is *not* "I went to the library last night."

— Gradually, the student must be helped to develop 1) the *competence* to discriminate between grammatical or well-formed sentences and ungrammatical ones and 2) the *performance* of the foreign language in consonance with his aptitude, motivation, and all other factors needed for learning.

3. Language teaching means familiarizing the students with the culture of the native speakers — including their gestures, distance maintained in speaking and formulas of expression. An intonation pattern may express anger in one language and delight in another. Opening formulas in English include "Well..." and "So..."; in Italian, "Beh!..." A nod in one language may mean "Yes"; in another, "No."

Dinner in the United States usually takes place about six or seven o'clock. In some regions of the United States, the noontime meal is called "lunch"; in others, it may be called "dinner." In Spain, one has "dinner" after 9:30.

— Since language is both a vehicle for communication and a reflection of the culture of its speakers, pupils should, of course, be helped to understand and talk about the target culture but they should also be enabled to talk about their native culture in the foreign language. This is essential for linguistic and psychological reasons.

If an Italian youngster is learning German and he has a German pen pal or meets a German, he may be asked by the German to explain the holiday on November 1 of which his friend may be unaware. By the same token, a German youngster studying a foreign language should be able to explain "Fasching" to any foreign speaker who asks him about it. Isn't that what "communication" is all about? The insistence in some recent texts and articles that only the foreign culture be talked about in the foreign language is thoroughly unrealistic. Such insistence may not only limit communication but it also violates an important principle of learning.

From the psychological sciences, teachers know that pupils learn material which they can associate with familiar experiences. The native cultural experiences of the learners can serve as a springboard for understanding the foreign culture because there are either similar or contrasting elements in them. Moreover, talking about what they had done during some native holiday, a content with which they are familiar, would supply the ideas for real, spontaneous communication among youngsters in a classroom.

In discussing the teaching of culture or of anything else, the watchwords should always be "judiciously" and "flexibly." No hard and fast rule should be allowed to dictate any phase of the teaching process unless the health and safety of our pupils are at stake. Since some controversial procedures are in fact psychologically sound, strengthen the bonds of association, take into account the experience the learners bring into class with them, or may serve as motivating devices, they should not be discarded simply at the whim of some "authority."

4. The fourth, but by no means unimportant, large area of language we must help our students acquire is its vocabulary.

— Within vocabulary (the *lexicon* of the language), we distinguish between *content* words (pen, school, go, pretty, well, etc.) and *function* or *structure* words (with, for, may, will, etc.). The function words must be learned as quickly as feasible in realistic situations which give them meaning (in a logical order and sequence, however). The content words should be taught gradually in manageable groups around "life" situations or centers of interest. At the beginning stages of language learning, the same words are generally used repeatedly to give practice in the new structures ("I want a pen"; "I'd like a pen"; "Will you buy me a pen?"; etc.).

— Although vocabulary is important, its study in the very early stages should be subordinated to that of the sounds and the structures (grammar) of the language. Vocabulary will accumulate quickly as the need arises later and as wider reading is begun after the basic sound and structure systems of the language have been learned.

—On the other hand, vocabulary items which are particularly relevant to the community in which your pupils are learning or which are needed to create interest in "real" conversations should be taught as needed. Moreover, when the foreign language is used as a medium of instruction, vocabulary related to the curriculum or work areas the learner needs will have to be given priority.

And now let us mention some other principles, not all of which are accepted by some educators but which should be made subjects of discussion with colleagues and other educators. Since the proof of the validity of any principle lies in its successful use in the classroom, it is essential that you, the teacher, discover for yourself as you work with various groups of students whether or not these are valid in your situation.

1. The listening, speaking, reading, and writing skills are generally taught in that order. There should be no fixed period, however, for teaching only the listening-speaking skills or the reading or writing skills. All of the factors within your particular school system and within your learners should determine the length of possible deferment of reading and writing. (This will be discussed at greater length in the chapter on reading.)

2. The native language of the learners should be used judiciously when comprehension is at a complete standstill and you have honestly made every effort to explain whatever needs explaining in the target language. There is nothing as frustrating to students as feeling completely left out of an entire lesson because they didn't understand something at the beginning of it. There is nothing which makes students feel that a teacher is more "unjust" than when they get a poor grade on a drill because they have not understood the directions.

If you are not familiar with the native language of the learners, or if your students come from many language backgrounds, you should ask a bilingual teacher or community member to give you the one or two words you may need to clarify an important direction.

3. It is generally recognized that older students, certainly those of about the age of ten and above, immediately think of the native language equivalent for a concept or word they are learning. This intermediate step of "translation" takes place whether or not we want it to. The art of the teacher lies in helping the student make an immediate association between referent and foreign language expression and extinguishing the intermediate native language step as quickly as possible.

4. Habit formation is extremely important. In the beginning stages, students should be placed in a position where most of their responses are correct. On the other hand, as quickly as possible, they must be

19

given some responsibility for selecting the correct forms, for placing words in arrangements permitted by the language, and for self-initiated communication. Some form of "free" communication should be encouraged from the very first day.

Each of these principles has definite implications for teaching procedure. However, before examining questions such as: How do pupils learn the sounds? How can we help them acquire control of the structure system? How is vocabulary taught? How is reading skill developed?, it is necessary to look at some of the characteristics of our learners and some of the school situations in which languages are taught.

## SOME FACTORS AFFECTING TEACHING AND LEARNING

### The Students

In order to teach effectively, it is important to learn as much as we can about our students, since some of our procedures will vary depending upon the students in our classes. Below are some factors within our students which cannot be ignored in teaching.

You will understand from your own reading and experience that chapters could be written about each. Our intention, however, is not to discuss any characteristic at length but, through questions, to make you more deeply aware, perhaps, of the complexity of teaching human beings a language. We hope too that you will bear in mind the answers to some of these questions as you consider your intermediate objectives, as you plan your lessons, and as you gather together the appropriate materials of instruction.

#### — Age

Are your students young children or adolescents who can imitate you more easily? Will they prefer to learn the language through games, songs, etc.? Are they adolescents whose native language habits are more deeply established? Are they young adults who will need greater help in pronouncing the new language, but who can analyze and structure information?

#### — Aptitude

Are there wide differences among the students in your class? How can you use the abilities of the bright students? How can you help the weaker students? Can you appeal to the ear alone? Do you need much concrete, visual material? Will students profit from grouping, individualized instruction, or special tracks?

## — Aspirations and needs

Particularly with young adults, do they need to learn the new language to get a job, do further study, conduct a business, or take a trip? Must they learn the language quickly to be able to understand other subjects which are being taught in it? Must they learn the language because they live in a community in which the language is spoken? What vocational use will they want to make of the new language? What "register," therefore, will have to be taught? Do they have to understand various dialects and styles of the language?

## — Motivation

Are the students highly motivated to learn the new language because they want to identify with speakers of the language? Do they want to learn the new language because they feel it will be useful to them educationally or professionally? Do their parents encourage them to learn it? Do their peers encourage them?

## — Native language*

Are there any similarities in sound, structure, and vocabulary with the new language? What are the basic *phonemic* (meaningful) features of the sound system of the students' native language? How do these contrast with the new language? What devices does the native language use to show meaning (intonation, word order, inflection, function words, etc.)? What writing system is used (alphabet, pictures)? How is the culture reflected in the language? For example, how many forms of address are used? What are these based on — sex, age, social status? How is the word "Good-bye" expressed? Do the two speakers use the same word?

## — Socio-economic status

Are students encouraged by their parents? Do they have to go to work before school in the morning or after school? Do they have any place to study at home? Do they get enough to eat? Can the hope of social mobility through language acquisition serve as an incentive?

## — Previous language experiences

Have the students studied any other foreign language? At what level of the target language are they? Did they study the language with methods and materials you might reasonably expect to be similar to those you use?

We could add many more questions. It is obvious that an effective teacher needs answers to these and to many similar questions. How can

---

* A simple checklist for comparing two languages will be found on pp. 260-61.

a teacher find the answers? Some of them are easily recognizable. Age and socio-economic status usually need no special study. In some situations and with young learners, however, it may be important to obtain results of general aptitude tests (if these exist in your school system) and also to find out the grades the students make in their native language studies, particularly in the language itself. These will offer some clues to any discouraging lack of progress. Is it due to low aptitude on their part, lack of motivation, poor previous teaching?

If you are teaching in a community where the target language is dominant, it is clear that your students must learn it as quickly as possible in order to participate in the life of the community. If your students are adults, it is very desirable (through an interpreter if you do not know their native language) to find out what their needs and aspirations are.

In order to learn about the native language of your students if you are not a native speaker of that language, you could:

1) Examine any studies that have been made comparing the target language and the native language of your students.

2) Ask someone (a teacher, perhaps) who speaks the native language of your students to tell you in broad terms how the language treats inflection, intonation, the writing system, etc.

3) Investigate cultural aspects which may impede or facilitate your teaching.

## The School and Community

In this section, as in the one above, it is impossible to explore the topic in depth. Again, we can only ask some questions, hoping that you will seek their answers by asking questions yourselves, by observing, by studying, and by examining records and other materials.

1) What is the duration of the language program? Is it an intensive program, for example? Is it a two-year, three-year, or four-year course?

2) What facilities exist in the school (language laboratory, library, television, auditorium)?

3) What instructional materials exist?

4) Is there a testing program (prognostic, proficiency, achievement)?

5) What kinds of pupil records are kept? How and where are they kept?

6) Are there provisions in the school for practicing and reinforcing the language (a newspaper, assembly programs, a language club)?

7) Does the community have large numbers of speakers of the target language?

8) What facilities and resources does the community have (library, museum, etc.)?

9) Is it an urban community or a rural community?

10) Are there people in the community who could be invited to speak to your class?

11) Are there newspapers, radio programs, television programs, or movies in the language your students are learning?

## THE CRUCIAL ROLE OF THE TEACHER

The role of the foreign language teacher is central to the learning process. While teachers of other disciplines are called upon to inculcate habits, attitudes, knowledge, or skills in a medium already familiar to their students, the foreign language teacher must bring about changes or modifications in behavior, habits, attitudes, knowledge, or skills in an unfamiliar medium requiring additional or different physiological activity. The organs of speech must be taught to move in unprecedented ways; the sounds striking the listener's ears must be perceived without distortion from or confusion with the known sounds of the native language.

The teacher has to be a combination of linguist, sociologist, anthropologist, and pedagogue.

What are some of the major dimensions of the teacher's task? He should modify curriculum content as he ascertains the strengths, weaknesses, and aspirations of his students. He should make every effort to help the students achieve their aspirations or to redirect them into attainable, realistic channels. With relation to aspirations, he must realize that what one student may consider success may not be success for another.

He should keep the motivation of his students at a high level, not only by varying his method of presentation or his instructional materials but also by giving students a sense of security, success, and achievement. Recent studies have shown, for example, that students experience great tension when they are taught with an audio-lingual approach exclusively for too long a time. They cannot be helped by the partial predictability clues we use in hearing speakers in our native language.

The teacher should provide for individual differences. Students have different learning capacities and may come to our classes with different degrees of skill. Individuals learn in different ways and at different rates. Some learn by intensive repetition and overlearning; some learn best by trial and error; and some learn by applying generalizations to new situations. The activities and experiences suggested in the curriculum as well as the methodology used by the teacher should reflect an awareness of these differences.

Individual differences among our students demand a variety of appropriate drills and materials not only related to their interests but also geared to their ability levels. These materials may need to focus on problems of phonology, structure, lexicon, reading, or writing. They may be needed for whole class presentation, for sub-groups within the class, or for individuals. Provision must be made for self-checking devices so that groups or individuals may sometimes work without the immediate supervision of the teacher.

Also important in giving students a feeling of achievement and in helping them grow toward the immediate and long-range objectives of the foreign language program is the teacher's attention to the following principles.

**He should:**

1. Organize the learning experiences carefully. In a grammar or vocabulary lesson, for example, language items for emphasis should be selected, graded, presented, and practiced in a manner which will facilitate the students' acquisition of them. More will be said about this on pages 84-85.

2. Plan in advance the situations through which the meaning of the new language items will be made clear to the students so that appropriate materials will be available.

3. Provide in each lesson not only systematic practice leading to habit formation but also meaningful use of the language in communication activities where language is generally used by native speakers.

In order to keep the students' interest high, teaching should generally proceed along two parallel streams. For example, dialogues — real conversational exchanges — are presented and dramatized from the very beginning of Level I* without waiting for the students to develop an active grasp of all the structures and vocabulary contained in them. In teaching reading, interesting passages are presented although students will not have a complete knowledge of all the sound-symbol relationships represented. The sound-symbol relationships will be taught gradually in small steps over a feasible period of time but reading of "real" material should not be deferred until all of them have been learned.

4. Keep previously learned materials alive through their judicious reintroduction in any logical phase of subsequent classroom (or laboratory) lessons.

5. Use the students' native language sparingly in the classroom,

_____

* Levels are defined on pp. 34-35.

but do not hesitate to use it to clarify instructions or to ensure that essential information has been understood.

6. Learn how to engage the students in full class, group, and individual recitation procedures as appropriate. While group recitation is desirable during many phases of the lesson because 1) it gives the learners a sense of initial security and 2) it enables all of them to produce speech much more frequently than would be possible otherwise, real communication is essentially an activity conducted by individuals.

7. Become accustomed to preparing or utilizing existing instructional materials which enable pairs of learners to practice language together.

8. Supplement the basic text where necessary by preparing drills, dialogues, or reading selections to lend variety to the lessons, to reinforce language items which have been presented, and to help the students grow toward real communicative ability.

9. Become skillful in preparing scripts for tapes, in voicing them, and in integrating laboratory practice and classroom activity.

10. Determine when beginning-level students are ready for reading and writing activities.

11. Plan reading lessons which will not only extend the pupils' knowledge of the language, but will also provide them with an aesthetic experience.

12. Incorporate writing activities which will lead gradually to more creative, "free" student expression as soon as possible.

13. Provide students with cultural insights into the foreign country both incidentally, as allusions met in the dialogues or reading materials are explained, and at later stages in more formal discussions.

14. Make sure that students retain their sense of individual dignity and national pride while learning to appreciate aspects of the culture of the country whose language is being learned. Both with relation to their own culture and that of the "foreign" country, it is essential that students sense the basic similarities of the human experience and that they realize that "different from" does not mean "better than" or "worse than."

15. Learn to select and use only the audio-visual aids which will help the students acquire a particular language item or cultural fact more efficiently.

16. Make and give frequent tests which will help 1) gauge the achievement of students; 2) diagnose individual learning problems; and 3) judge the effectiveness of his teaching.

The good teacher recognizes the importance of integrating discrete language skills into communication situations which simulate or duplicate the real situations in which students will need to use the foreign language.

The skillful teacher integrates students' out-of-class work or possible community experiences with classroom recitation. In particular, those activities which the teacher has assigned, such as a visit to the language laboratory or listening to recordings or studying from programmed texts, should be referred to and taken into account in the classroom.

The master teacher recognizes that students will want to use the foreign language both as a tool and as a means of identifying with a new community of human beings — what Lambert and his co-workers call "instrumental and integrative" orientation. A curriculum implemented in an encouraging classroom climate in which both orientations are fostered should be the desideratum of any foreign language program.

Finally, the superior teacher knows how to "exploit" all facets of the learning situation to enhance students' motivation; to ensure that learning will be more effective; and to make his teaching more effective.

• For example, he learns the interests of his students by exploring the community in which he teaches and by judiciously questioning the students.

• He creates an opportunity for learning resulting from an incidental happening in the class, school, or immediate vicinity.

• He utilizes the strengths of his students by having them help in the numerous tasks of the classroom, such as preparing instructional materials, checking homework or test papers, serving as "teachers" in asking questions, correcting blackboard work, or helping fellow students who may have been absent or who have fallen behind in some aspect of the work.

• He uses the same piece of material — a dialogue, a reading selection, a set of flashcards or some pictures — for multiple purposes. For example, although a reading selection may be useful for expanding vocabulary, for teaching skills of comprehension or motivating the presentation of a grammatical structure, it should also be used as a source for aural comprehension, for dictation, or for the study of model paragraphs leading to written composition.

A picture may be used not only to identify or to practice vocabulary, but it should also be used to advantage in teaching or reinforcing various structures, in oral conversational exercises, and in written composition.

• He enhances learning by utilizing the resources, people, and places in the community.

No one is born a superior teacher; everyone can hope to become one. In addition to continuous, wide reading in the field of foreign language teaching and also in any other which at first glance may seem to have only the most remote connection to foreign language teaching; to observation of other teachers, even of poor ones; and to a sincere interest in his students, the teacher who would be "superior" must have the courage to use his intuition, to experiment boldly, to question dogmatic statements, and to realize that he, too, is a unique individual with his own strengths and perhaps his own idiosyncrasies.

Whether or not all segments of society recognize the fact, it is the teacher who will eventually shape the future of our nations and of our world. It is in the classroom that the majority of us acquire the knowledge, skills, and attitudes which, to a large extent, will shape the kind of individual we will become. A positive attitude resulting from a successful, happy experience may determine if the study of foreign languages will be encouraged and, even more important, if our attitudes toward other nations will be marked by a desire for peaceful coexistence and cultural rapprochement.

It may be useful for all teachers to familiarize themselves with the standards for foreign language teachers prepared by the Modern Language Association of America.


## Qualifications for Secondary Teachers of Modern Foreign Languages*

It is vitally important that teachers of modern foreign languages be adequately prepared for their task. Though a majority of the language teachers in our schools are well-trained, many have been poorly or inadequately prepared, often through no fault of their own.

It should be understood that teaching by persons who cannot meet these minimal standards will not produce results which our profession can endorse as making a distinctive contribution to language learning.

The lowest level of preparation is not recommended. It is here stated only as a point of departure which carries with it the responsibility for continued study and self-improvement, through graduate and in-service training, toward the levels of good and superior preparation.

Those who subscribe to this statement hope that the teacher of foreign languages 1) will have the personal qualities which make an effective teacher; 2) has received a well-balanced education, including a knowledge of his own culture; and 3) has received the appropriate training in professional education, psychology, and secondary school methods. It is not our purpose to define further these criteria. We are concerned here with the specific qualifications for a teacher of modern foreign languages.

---

* Adapted from a statement prepared by the Steering Committee of the Modern Language Association.

### Aural understanding:

*Minimal* — The ability to get the sense of what an educated native says when he is enunciating carefully and speaking simply on a general subject.

*Good* — The ability to understand conversation at average tempo, lectures, and news broadcasts.

*Superior* — The ability to follow closely and with ease all types of standard speech, such as rapid or group conversation, plays, and movies.

### Speaking:

*Minimal* — The ability to speak on prepared topics (e.g., for classroom situations) without obvious faltering, to use the common expressions needed for getting around in the foreign country, and to speak with pronunciation readily understandable to a native.

*Good* — The ability to talk with a native without making glaring mistakes, and with a command of vocabulary and syntax sufficient to express one's thoughts in sustained conversation. This implies speech at normal speed with good pronunciation and intonation.

*Superior* — The ability to approximate native speech in vocabulary, intonation, and pronunciation (e.g., the ability to exchange ideas and be at ease in social situations).

### Reading:

*Minimal* — The ability to grasp directly (i.e., without translation) the meaning of simple, non-technical prose, except for an occasional word.

*Good* — The ability to read with immediate comprehension prose and verse of average difficulty and mature content.

*Superior* — The ability to read, almost as easily as in the native tongue, material of considerable difficulty, such as essays and literary criticism.

### Writing:

*Minimal* — The ability to write correct sentences or paragraphs such as would be developed orally for classroom situations, and the ability to write a short, simple letter.

*Good* — The ability to write a simple "free composition" with clarity and correctness in vocabulary, idiom, and syntax.

*Superior* — The ability to write on a variety of subjects with idiomatic naturalness, ease of expression, and some feeling for the style of the language.

### Language analysis:

*Minimal* — A working command of the sound patterns and grammar patterns of the foreign language, and a knowledge of its main differences from the native language of the learners.

*Good* — A basic knowledge of the historical development and present characteristics of the language, and an awareness of the difference between the language as spoken and as written.

*Superior* — The ability to apply knowledge of descriptive, comparative, and historical linguistics to the language-teaching situation.

### Culture:

*Minimal* — An awareness of language as an essential element among the learned and shared experiences that combine to form a particular culture, and a rudimentary knowledge of the geography, history, literature, art, social customs, and contemporary civilization of the foreign people.

*Good* — First-hand knowledge of some literary masterpieces, an understanding of the principal ways in which the foreign culture resembles and differs from our own, and possession of an organized body of information on the foreign people and their civilization.

*Superior* — An enlightened understanding of the foreign people and their culture achieved through personal contact, preferably by travel and residence abroad, through study of systematic descriptions of the foreign culture, and through study of literature and the arts.

### Professional preparation:

*Minimal* — Some knowledge of effective methods and techniques of language teaching.

*Good* — The ability to apply knowledge of methods and techniques to the teaching situation (e.g., audio-visual techniques) and to relate one's teaching of the language to other areas of the curriculum.

*Superior* — A mastery of recognized teaching methods, and the ability to experiment with and evaluate new methods and techniques.

### Suggestions

— Select ten common everyday expressions in your native language or that of your students; e.g., English: "He's ten years old." French: "Il a dix ans." Spanish: "Tiene diez años." Italian: "Ha dieci anni." German: "Er ist zehn Jahre alt."

Indicate potential difficulties for your students in learning to use the expressions.

— Observe a friend or a member of your family for a week as he is engaged in conversation. List the non-linguistic features of the speech

29

act (e.g., gestures). Note, too, in which type of conversational situation the same features become more prominent.

— Which sounds cluster in your native language? Which sounds cluster in the target language? Give examples.

— Select one use of a language item (e.g., the simple present of a verb) and show how it is systematic in your native language.

— List the major sentence types in the target language.

— From several pages of prose, select five sentences which might be ambiguous out of context. Indicate the underlying (deep) structure(s) of each sentence.

— Collect five expressions in other languages equivalent to "cock-a-doodle-do."

— Select words in your native language which are now considered archaic or obsolete. Trace their origin, use, reason for obsolescence, etc.

— Study the speech of a two-year-old child over a period of about a month. What words does the child pronounce? What vowels or consonants cause difficulty? What intonation patterns do you detect? What word combinations do you note (noun + verb; verb + noun + adjective + noun; etc.)?

If possible, tell how the child's speech acts were reinforced (playmate, adult, etc.).

— Discuss the relevance of language theory to language teaching.

— Learn a ten line poem by heart. How did you learn it (line by line, whole method, combination)? Put it aside for a month. How much of it did you remember after a month?

— If you are teaching or observing other teachers, try to keep a one-week record of the number of times a word or expression is reintroduced — either alone or in combination with other expressions.

— Make a list of about fifty words borrowed from the foreign language and used extensively in your native tongue.

— Make a similar list of words in your native tongue used in your target language.

### Additional Reading*

SAPIR, E. *Language*. New York: Harcourt Brace, 1931.
BLOOMFIELD, L. *Language*. New York: Henry Holt, 1933.

---

* References in this chapter are given in chronological order so that readers can note progressive development in theory.

Many of the books suggested for further study in this and other chapters have been published in the United States or in England. You should prepare similar lists for books published in your native and target countries.

For extensive bibliographical help, see Mackey, W., *Language Teaching Analysis* as well as Birkmaier, E. and Lange, D., *A Selective Bibliography on the Teaching of Foreign Languages*. N.Y.: MLA, ACTFL, 1968.

FRIES, C. *Teaching and Learning English as a Foreign Language.* Ann Arbor, Mich: U. of Michigan Press, 1948.

CARROLL, J. B. *The Study of Language.* Cambridge, Mass.: Harvard U. Press, 1953.

LADO, R. *Linguistics Across Cultures.* Ann Arbor, Mich: U. of Michigan Press, 1957.

SKINNER, B. F. *Verbal Behavior.* New York: Appleton, 1957.

HILL, A. *Introduction to Linguistic Structures.* New York: Harcourt Brace, 1958.

HOCKETT, C. F. *A Course in Modern Linguistics.* New York: Macmillan, 1958.

PIKE, K. *Language in Relation to a Unified Theory of the Structure of Human Behavior.* Santa Ana, Calif.: Summer Institute of Linguistics, 1960.

MOULTON, W. "Applied Linguistics in the Classroom," *PMLA*, Vol. LXXVI, May 1961.

MARTINET, A. *A Functional View of Language.* London: Oxford U. Press, 1962.

VYGOTSKI, L. *Thought and Language.* New York: Wiley, 1962.

BROOKS, N. *Language and Language Learning.* New York: Harcourt Brace & World, 1964.

CARROLL, J. B. *Language and Thought.* Englewood Cliffs, N.J.: Prentice-Hall, 1964.

PEI, M. *Invitation to Linguistics.* Garden City, N.Y.: Doubleday, 1964.

CHOMSKY, N. *Aspects of the Theory of Syntax.* Cambridge, Mass.: The M.I.T. Press, 1965.

HALL, R. *Introduction to Linguistics.* Philadelphia: Chilton, 1965.

HALLIDAY, M., MCINTOSH, and STREVENS. *The Language Sciences and Language Teaching.* London: Longmans Green, 1964.

MACKEY, W. *Language Teaching Analysis.* London: Longmans Green, 1965.

POLITZER, R. *Foreign Language Learning: A Linguistic Introduction.* Englewood Cliffs, N.J.: Prentice-Hall, 1965.

RIVERS, W. *The Psychologist and the Language Teacher.* Chicago: U. of Chicago Press, 1965.

LAMBERT, W. "On Learning and Thinking and Human Ability," *MLJ*,* 1965.

BOLINGER, D. *Aspects of Language.* New York: Harcourt, Brace & World, 1968.

BIRKMAIER, E. (ed.). *The Britannica Review of Foreign Language Education.* Chicago: Encyclopedia Britannica, Inc., 1968.

CHOMSKY, N. *Language & Mind.* New York: Harcourt, Brace & World, 1968.

JAKOBOVITS, L. *Foreign Language Learning: A Psycholinguistic Analysis of the Issues.* Rowley, Mass.: Newbury House, 1970.

DIPIETRO, R. *Language Structure in Contrast.* Rowley, Mass.: Newbury House, 1971.

---

* See p. 300 for full title.

# II

# Developing a Curriculum

If you are asked to teach a foreign language in a school where no curriculum guide exists, if there is need to revise the existing curriculum, or if you cannot obtain graded textbooks, the material in this chapter should be of particular interest to you. In most situations, however, the school will make available a syllabus or teaching guide and a series of textbooks for each level of learning. You would, then, present as much of the material in each book as is recommended for each level or as much as your students can assimilate. Even where a curriculum and textbooks exist, however, you may wish to round out the content of your program by considering the principles and suggestions in this chapter.

## SOME BASIC PREMISES

— A curriculum guide usually includes the following:

1) an analysis of the overall aims of the program (in other words, the terminal behavior which the students will be expected to have achieved at the end of the program) ;*

2) a list of the intermediate goals; (that is, the desired outcome at the end of each learning level in terms of the skills of listening, speaking, reading, and writing — and cultural appreciation) ;*

3) a list of items (within phonology, grammar, and vocabulary) and of the language operations or transformations to be taught at each level;

4) a list of the cultural concepts to be emphasized;

5) a description of the situations and activities through which language items and skills can be introduced and practiced;

6) suggestions for evaluation (testing) of the pupils' growth;

7) sources for teacher reference and pupils' texts.

---

* These are often stated in terms of "performance objectives" in which four basic components are given in detail: 1) the purpose for learning the item or skill; 2) the outcome (terminal behavior) expected; 3) the condition under which the student is expected to learn (the number of items he is to study, the time he will have, etc.) ; 4) the means whereby the performance will be evaluated and the degree of "mastery" desired.

— The content of the curriculum at any level will depend on several factors: the *age* of the pupils, the *number of years* the total program will last, and the *aims* and *scope* of the program. For example, will there be emphasis on listening and speaking, emphasis on reading (for those in need of reading scientific journals, etc.)? What degree of "mastery" will be expected?

— With these considerations in mind, curriculum writers select and grade the material for each level, determine the number of items and patterns to be learned, and weigh the relative emphases of the skills. (How much listening and speaking will be done at Level I? How much reading? How much writing? Will the same proportions in skill development be maintained after the first level?)

The theoretical "school" the curriculum writer subscribes to may be a determining factor in the sequence of material taught. Some writers may prefer to teach all the sounds thoroughly first with limited vocabulary and structures. Others may prefer to start with basic kernel sentences, not teaching simple questions, for example, for several months since questions are "transforms" of kernels.

Whatever the "school," the pronunciation features, grammar, vocabulary, and cultural information needed to achieve the terminal behavior desired should be carefully listed and then apportioned judiciously over the number of levels in the program. One way of sequencing the broad grammatical categories and operations is not necessarily better than another. The steps within the categories and operations and the methods of presentation of each step as well as the other principles noted here are more important than the possible starting points.

— Since language learning is cumulative, provision is made to relate all new language learning to that which the students learned at previous levels or in previous units in listening, speaking, reading, or writing activities.

— No skill which has been developed (listening or speaking, for example) is (nor should it be) ever neglected even when another skill (e.g., reading) is being emphasized in teaching.

— Although each facet of a skill or feature of the language may be practiced separately, these are brought together in communication activities constantly so that pupils are made increasingly aware of their interdependence in actual use.

— The curriculum of the language program is so designed that it enables the pupils, after a reasonable period of learning, to continue to study and read by themselves, to increase their listening-speaking skills, and to engage in an area of specialization if so desired.

— Unless there is some urgent reason to change the order, priority in the curriculum is given to: 1) the sounds and other features of the pronunciation system; 2) the basic sentence patterns; 3) the function words; 4) the inflections which are most frequent; 5) the vocabulary which will: a) enable the students to practice the basic patterns; b) be useful in helping them talk about their lives and their experiences; and c) strengthen their conviction that the foreign language can be used to express the same ideas they express in their native tongue and that it is something worth knowing.

— The oral language activities which are written into the curriculum afford the students practice in understanding and in answering questions; in making statements in the affirmative and in the negative with long or short answers; in responding by carrying out directions; in making comments (of agreement, of disagreement, of surprise, etc.) ; in asking questions; or in summarizing. The oral practice activities should enable them gradually, but with perceptible progress, to carry on a conversation about things they would ordinarily talk about in their own language with people of their age group.

— The situational content for all learning starts with the students themselves and their environment. It is only by relating it to their own experience that a new item or concept becomes meaningful to them. If, for example, the reading material in your text refers to a holiday in the target country, it is desirable to discuss holidays *as your students know them and live them* before proceeding to the unfamiliar concept.

— Reading and writing activities are introduced judiciously soon after students acquire a reasonable facility in basic listening-speaking activities. (This is discussed more fully in Chapter IV.)

— Reading and writing activities are designed to reinforce the listening and speaking activities as well as to develop the abilities to read and write for educational, recreational, or aesthetic purposes.

—The culture which may be implicit in the dialogues or reading passages is made explicit by the teacher. For example, "I'll meet you for a snack at six," if spoken by Italians or Spaniards would have to be explained to English speakers who would generally be getting ready for dinner at that time.

— In addition to such incidental explanations, entire lessons or parts of lessons are devoted to the systematic presentation of cultural topics during the intermediate and advanced levels of study or at other times, as needed.

## Aims and Levels

Two words which have been used, aims and levels, need further explanation. What should be the *aims* of the program? What do we mean by *levels*?

In the usual language program, whether it starts in the elementary or secondary school or at the university, we usually talk about *five* principal aims.[1] We aim to give each student:

— The progressive ability to understand the new language on topics in harmony with his age level when spoken by a native speaker. (By native speaker we mean a person who either was born and learned the language in the country where it is spoken or a person who has learned it well enough to be mistaken for a native speaker.)

— The progressive ability to carry on a conversation with a native speaker on topics of interest to persons of his age group.

— The progressive ability to read material in the new language with comprehension, ease, and enjoyment.

— The progressive ability to write correctly, expressing his own thoughts and emotions.

— The information, knowledge, attitude, and insight to appreciate the similarities and differences (if such exist) between his culture and that of the speakers of the target language.

A brief comment should be made here. As noted above, at the beginning level the culture need not and should not be taught systematically. When a word or concept arises which needs special explanation, you should give it by all means. But since language is the central feature of culture, certain aspects of culture are learned automatically as the language is developed. More will be said about this below.

And now, what is meant by *level*? Since a language-learning program may start in the elementary school, the secondary school, or the university, it is desirable to talk about *levels*[2] of learning. The first level is the *beginning* level of language learning; the second level is the *intermediate* level; and the third and fourth levels may be considered the *advanced* level. In the usual secondary school (high school) program, the first level is the first year of high school. If the language is begun in the junior high school,[3] the first level may be the first two years of the junior high school. In that case, a student who has begun the language at the junior high school may enter the second, or intermediate, level in the high school. When language is started in the elementary school, the first level may be spread over the three or four

---

[1] Two more formal statements related to the aims and values of foreign language study are appended to this chapter.

[2] Here are two definitions for your consideration: A stage of learning; the time segment on the continuum of learning at which a student can learn a segment of material because 1) he has already acquired the background knowledge and skills needed to learn it and 2) it is appropriate to his age and maturity level. In other words, the level may be considered the period of time when a learner is educationally, linguistically, and emotionally ready to absorb the material prescribed for that level.

[3] The three- or four-year period of schooling which comes after a five- or six-year elementary school program.

years of foreign language instruction in the elementary school. At the university, the first level may be of only one semester's duration. All the factors which have been discussed (age, length, type of course, etc.) must be considered in talking about levels.

## Curriculum Planning

At any rate, whatever the name of the level, several things in curriculum planning, in addition to those already mentioned, are important:

1. The material should be carefully graded. For example, we would start with one modifier of a noun before giving two modifiers together; we would teach a regular plural sound and form before teaching the "exceptions"; we would focus on one common sound-spelling relationship before giving the more unusual ones.

2. There should be systematic provision in language drills, in dialogues, in reading passages, and in dictations for the constant reintroduction of all the material which has been taught with the new material we are teaching.

3. We shouldn't try to teach all the vocabulary around a topic or "center of interest" or all the forms, meanings, or uses of an item of structure at one time. Instead, we should use what is called a "spiral approach."

Let us study an example of the "spiral approach" within a cultural topic. The first time (at the first level) we speak of "family," we may present the names of immediate family members: "father," "mother," "brother," "sister." At the second level, we may add to the family members the words "grandmother," "grandfather," "relatives," "uncle," "aunt," "cousins." At the third level, perhaps, we may want to teach "mother-in-law," "son-in-law," "great-aunt," etc.; at the fourth, "second cousin," "distant relations," etc.

Now let us look at an example within an item of structure — the inflection of pronouns in English, for example. At Level I, we might teach, "*I* have a book" and "This is *my* book"; at Level II, we might teach "Give *me my* book" ("Give *him his* book"); at Level III, "This isn't *mine*. It's *theirs*"; at Level IV, "I saw it *myself*"; etc.

The arrangement of items should be flexible. The situation in which the language is being learned and the communication needs of the students should determine the selection and gradation of the items within each category.

4. The curriculum should reflect realistic objectives. This should be based on such considerations as the length of the program — eighty hours, one year, two years, four years — and the aspirations and needs of the students. In addition to their general purpose for language study,

36

it is important to consider in writing or implementing a curriculum those language-learning activities and experiences which take cognizance of the use to which the students might put their knowledge, at least in the immediately foreseeable future.

5. The curriculum should provide for continuity of instruction both horizontally and vertically. All teachers on the same level should present and practice the same corpus of material. Provision for the normal integration of the language abilities (another form of horizontal articulation) — listening, speaking, reading, and writing — should also be made. Continuity of instruction on a vertical level is also essential. It would be helpful, therefore, to have a curriculum for each learning level explicitly spelled out and for all staff members to be made aware not only of the probable content, activities, and experiences of students who come to them from less advanced levels but also of the expectations of instructors who will teach their students at the next higher level.

6. The curriculum should provide integrative experiences in which all students on a level learn a given body of content. For example, all students should be given enough practice in the phonological aspects of the foreign language to be understood. All might be taught to use contextual clues to understand unfamiliar reading material. All should learn the language utterances they need to engage in the give-and-take of real conversation. All might learn to write letters of thanks or of inquiry, and eventually even of love.

The curriculum, however, should also provide for the inclusion of differentiating experiences which recognize the uniqueness of each individual. Not all of the students should be expected to create plays or write essays on abstract topics. We know that few native speakers are capable of doing that. Not all of the students need to understand or produce various intonation patterns unless they're going to be broadcasters or teachers. It is imperative, however, that enrichment experiences be offered to individuals who have potential and will be engaged in teaching, broadcasting, playwriting, or the like.

7. The curriculum should provide for flexibility in methodology. It is unrealistic to expect that all students will profit from any one method or technique. Since we do not really know how learning takes place in the human organism, we do students an injustice when we adhere strictly to unproved language-learning assumptions, practices, or clichés, such as those advocating that students should never talk about the language, that reading should be deferred for X number of hours, that long dialogues need to be memorized, that the use of the students' native language may be harmful, that a prescribed sequence of learning must be followed without deviation, that rules or generalizations should never be given, that all grammar should be taught only through trans-

formation rules, etc. Flexibility in methodology also requires adaptation based on the known experiences of students outside the classroom. Outside visits, use of programmed texts, or language laboratory work should be integrated into the classroom period. Television viewing or participation in sports should be woven into the lessons.

8. The curriculum should make provision for continuous evaluation not only of the students' growth but also of the curriculum itself (activities and experiences, related instructional materials), and testing procedures.

Imbalance in the curriculum may stem from objectives which are not clearly defined, from content which is insufficient or not geared to the students' abilities or needs, or from language activities which over-emphasize one feature or skill to the neglect and detriment of another. As we have noted, experimentation in this regard proves what good teachers know, namely that we learn what we practice. Students learn to construct new sentences when they are given varied, systematic practice in doing so; they learn to respond to a communication stimulus when they have been given many opportunities in class to do so; and they learn to read when they are taught to read.

Imbalance, of course, may be the result of factors within the students themselves. Innate intelligence, the native language spoken, attitudes of prejudice for whatever social or political reason, and psychological problems cannot help but affect the curriculum.

As teachers, we may be the cause of any imbalance due to our fear of trying new techniques or because we accept practices or procedures without seeking the rationale behind them or asking ourselves whether they can work with our students, with our teaching personalities, in our schools, and in our communities.

Lack of facilities in the school for reinforcing learning, administrative indifference, or any lack of know-how will have some impact on what goes on in each classroom where the curriculum is put to the acid test. It is up to the conscientious teacher to redouble his efforts to overcome weaknesses in the school program.

Following are two statements related to the values and goals of modern language study:

## A. Values of Foreign Language Study*

The study of a foreign language, like that of most other basic disciplines, is both a progressive experience and the progressive acquisition of a skill. At no point can the experience be considered complete

---

* Adapted from a statement of the Steering Committee for the Foreign Language Program of the Modern Language Association of America issued in 1956.

or the skill perfect. Many pupils study a foreign language only two years; longer time is, of course, needed to approach mastery. At any point, however, the progress made in a language, when properly taught, will have positive value and lay a foundation upon which further progress can be built. Therefore, the value derived from language study must be relative to the amount of time and effort devoted to it.

The study of a foreign language, skillfully taught under proper conditions, provides a new experience, progressively enlarging the pupil's horizons through his introduction to a new medium of communication and a new culture pattern, and adding to his sense of pleasurable achievement. This experience involves:

1. The acquisition of a set of *skills,* which can become real mastery for unlimited use when practiced long enough. The international contacts and responsibilities of all nations make the possession of these skills by more and more (Americans) a matter of national urgency. These skills include:

a) The increasing ability to *understand* a foreign language when spoken, making possible greater profit and enjoyment in such steadily expanding activities as foreign travel, business abroad, and foreign language movies and broadcasts.

b) The increasing ability to *speak* a foreign language in direct communication with people of another culture, either for business or for pleasure.

c) The ability to *read* the foreign language with progressively greater ease and enjoyment, making possible the broadening effects of direct acquaintance with the recorded thoughts of another people, or making possible study for vocational or professional (e.g., scientific or journalistic) purposes.

2. A new understanding of language, revealing to the pupil the structure of language and giving him a new perspective on his native language as well as increased vocabulary and greater effectiveness in self-expression.

3. A gradually expanding and deepening knowledge of a foreign country — its geography, history, social organization, literature, and culture — and, as a consequence, a better perspective on his own culture and a more enlightened nationalism through adjustment to the concept of differences between cultures.

Progress in any one of these experiences is relative to the emphasis given it in the instructional program and to the interests and aptitude of the learner. Language skills, like all practical skills, may never be perfected and may later be forgotten, yet the enlarging and enriching results of the cultural experience endure throughout life.

## B. Goals of Modern Foreign Language Study

The following excerpt (slightly adapted), taken from Guidelines for NDEA Title III, issued by the United States Department of Health, Education, and Welfare in January 1965, will also be of interest to those concerned with language instruction:

The overall goals of modern foreign language study are effective communication and cultural understanding. The specific goals are:

1. To *understand* a foreign language when spoken at normal speed on a subject within the range of the student's experience;

2. To *speak* well enough to communicate directly with a native speaker on a subject within the range of the student's experience;

3. To *read* with direct understanding, without recourse to native language translation, material on a general subject;

4. To *write,* using authentic patterns of the language;

5. To *understand* linguistic concepts, such as the nature of language and how it functions through its structural system;

6. To *understand,* through the foreign language, the contemporary values and behavior patterns of the people whose language is being studied;

7. To *acquire* knowledge of the significant features of the country or area where the language is spoken (geographic, economic, political, etc.);

8. To *develop* an understanding of the literary and cultural heritage of the people whose language is studied.

## INTRODUCTORY NOTES ON CONTENT

### The Linguistic and Cultural Content

The sequence of presentation of the linguistic content will depend in part, as we have mentioned, on the language system to which the curriculum writers in your schools or school system subscribe or on which the textbooks you are using are based.

There are several ways, of course, to describe a language. The two most common today are:

1. *Structural* — working from the phonemes of the language; that is, from the minimal units of meaningful sounds, to the morphology (the form of words), and then to the syntax (the arrangement of words).

2. *Generative-transformational* — working from the kernel or base sentences to the surface structures, which may still consist of the kernel sentences or of transforms of these.

Whichever description is used, the terminal behavior expected of our learners is still the ability to listen to a flow of speech with understanding, to produce a flow of speech, and to read and write.

40

Each of these abilities requires a knowledge of four basic sub-systems of language:

1. *The sound system,* including the pronunciation of vowels and consonants, the intonation patterns, rhythm, stress, and pause.

2. *The grammar system,* including:

a) a knowledge of morphology, the forms of words which may be modified through *inflections* for plurality, possession, tense, etc., or through *derivation* — that is, through the changes produced by affixes (prefixes [kind/unkind] and suffixes [kind/kinder]) or infixes (internal changes [Carlos, Carlitos]).

b) syntax, the order of words, phrases, or clauses in an utterance.

c) morphophonemics (a term which straddles or cuts across the sound and grammar systems), which refers to the sound changes in an utterance brought about by some grammatical (morphological or syntactic) phenomenon and/or by the environment in which a sound occurs (e.g., English: singular *wife*, plural *wives*; French: "Il en a dix [dis]," "Il a dix ans [diz a]," "Il a dix [di] francs.").

3. *The lexical system,* including the content words (nouns, verbs, adjectives, and adverbs) and the structure or function words (such as the articles and other determiners, prepositions, auxiliaries, modals, and conjunctions).

4. *The cultural system,* including those aspects which are reflected in the language items and in the lexical system. Ask yourself how many forms of address there are to note the interrelationship of culture and lexicon. English has one, the form "you"; French has two; Spanish and Italian have four; German has three; Russian has two. Some aspects of culture are not found in the language items per se but may determine the content and tone of our verbal responses and our physical responses (e.g., What distance do two speakers maintain when they are holding a conversation? Which gestures or facial expressions connote which emotions?).

*All of these sub-systems are interrelated.* To express any idea — even a one word utterance — all of the sub-systems come into play. If, for example, someone has made a surprising statement about "Robert," and you answer, "Robert," using a rising intonation, you are using vowels and consonants; a particular intonation pattern; word stress; grammar (you did not say "Robert's" or "to Robert"); and a lexical item. Since Robert is the first name of a male person and a feature of the culture, both you and the first speaker are either talking about a young person or about someone you both know well or you would have been required to say, "Mr. ........................."

It is obvious that whatever linguistic school one "prefers," whatever the starting point — phonemes or kernel sentences — students must learn the items within the various sub-systems of the language and they must learn how the sub-systems are related to each other in listening, speaking, reading, and writing. The meaning of any utterance is the combination of the sound, grammar, lexical, and cultural systems reflected in it.

*Interrelationships of Linguistic and Cultural Sub-Systems:*

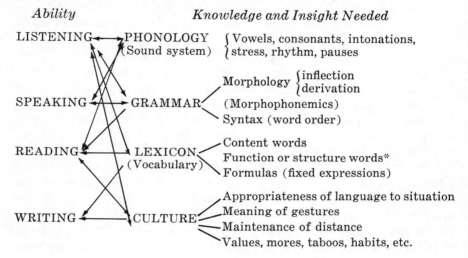

*Ability*

*Knowledge and Insight Needed*

LISTENING — PHONOLOGY (Sound system) { Vowels, consonants, intonations, stress, rhythm, pauses

SPEAKING — GRAMMAR — Morphology { inflection derivation
(Morphophonemics)
Syntax (word order)

READING — LEXICON (Vocabulary) — Content words
Function or structure words*
Formulas (fixed expressions)

WRITING — CULTURE — Appropriateness of language to situation
Meaning of gestures
Maintenance of distance
Values, mores, taboos, habits, etc.

## SOME FEATURES OF LANGUAGE

Only the briefest description, in very simple terms, will be given. Suggestions for further study will be found in the Bibliography at the end of this chapter. The texts recommended are primarily those published in America and England and are generally available throughout the world. The examples given are in English since most of our studies have been in English. It is urged that you prepare similar materials for the language you are teaching.

Another statement may be in order before proceeding. Linguistics is a comparatively young science. Many experiments in the field are still in progress. Their results may not be known for years to come. It is natural, therefore, that some controversies exist among linguists about some symbols, terms, and even concepts. The facts given below are those generally accepted by a majority of linguists.

---

* Some linguists prefer to consider function words as part of the grammar system since many of them signal grammatical meaning rather than lexical meaning.

## The Sound System

Since we will have occasion to refer to them several times in this Guide, the organs of speech, or *vocal organs*, are indicated on the following diagram:

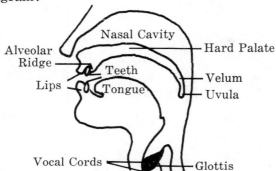

You should learn to sketch the vocal organs quickly at the chalkboard or on a chart and to indicate the changing position of the tongue in producing the various sounds.

Below are shown two sets of symbols representing only the significant sounds of the English language. These sounds, the *phonemes*, are those which produce a difference in meaning.

The first column (headed *IPA*) gives symbols of the widely accepted International Phonetic Alphabet with slight modifications (for example, a for ɑ; y for j). The second column (headed *T & S*) gives the symbols used by Trager and Smith in their text, *An Outline of English Structure*, and adopted by many American linguists with various modifications (e.g., ɑw for aw, ɔy for oy).

### CONSONANTS

| *IPA* | *T & S* | *English Word* | *IPA* | *T & S* | *English Word* |
|-------|---------|----------------|-------|---------|----------------|
| b | b | boy | s | s | soap |
| d | d | do | ʃ | š | ship |
| f | f | first | t | t | tie |
| g | g | go | θ | θ | thin |
| h | h | hit | ð | ð | then |
| k | k | cook | v | v | very |
| l | l | let | w | w | water |
| m | m | man | y | y | yes |
| n | n | no | z | z | rose |
| ŋ | ŋ | sing | ʒ | ž | pleasure |
| p | p | put | tʃ | č | cheese |
| r | r | robe | dʒ | j | judge |

43

## Vowels

| | | | | | |
|---|---|---|---|---|---|
| a | a | hot | ɔ | ɔ | law |
| æ | æ | map | o | ow | hope |
| e | ey | made | u | uw | spoon |
| ɛ | e | let | ʊ | u | foot |
| i | iy | eat | ə | ə | but |
| ɪ | i | sit | ə | ə | above |

## Diphthongs

| | | |
|---|---|---|
| aɪ | ay | tie |
| aʊ | aw | how |
| ɔɪ | oy | boy |

In addition to the symbols shown here, many texts contain other variations of these two systems. It is important, therefore, that you study carefully the pronunciation symbols in any text that you use.

Since the IPA has been the basis of many transcription systems and is widely known throughout the world, we will use its symbols in future examples in this Guide. The symbols will be within slant lines // to indicate that they represent the phonemes of the language. Phonetic symbols covering the phonemes plus the non-meaningful variations of them are generally enclosed in brackets []. For example, the phoneme /p/ is pronounced in a slightly different manner if it is in initial position; if it is the second consonant in a cluster (e.g., sport) ; or if it is in final position. These variations of the phonemes are called *allophones*.

In working with phonetic and phonemic symbols, it is important to remember that no symbols can help a student produce a sound. What is significant is that we, the teachers, know 1) the *sound* associated with the symbol and 2) the techniques to help our students *hear* and *produce* the sound and distinguish it from all others. It is also essential that we and our students attach the same sound to a symbol or a gesture. Symbols can serve as memory clues when the students do their assignments or as aids to them when they look a word up in a dictionary.

We should know all we can about the sound system of the language we are teaching and how the sounds are produced, particularly those which could cause a difference in meaning in the language. The sounds /i/ and /ɪ/ between /b/ and /t/ in *beat* and *bit*, for example, are phonemes because they alone make the meaning difference in the two words. We know that /p/ and /b/ are phonemes because in the words *pit* and *bit* only the sounds /p/ and /b/ make the meaning difference.

Each language has its own phonemes. In some cases, however, a similar phoneme may exist in the native language of your learners and in the language you are teaching, but it may be articulated differently or it may exist in a different position within a word. In English we can put together (cluster) /sk/ at the beginning of a word (e.g., school). Spanish speakers never have that cluster in one syllable at the beginning of a word and therefore will find it difficult to produce. (The terminal "s" sound in a syllable is always preceded by a vowel.)

Phonemic too, as we shall see, are stress, intonation, and pause (juncture). To illustrate, let us examine each of the components of the English phonemic system in turn. We will start with the sounds: the "vowels" and "consonants."

What makes a difference in sounds? Several things:

1. The vibration of the vocal cords. Pronounce /b/ several times putting your hands on your throat. Now pronounce /p/ several times. They were vibrating for /b/. They were not vibrating for /p/, were they? We call sounds which are made with the vocal cords vibrating *voiced* sounds. All vowels are voiced. When the vocal cords do not vibrate, we say the sounds are *voiceless* or *unvoiced*.

The *voiced consonant phonemes* in IPA symbols are /b/, /d/, /g/, /l/, /m/, /n/, /ŋ/, /r/, /ð/, /v/, /w/, /y/, /z/, /ʒ/, /dʒ/.

The *voiceless consonants* are /f/, /h/, /k/, /p/, /s/, /ʃ/, /t/, /θ/, /tʃ/.

Notice the pairs of voiced and unvoiced consonants (the voiced consonant is first): b/p; d/t; g/k; ð/θ; v/f; z/s; ʒ/ʃ; dʒ/tʃ.

2. Does the breath come out of the mouth or the nose? In the nasal sounds /m/, /n/, and /ŋ/, the breath comes out of the nose, doesn't it?

3. Is the air stopped in our mouths as we make a sound? Could it continue? Where is it stopped? (If it is stopped, for example, we may call the sound a *stop*.) *T* is a stop. (Try it!) *M* is a *continuant*.

4. What happens to the position of the vocal organs as we make a sound? Where do the vocal organs come together? To what other position do they move? What is the position of the tongue, of the lips, of the teeth? In other words, what about the *articulation?*

Let us examine the *vowels*:

We studied French with a vowel triangle like this. It is just as useful in the study of other foreign languages. Notice how your tongue moves from front to back; notice how your lips become more rounded or less rounded as your jaw opens and closes.

45

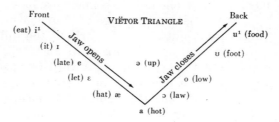

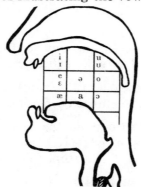

The following vowel chart, although in another form, gives the same information about the tongue position for the phonemes shown and will help you to help your students make the sounds.

| The highest part of the tongue is | | front | central part | back | |
|---|---|---|---|---|---|
| high | in the | i¹<br>ɪ | | u¹<br>ʊ | of the mouth |
| mid | | e<br>ɛ | ə | o | |
| low | | æ | a | ɔ | |

Still another way of illustrating the vowels is this:

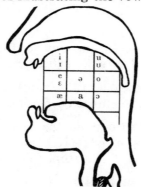

As you make each vowel sound, study the position of your lips carefully. Are they rounded or stretched back?

All the simple vowels (above) can occur alone or with /y/, /w/, or /h/² so that the tongue glides (goes) from the vowel position to the /y/, /w/, or /h/ or from the /y/, /w/, or /h/ to the vowel position. Pronounce: toy/tɔɪ/; ice/aɪs/; how/haʊ/; hoop/hup/.

---

¹ Simple /i/ and /u/ are not considered phonemic by some linguists because some English speakers do not use them in their dialects.

² /y/, /w/, and /h/ are sometimes called semi-vowels. These combinations with /y/, /w/, and /h/ are sometimes called "complex vowel nuclei."

46

We know, then, that: 1) The vowels are voiced. 2) The differences in sounds are produced by the shape and position of the tongue in the mouth. The tongue may be pushed toward the front, center, or back of the mouth but its center may be relatively high, mid, or low. 3) The shape of the lips — rounded or stretched — also brings about differences in sound.

Let us turn our attention to the *consonants*. We will examine, as we have pointed out, whether these are voiced or unvoiced; what happens to the air in the mouth; what the positions of the tongue, lips, and teeth are.

Study this chart carefully. We have purposely indicated simple terminology that you could use in teaching your students.

| Passage of air | Vibration of Vocal Cords | Two Lips | Lower Lip-Upper Teeth | Tip of Tongue-Upper Teeth | Tip of Tongue-Back of Upper Teeth | Front of Tongue-Front of Palate | Back of Tongue-Soft Palate | The Vocal Cords |
|---|---|---|---|---|---|---|---|---|
| Completely stopped | No — Voiceless | p | | | t | | k | |
| | Yes — Voiced | b | | | d | | g | |
| Two sounds: A stop followed by a continuant | No — Voiceless | | | | | tʃ | | |
| | Yes — Voiced | | | | | dʒ | | |
| Through a narrow opening | No — Voiceless | | f | θ | s | ʃ | | |
| | Yes — Voiced | | v | ð | z | ʒ | | |
| Through side of tongue | No — Voiceless | | | | | | | |
| | Yes — Voiced | | | | l | | | |
| Through nose | No — Voiceless | | | | | | | |
| | Yes — Voiced | m | | | n | ŋ | | |
| No stoppage | No — Voiceless | | | | | | | h |
| | Yes — Voiced | w | | | r* | y | | |

Three factors enter into the formation of a consonant: 1) the vibration or lack of vibration of the vocal cords; 2) the point of obstruction of air in the mouth, if at all; and 3) the points of meeting (the *articulation*) of the lips and the relation of the tongue to the teeth and the palate.

---

* Tongue curls toward back.

And now, let us look at *stress, intonation,* and *pause (juncture),* which also produce differences in meaning.

### Stress

*Stress* is the name given to the relative degree of loudness of a part (syllable) of a word, or of a whole word, or of a syllable within an utterance.

In English we may distinguish two kinds of stress. There is *word stress* and *sentence stress.* Each word or word phrase has one primary stress. We say agaín, néver, ápple tree, bús route, goodbýe, go ín, try ón, come báck. Word stress can be phonemic. Study, for example, "cóntract" (noun) and "contráct" (verb). Word stress is often called "accent."

There are four possible phrase* stresses in English:
1) the loudest — called primary — usually marked ´
2) next to the loudest — called secondary — usually marked ʌ
3) the third loudest or medium soft — called tertiary — usually marked ˋ
4) the least loud — called weak — usually marked ᴜ
(Many books, however, do not mark weak stress.)

Let us examine *sentence stress.* In a sentence like "I'm studying English," the stress is on the *E* of English, isn't it? Every sentence has at least one stress, but it may have two or more, depending on the length of the sentence or the meaning the speaker wants to convey. A sentence like "What are you doing?," for example, may have stress on *What* and stress on *do.* A short answer such as "Yes, I did" may have stress on *Yes* and on *did.* Almost any word in an English sentence can be stressed depending upon the situation and on the meaning one wishes to convey.

Stressed syllables are usually *longer* and *louder,* thus giving English the rhythm we say is characteristic of the language.

While rhythm is not phonemic, it is a most important feature of connected speech. Rhythm, which depends on the accented syllables in each utterance, is rather regularly spaced in English. In speaking, we try to maintain the same time between one stressed syllable and the next stressed syllable in the utterance. In order to maintain the rhythm, we say the unstressed (unaccented) syllables faster. We do this by crowding the unstressed syllables together and by pronouncing all or most of the unstressed vowels as /ə/ or not pronouncing them at all. Notice how people normally say a sentence like:
"What are you going to do?" /wat ə yə goɪŋ tə du/

---

* No single word has four stresses, but word combinations or phrases do; e.g., élĕvătŏr ŏpĕrătŏr.

## *Intonation*

Intonation is the name given to the levels of pitch (the relative height of the voice) in a sentence. When we talk about intonation, we include, too, the rising of the voice or the fading of the voice into silence at the end of an utterance as well as the sustained pitch of the voice in certain sentences we will examine later.[1]

There are four relative levels of pitch in English.[2] (We use the term "relative" because the height to which the voice rises varies from speaker to speaker.) These are marked in different ways by various linguists. Some use 1 for the lowest pitch; some use 1 for the highest pitch. Some use lines. Some use arrows. We will use lines and numbers (to reinforce the lines). Most people start to speak at pitch level 2. Pitch level 2 is *normal* level. The voice then usually rises to 3 and then remains at 3 in certain types of questions, or falls to 1. Level 3 is *above normal;* level 1 is *below normal.* Level 3 is usually (but not necessarily) the level of the stressed part of the sentence. Level 4 is way above normal. It is usually used to express emotion, anger, surprise, delight, etc.

This is how we will mark our examples:

$_2$What are you| do‌ng ? ³ ‾|₁

When the word on which there is stress is the *last* word in the sentence and is a *one-syllable* word, we use a *diagonal* line to show that the voice glides from one position to another. Notice:

$_2$When did he| le‌ave ? ³ ‾₁

There are *two* important intonation patterns in English. It is desirable to concentrate *only* on these two in teaching English as a second or foreign language at the beginning and intermediate levels of the elementary and secondary schools and at the beginning college level.

1) We use *rising-falling* intonation in —
   a) Simple statements
   $_2$ He came to| see| me. ³ ‾₁
   b) Commands
   $_2$ Go to the| do‌or. ³ ‾₁

---

[1] Some linguists prefer to call these "terminal contours" since they mark the end or termination of an utterance.

[2] In tone languages (e.g., Mandarin Chinese) the pitch or voice level *within a word* or within a syllable can be phonemic. For example, *shih* with a high rising tone means "ten"; with a low falling tone it means "scholar."

c) Question-word questions

$_2$ Why did he leave? $^3$ $_1$

d) Attached (tag) questions* sometimes (when we're *not* asking for information).

$_2$ He didn't go, did he? $^3$ $^3$ $_1$

The fall and fade-out of the voice is often designated by a /#/ (double cross).

e.g., $_2$ Why did he leave # $^3$ $_1$

2) We use *rising* intonation at the end of questions which do *not* begin with a question word.

Examples: $_2$ Is he there? $^3$

$_2$ Can you get it for me? $^3$

Notice that in sentences with *rising* intonation, everything that follows the *rise* (the stressed syllable) is also pronounced on the high pitch or level.

The rise and fade-out of the voice is often designated by a /||/ (double bar).

e.g., $_2$ Can you get it for me || $^3$

We also use *rising* intonation in direct address and in introductions. Notice:

$_2$ Mr. Brown, $_2$ this is Miss Jones. $^3$ $^3$

$_2$ How are you, $_2$ Mrs. Jones? $^3$ $^3$ $_1$

In a *series*, we use *rising* intonation until the last item where we use *rising-falling* intonation.

$_2$ I need books, $_2$ pencils, $_2$ and crayons. $^3$ $^3$ $^3$ $_1$

Sustained pitch in utterances is designated by a /|/ (single bar). It is used where, in *writing*, we would ordinarily place a comma or a dash. Notice:

$_2$ Are you there | John? $^3$ $^3$

The pitch of *there* and the pitch of *John* are the same, but if you

---

* In attached (tag) questions, when we're *asking for information*, we use *rising* intonation. Notice:

$_2$ He didn't go, $_2$ did he? $^3$ $^3$

50

say the sentence aloud, you will note that you have prolonged the sound of *there* more than if the sentence had been "Are you there?"

One last brief word before we leave the important subject of intonation. A contrast such as ₂Was he‾ angry? and ₂Was‾he angry!₁ will show immediately that *intonation* is phonemic.

### Internal juncture or pause

Another important feature of the English sound system which makes a difference in meaning is *internal juncture*. The word *pause* is often used to indicate juncture.

Say: The night rate /naɪt + ret/ is cheap.
The nitrate /naɪtret/ is cheap.

Say: Ice cream /aɪs + krim/
I scream /aɪ + skrim/

We would say that, in the first sentence, there is *plus juncture* between *night* and *rate*. In the second pair of utterances, the *plus juncture* comes between *ice* and *cream* in example 1; it comes between *I* and *scream* in example 2. There is no difference in the pronunciation of the other sounds, is there? The difference in meaning is caused *only* by the slight pause.

There are other features of the sound system which should be taught, of course, along with dialogue dramatization and oral reading, where appropriate. Sarcasm, anger, joy, disappointment, sorrow, and the entire gamut of emotions will be learned as students hear teachers or others convey such emotional tones or as they listen to recordings.

One other remark needs to be made about the sound system. As far as speech is concerned, what is considered a sentence? Look at this example:

Question: "Where did you go yesterday?"
Possible answer: "To the movies."

For the purposes of *speech* ₂To the‾movies,₁ where there is a complete fading out of the voice after ₁, may be considered a sentence.

Some linguists distinguish between *sentences* (a group of words with a subject and predicate) and *nonsentences*. In order to avoid discussion, the term "utterance" is used more and more frequently. An utterance is the name given to any meaningful act of speech which includes the features of the sound system we have been discussing (i.e., pitch, rising or fading of the voice, stress, or pause). For example, in an exchange such as "Who came in?" . . . "John," *John* is an utterance.

We have seen that *sound, stress, juncture, rhythm,* and *intonation* are at the very core of spoken language. All are important in understanding and speaking a foreign language and all of them must be taught. Since the teacher must be concerned with helping his students learn these features, we will have more to say about the method of teaching them in Chapter III.

### Some Remarks on Grammar

In this section we will confine ourselves to pointing out only some of the basic features of the English system. We will do so by presenting some examples of speech and posing some questions.

— We had indicated earlier that an important aspect of the system is the use of *word order.*

*Compare:* Mary is home. Is Mary home?
*Can you say:* "Spoke to I him" and be understood?
*Where is your word 'not,'* before or after 'is'?:
He is not (or He isn't) an American.
Wouldn't "I go every morning to the park" sound "foreign" to the ears of an English speaker?
Is *a station bus* the same as *a bus station?*

— English uses *inflection;* that is, it may add or take away something from a word or change the form of the word to indicate number (singular or plural), tense (present or past),* possession, etc.

Notice: The *boy* is here. The *boys* are here.
The *boy* is in the classroom. The *boy's* book is in the classroom.
This is *my* book. This is *mine.*
*I* gave *him* a book. *He* gave *me* a book.
I *talk* to John every day. I *talked* to John yesterday.
I *sing* every day. I *sang* yesterday.
Sally is *pretty* but Joan is prett*ier.*

—*Derivation* is also an important linguistic phenomenon. Notice how the *slot* into which the derived words fit changes.
1. The *code* is not clear.
2. Will you *encode* the message?

1. He's a *kind* man.
2. *Kindness* is a virtue.
3. He spoke *kindly.*

— Most languages use *function* or *structure words* to express

---

* Linguists today prefer to talk about two *tenses* only. They consider expressions like "I've talked (to John)" or "I had talked (to John)" *verb phrases.*

relationships or meanings. There are about 154 function words in English. Some of those used most frequently are:

1. *Determiners:* a, an, the;* this, some, etc.
   > Give me *a* book (any). Give me *the* book (one already mentioned).
2. *Auxiliaries:* do, have, be.
   > I want to go. I *don't* want to go.
   > I saw him. I*'ve* seen him many times.
   > John wrote the letter. The letter *was* written by John.
3. *Prepositions:* at, by, for, from, of, on, in, with (the most frequent).
   > The book is *on* the desk. The book is *in* the desk.
4. *Conjunctions* (coordinating and subordinating) : and, but, until, although.
   > I want the book *and* the pencil.
   > I want the book *but* I don't want the pencil.
   > I'll wait *until* he comes.
5. *Interrogatives:* when, where, etc. (often called "Wh" words)
   > *When* did you go? *Where* did you go?
6. *Degree words* and *intensifiers:* more, most, very, too.
   > May I have *more* bread?
   > It's *very* hot today. It's *too* hot to go out today.
7. *Modals:* English uses *modals* — may, etc. — with verbs to indicate different degrees of reality or possibility.
   Consider:
   > I *may* go to the movies.
   > I *might* go. (a little less probable)
   > I *can* go.
   > I *should* go. I *ought* to go.
   > I *must* go. I *have* to go.

Notice these additional examples of features of English grammar:

1. I like *cheese.*     Give me a *cheese sandwich.*
2. Give me the *lamp oil.*     Give me the *oil lamp.*
3. It's a *long foot.*     It's a *foot long.*
4. He walked *along the street.*     He *walked along.*
5. He *took* his coat.     He *took off* his coat.
6. *Look! There's* an airplane.     *There's* an airplane in the sky.
7. *It's* cold today.     Poor dog. *It's* cold.
8. *Go* to the shop every day.     *I go* to the shop every day.
9. *Sing.*     *Let's sing.*

---

\* *A, an,* and *the* are generally called "articles."

| | |
|---|---|
| 10. The *man's legs* are long. | The *legs of the table* are high. |
| 11. The boy is *tall.* | The boys are *tall.* |
| 12. He's a *tall* boy. | He's a *very tall* boy. |
| 13. *You're* going, *aren't* you? | You're *not* going, *are you?* |
| 14. *One* never knows. | Let me have the *one* in the window. |

Notice these responses:

| | |
|---|---|
| 1. Are you going to be a doctor? | Yes, I *am.* |
| 2. What did you do yesterday? | I *studied.* |
| 3. Do you think it's going to rain? | I think *so.* |
| 4. Do you have *any pencils?* | Yes, here's *one.* |
| 5. Who*'s* at the door? | Mary *and* John. |
| 6. You like rice, *don't you?* | Yes, I *do.* |

The basic sentence types in English are the following:

*Two parts:* Boys / eat.
The little boys at school / like to eat all the time.

*Three parts:* John / wrote / a letter. (This is a favorite sentence type.)
The men in the office / have had to write / long letters to their clients.

*Four parts:* John / wrote / me / a letter.
The women of the Colonial Association / are going to write / all the people they know / several letters.

Kernel (basic) sentences are *declarative, simple, active* (e.g., "The owner built a garage."). Kernel sentences may undergo many transformations and they may be combined with other kernel sentences and again transformed. Notice some derived sentences possible from the sentence above, either alone or in combination with others.

The *(new)** owner built a garage.
The owner built a *(large)* garage.
The owner *(may)* build a garage.
The owner (may) *have* built a garage.
*There's* the garage — over there.
*There's a new* garage on (his) property.
*Did* the owner *build* a garage?
*Who* built a garage?
*What* did the owner *build?*
The garage *was built* by the new owner.
*By whom was* the garage *built?*

---

* The parentheses indicate that other words might be used.

54

The owner built a garage (*quickly*).
The owner built a garage on *his* property.
*He* built a garage on his property.
The owner *who built the garage* had just bought the property.
*Having built* the garage, the owner decided to sell it.
*Building* the garage was *very* expensive for the new owner.
The owner built the garage *but* he sold it right away.
Let's look at the garage *which the* new owner built.
He said: "*Build* a garage for me."
He said: "*Let's build* a garage."
He asked that a garage *be built*.
He said that he *wanted* a garage *built*.
    etc., etc.

These examples were obviously not intended to cover all the features of language. They will serve, however, to point up, particularly to native speakers who have never had to think about form, order, inflection, or function, some of the more important characteristics of language which signal meaning, and the relationships which exist in many languages between deep structures and surface structures.

The following brief alphabetical listing of grammatical categories, functions, and transformation operations found in many languages includes some already noted in the examples above. It is placed here for your convenience in preparing drills and dialogues and as a reminder to you of material you may have presented which should be reintroduced wherever and whenever logical and feasible. Some of these categories, functions, and operations may not exist in the language you are teaching while others not included here may exist. Add, delete, combine. Use this list in the way it best suits you.

### Grammatical Categories and Functions:

Adjectives (e.g., comparative, indefinite, interrogative)
Adverbs (e.g., of frequency, manner, place, time)
Articles (e.g., definite, indefinite, partitive)
Auxiliary verbs
Clauses (e.g., conditional, coordinate, subordinate)
Commands
Comparisons
Compound sentences
Conditional sentences
Conjunctions (coordinating, subordinating)
Demonstratives
Determiners (e.g., articles, indefinites, possessives)
Direct objects

Emphatic statements or utterances
Exclamatory statements or utterances
Family names
Frequency adverbs
Future
Gerunds
Impersonal pronouns
Indirect objects
Indirect speech (e.g., commands, questions, statements)
Intensifiers
Interrogative sentences, utterances and words
Modals
Modifiers
Nouns (e.g., as modifiers of nouns, countable, non-countable, expressing possession, proper names)
Numerals (cardinal, ordinal)
Objects (direct, indirect, of prepositions)
Participles
Partitives
Passive voice
Past tense
Phrases (adjectival, adverbial)
Possessives
Prepositions (e.g., accompaniment, direction)
Present (continuous, perfect, simple)
Progressives
Pronouns (e.g., demonstratives, indefinite, interrogative, reciprocal, reflexive, relative)
Questions (e.g., attached, inverted, *Wh*)
Reciprocal words
Requests
Statements
Subjects (e.g., agreement with verbs, contractions)
There (in unstressed position)
Verbals (e.g., gerund, infinitive, participle)
Verbs (e.g., aspects, moods, orthographic changing, sequence of tenses, tenses, two-word, three-word)

*Some basic transformations* (with English examples)

1. Affirmative — He's not a student. Yes, *he is* a student.
2. Emphatic — I *do have* a book.
3. Negative — I'm *not* thirsty.
4. Passive — The house *was built* by Jack.
5. Questions — *Is he* a student?

56

6. *Wh* — (*Who*) is he?
7. *There* (unstressed) — *There's a* book on the table.

*Two-String transformations* (derived from *two* kernel sentences)
1. Adjectival — He's a *rich* man.
2. Adverbial — He went *there in a hurry.*
3. Complement — He saw *Mary* singing.
4. Conjunctive — The man *and* his friend were walking.
5. Embedded *Wh* — I'm not sure *where* the teacher may be.
6. Gerundive — *Swimming* is a sport Harry enjoys.
7. Indirect object — He gave *us* the book.
8. Infinitive — Harry likes to *swim. To know* him is *to love* him.
9. Modal — You *must* take the medicine.
10. Relative — The suit *(that)* I like had wide lapels.
11. Subordinate — I'll go *unless* it rains. I'll go *after* the rain stops.
12. That — *That* she's over seventy is obvious.

## Lexicon

Following are several comments with respect to the *lexicon,* or the vocabulary of the language:

Content words become meaningful only when studied and considered in context with all the other words which surround them and which help give them their meaning. (This is one aspect of the science of semantics.) Note, for example:

Show me your hand.
Hand in your papers.
Language is handed down from mother to child.

Notice some possibilities with the word "time":

What *time* is it?
It's *time* to leave.
Have a good *time.*
He's gone there several *times.*
He fell on hard *times.*
Four *times* two is eight.
I'll *time* the race.
etc., etc.

Linguistic science has underscored the fact that some of the traditional definitions such as "A noun is the name of a person, place, or thing" are not accurate. Is *hand* a noun in the sentence above? What part of speech is *time?*

The word *get,* for example, has over two hundred meanings. Notice:  Here's five cents. Get the paper.
Get the paper. It's on the table.
He got a good mark on the test.

In *Teaching and Learning English as a Foreign Language,* Fries divided the context words of language into *things, actions,* and *qualities.* He further subdivided words into *simple, compound,* and *derived.* Let us examine several samples:

*Content words*

Things:
    Simple     — door
    Compound — doorknob
    Derived    — arrival, goodness, ability

Actions:
    Simple     — run, walk
    Compound — call up, take off, put on
    Derived    — enjoy, soften, harden

Qualities:
    Simple     — true, false
    Derived    — misty, childish, broken

In addition, many languages have two- and three-word verb combinations and idioms whose meanings cannot be derived from the meaning of the individual words and which may present special problems. Notice: (1) The women *made up.* (They put on powder and lipstick, or They resumed pleasant relations after a quarrel.) (2) He *took off* his coat. He *took* his coat *off.* (We can say, He *took* it *off* but not He took off it.)

## SOME ASPECTS OF CULTURE

Before discussing the more formal, systematic aspects of culture to be included in the curriculum, it may be desirable to examine definitions of the term "culture" as it is used today by scientists — not only by anthropologists whose main concern is the study of culture (and language as it reflects culture), but also by sociologists, linguists, and psychologists.

— "Culture is that complex whole which includes knowledge, beliefs, art, morals, customs, and any other capacities and habits acquired by man as a member of society." [1]

— "All those historically created designs for living, explicit, implicit, rational, irrational, and non-rational." [2]

Many students of culture acknowledge that culture like language — one of the components of culture — is a *structured* system of actions

---

[1] Taylor, A., in *Language in Culture.* H. Hoijer (ed.).
[2] Kluckhohn, C. *Mirror for Man.*

or patterned behavior. But just as in language, we distinguish between the code — "la langue" — and the idiolect — "la parole" — each individual's personal use of the code — so, in culture it is important that we help our students distinguish between the cultural norms, beliefs, or habits of the majority within the speech community and the individual or group deviations from some of these norms.

A simple diagram may bring this fact home to our students:

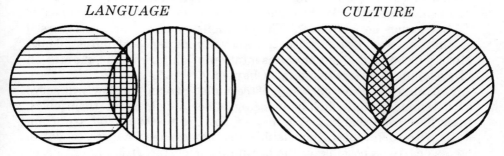

LANGUAGE                    CULTURE

Several brief observations should be made before we list cultural topics from several sources:

1. Culture embodies the human being's way of adjusting to his environment. Since many features of nature are "similar" in many parts of the world and since "homo loquens" is a member of the human race, it is not surprising to find that all human beings in the world share seventy-five traits in common![1] To dwell only on cultural differences in the classroom is to negate or weaken one of the major values of foreign language study, which is to make students aware of the *universality of human experience.*

2. The literature of the foreign country is perhaps the best bridge to an understanding of the foreign country. The environment, the characters' adjustments to that environment, the thoughts, ideals, values, habits, and speech of those who people a literary work are all reflected in it. Since at the secondary school level it is unrealistic in most cases to expect our students to read a piece of literature in the unadapted original, might it not be desirable to study translations of the masterpieces but to encourage oral and written book reports in the *target* language? Again, it is a question of being flexible and judicious and asking ourselves: "What values derived from such a procedure will accrue to our students?" "Would positive, motivating attitudes be engendered?"

3. In harmony with our belief[2] that students should be enabled

---

[1] Carroll, J. B., *Language and Thought.*
[2] See pp. 17-18.

to discuss their native culture with their foreign-speaking friends at the same time that they are provided with a real experiential content through which and around which they can make use of their knowledge of the foreign language, we are including topics related to any native culture. These should also be made part of the curriculum. At the beginning level of learning in particular, culture should be presented, discussed, or merely alluded to in two parallel streams: e.g., "What does X (the foreign boy) have for breakfast?" "What do you usually have?" "What games do the students play after school?" "What games do you play?" The questions could, in fact, be reversed so that we would start with the known experience of our students. More will be said about the presentation of culture in the chapter on "Developing Cultural Insights," Chapter V.

4. Many of the topics suggested under Stream I below will serve as a reminder that all human beings like to talk about themselves, their likes, and dislikes. Whether or not the textbook you are using deals with such topics, you should teach names, ages, addresses, dates, etc., as early as possible in the beginning semester. It is important, of course, that you help students recognize "taboos" related to any of these aspects as, for example, in asking a woman her age.

What should be included in the curriculum?

*Stream I* — Aspects of native culture for *conversation* and for *comparison* or *contrast* with similar aspects in the target culture

1. Introductions and identification
   a) Greetings, leave-takings, introductions
   b) Identification of self and others
   c) Address and age
2. The immediate classroom
   a) Names and location of parts of the room
   b) Names of instructional materials
   c) Identification of activities (reading, writing, etc.)
   d) The program (hours for various subject areas, activities in and out of class)
   e) Common classroom expressions
3. The school
   a) Location of rooms and special places in the building
   b) People in the building (names, functions, special services)
   c) Rules and regulations (fire drills, time of arrival, use of stairs)
   d) School activities such as club programs, general organization, assembly programs, newspapers, magazine
4. The family
   a) Members

b) Relationships and ages
c) The home
　　1) Rooms and their uses
　　2) Furnishings
　　3) Cleanliness (how, who)
　　4) Safety
d) Occupations of various members
e) Meals (table setting, formulas)
f) Daily health routines
g) Clothing (including seasonal changes necessary)
h) Recreational activities
5. The immediate community of the school and home
　a) Homes
　b) Non-residential buildings (offices, movies, library, etc.)
　c) Transportation facilities (directions, tickets)
　d) Communication facilities (telephone, mail, newspaper, radio, television)
　e) Consumer services (stores, banks, etc.)
　f) Local government agencies (post office, police station, firehouse)
　g) Places of recreational interest (parks, libraries, community centers, movies, theaters, outdoor cafés)
　h) Educational opportunities (for parents as well)
　i) Places of worship
　j) Formulas used in telephoning
　k) Current events
6. The wider community
　a) Health services
　b) Transportation and communication
　c) Government — city, state, national
　d) Nearby centers — rural and urban
　e) Current events
　f) Places of recreation
7. Our cultural heritage
　a) Holidays
　b) Heroes and history
　c) Historical documents and speeches
　d) Songs, rhymes, proverbs
　e) Music, literature, and art forms
　f) Scientific developments
8. Personal guidance (This topic is treated in greater detail because of its importance to secondary school students.)
　a) Social:
　　1) Recreational facilities (addresses, special features, fees or qualifications for admission)

2) Social relations — living together, working together, and playing together with others in the school and community
3) Customs:
   a) Greetings and leave-takings (with peers, elders, children)
   b) Foods — time for meals, types of restaurants, special types
   c) Holidays — dates, gifts, visiting, greeting cards
   d) Dress — seasonal, formal, informal, special occasion
   e) Communication — letters, telegrams, telephones
   f) Transportation — reservations, importance of arrival time
   g) Business forms and legal practices
   h) Courtship and marriage
   i) Behavior patterns in various situations — social, educational, vocational
   j) Consumer education — installment buying, credit borrowing
   k) Social amenities in different situations
b) Educational:
   1) Opportunities for advanced study (college and university orientation)
   2) Requirements for admission to institutions of higher learning (physical, educational, other)
   3) Scholarships
   4) Training for specialized careers
   5) Adult education
   6) Library, museum, and other facilities
c) Vocational:
   1) Opportunities for employment after graduation (part-time employment)
   2) Requirements for various types of employment
   3) Means of finding employment (agencies, newspapers, governmental agencies, letters, friends, etc.)
   4) Filling out forms such as applications for employment, social security, pension
   5) Getting a job (dress and conduct at interview)
   6) Holding a job (punctuality, performance, human relationships)
   7) Labor laws, taxes, pension, rights and responsibilities
   8) Specialized vocabulary
d) Leisure-time activities:
   1) Community facilities
   2) Hobbies — kinds (indoor, outdoor)
   3) Arts, crafts, dancing, sports — where to learn, cost, etc.
   4) Private recreational facilities and clubs

     5) Popular sports in the community or city (participant or spectator)
     6) Club programs in schools
  e) Moral and spiritual values:
     1) Principles of human dignity
     2) Individual rights and responsibilities
     3) Places of worship — addresses, denominations, special language services (if these exist)

9. Miscellaneous
  a) Expressions of time
  b) Days of the week
  c) Months of the year
  d) Weather and safety
  e) Seasons
  f) Weights, sizes, measurements, money
  g) Formulas of courtesy, agreement, disagreement, regret, surprise, excitement, pleasure, etc.

*Stream II* — The target culture

We are including several lists of cultural topics for your consideration. You will undoubtedly find many others which will also suggest areas of interest, study, and emphasis.

1. Brooks Profile[1]
  a) Symbolism (language, literature, art, religion)
  b) Values (conscience, philosophy)
  c) Authority
  d) Order
  e) Ceremony
  f) Love
  g) Honor (standards of personal conduct)
  h) Humor
  i) Beauty
  j) Spirit (man's awareness of man)

2. Cadoux[2] topics (abridged and adapted) — Substitute your target country.

    Theme I — (France) in the Contemporary World
      I) The influence of (France) on your culture
        A) Contemporary Culture

---

[1] Brooks, Nelson, "Teaching Culture in the Foreign Language Classroom."
[2] Cadoux, R., *French for Secondary Schools.*

63

a) Products imported
b) Social customs, dress, furniture, language
B) Our heritage
a) The role of (France)
b) Place names, areas where (French) is spoken
c) Great men in our country of (French) descent

II) Areas of the world where (French) is the official language

III) (France), the nation
A) Geography (physical, economic)
B) The capital (location, importance)
C) Widely known social customs (the café, holidays)

Theme II — The (France) of the (French)

I) The (French) way of life
A) Daily life in (France)
a) Houses and apartments:
1) Types of construction (rooms, gardens, elevators, concierge)
2) The streets and residential areas
b) Family life:
1) Members of the family
2) Family meals and recreational activities
3) Marriage
c) Education in (France):
1) General attitude toward education
2) Free and compulsory education
3) Government control of education
4) Various types of schools (elementary schools, secondary school, specialized schools, etc.)
5) The school day in elementary and secondary schools
6) The examination system
7) Recreational activities
8) Universities and special schools for art and technical education
d) Recreation:
1) The family as the center of social life
2) The social visit
3) The café as principal meeting place
4) Theaters, concerts, festivals of music, radio, and television

5) Newspapers, magazines, and books
6) Sports (football, cricket, tennis, etc.)
7) Vacations and resort areas

e) The (French) worker:
1) General attitude toward work
2) The "artisan"
3) The industrial worker (hours of work, unions, protection by legislation)
4) The agricultural worker (including ownership of small or large farms)
5) General social security benefits

f) Holidays and customs:
1) Legal holidays and others
2) Fairs
3) Folk dances

g) Cuisine:
1) Importance of culinary art in (French) life
2) Characteristic dishes and drinks
3) Breakfast, lunch, and dinner
4) Specialties of local regions

h) Transportation and communication
i) The money system
j) The metric system
k) Religion

II) Highlights in the history of the country
A) Early invaders and their influence on the ethnic composition
B) Great personalities
C) Outstanding events

III) Historical monuments
A) In the capital and in its environs
B) In the provinces

IV) The language
A) Its origins
B) The influences of other languages

V) The government of (France)
A) Its actual form
a) The legislative bodies
b) Local government (its composition and principal officers)

B) The community
  a) Important departments, territories, and member states
  b) Their relationships to the central government
  c) Products important to the economy
C) The citizens (voting and taxation)

Theme III — (France) in the Development of Civilization
  I) Contributions to civilization
    A) Literature
      a) Important writers and their works
      b) Outstanding schools and trends
      c) The major literary prizes
      d) Nobel prize winners of recent years
    B) The arts (painting, sculpture, architecture, etc.)
      a) Outstanding personalities (their works and contributions)
      b) Important schools of art (classic, romantic, impressionists, etc.)
      c) Famous museums and art galleries
    C) The dramatic arts
      a) The outstanding plays and playwrights
      b) Internationally known films (directors, inventors)
    D) Music
      a) Outstanding composers (their compositions and contributions to the development of music)
      b) Famous performers and conductors
      c) Popular music and light opera or concert music
    E) Science (chemistry, biology, medicine, mathematics, physics, etc.)
      a) Outstanding scientists
      b) Practical inventions (in motors, industrial machines, aviation, etc.)
      c) Atomic science today
  II) The (French) community
    A) The use of the language
    B) The establishment of schools, institutes, universities
    C) The spread of cultural patterns
  III) Institutions to promote the spread of culture
    State-subsidized centers (theaters, concert groups), schools and their implication in spreading the (French) culture at home and abroad

IV) Democratic ideas and institutions
   A) The revolutionary period
      a) Great thinkers
      b) Declaration of the rights of man
   B) The Parliament, voting, civil rights
   C) The many political parties

V) Institutions to promote research and to set standards

3. Hall and Trager Profile[1]
   a) Interaction
   b) Association
   c) Subsistence
   d) Bisexuality
   e) Temporality
   f) Territoriality
   g) Learning
   h) Play
   i) Defense
   j) Exploitation (of resources)

4. Nostrand Topics[2] (abridged and adapted)
   a) Biological and psychological integration of the human organism and its interaction with the environment
   b) Personality structure (thoughts, feelings)
   c) Organization of the society (shared norms of behavior)
   d) Shared patterns of meaning (system of values, problem-solving techniques)
   e) Historic achievements of people in philosophy and religion
   f) Achievements in sciences and mathematics
   g) Gestures, intonation, distances maintained
   h) Humor
   i) Art forms (literature)
   j) Social institutions
   k) Society's adaptation to the geography and climate

Suggestions for presenting the topics and for correlating them with other subjects in the school-wide curriculum will be discussed in Chapter V.

---

[1] Hall, E. and Trager, G., in Brooks, "Teaching Culture in the Foreign Language Classroom."

[2] Nostrand, H., "A Second Culture: New Imperatives for American Education," in *Foreign Language Teaching*, J. Michel (ed.).

## Suggestions

— Prepare ten facial diagrams in profile. Indicate the speech organs.

— Indicate the vowel positions in the target language on a facial profile.

— On several facial front diagrams, indicate the spread of the lips in the pronunciation of vowels in the target language.

— Indicate the vowel positions in the target language on the Viëtor Triangle.

— Make an inventory of the vowels in your students' native language. Contrast them with those of the target language.

— Make an inventory of the consonants in your students' native language. Contrast them with those of the target language.

— Prepare a chart similar to that on page 47 indicating the points of articulation for all the consonants in the target language.

— What are the main types of intonation in the target language? Give two examples of each. Mark the intonation in such a way that the melody of the voice would be immediately apparent to a learner.

— Select five lines of prose. Transcribe them in IPA symbols.

— Describe the articulation of five consonants in the target language.

— Describe the pronunciation of five vowels in the target language.

— Select five consonants which exist in different positions in the target language. Indicate the sequence (with examples) in which you would teach them.

— How is negation expressed in your native language? In the target language? Give five examples.

— Is derivation a feature of your target language? If so, select ten words and indicate possibly related words which can be derived from them.

— Show by using the words above in utterances that derivation also brings with it a functional shift — in other words, that the slots in which the derived words could be used differ.

— Select a word (e.g., "head"). Use it in several sentences. Indicate how its meaning depends on the context.

— List the most important function words in your target language.

— Using a common function word, give five examples of its use in authentic utterances. In what sequence would you present these uses? Which might be taught together?

— Prepare lists of ten words each in the foreign language used in special jobs or professions.

— Indicate ten *overt* cultural features shared by the majority of persons in your community.

— Indicate several beliefs held by the members of your community which might influence their attitude toward members of the target culture.

— Observe — and if possible speak to — five individual members of your community living in different social conditions. Find out what each has for breakfast on a work day, for example.

## Additional Reading

BROOKS, N. *Language and Language Learning.* New York: Harcourt, Brace & World, 1964.

FRIES, C. *Teaching and Learning English as a Foreign Language.* Ann Arbor, Mich.: U. of Michigan Press, 1948.

HALL, E. *The Silent Language.* Garden City, N.Y.: Doubleday, 1959.

HILL, A. *Introduction to Linguistic Structures.* New York: Harcourt, Brace & World, 1958.

KLUCKHOHN, C. *Mirror for Man.* New York: McGraw-Hill, 1949.

MEAD, M. *Continuity in Cultural Evolution.* New Haven, Conn.: Yale U. Press, 1964.

*Meaning and Role of Culture in Language Teaching.* Washington, D.C.: Georgetown U. Press, 1961.

STEVICK, E. *A Workbook in Language Teaching.* Nashville, Tenn.: Abingdon Press, 1964.

UNESCO. *The Teaching of Modern Languages.* Paris: UNESCO, 1955.

WYLIE, L., ed. "Six Cultures," in *Reports and Surveys in the Teaching of Modern Foreign Languages.* New York: MLA, 1962.

# III

# Teaching the Features
# of Language

## USING A VARIETY OF TECHNIQUES

While it is essential to teach the items of language and to develop communication abilities with attention to sequence and gradation, there is no one best way of introducing and giving practice in them. On the contrary, there are many generally accepted ways of introducing the sounds, structure, and vocabulary of the language, the normal forms of conversation, and the four communication skills.

Some teachers prefer to start by having students learn and dramatize a conversation or a dialogue in which the language items to be presented are included; some prefer to start by helping them read an advertisement, a comic strip, a letter, a diary, or interesting material of one kind or another; some start directly by giving the new structure in authentic utterances which are later included in a conversation; some start by telling well-known stories (fairy or folk tales) preferably with a repetitive motif; some may start by dramatizing an Action (a Gouin) Series, such as "I'm getting up; I'm going to the door; I'm opening the door," etc. You will notice that listening, speaking, and reading skills may be introduced and developed not only as a bridge to the understanding of the language items but also to make students aware of the place of the individual features within the language system and of their importance in normal communication.

The majority of teachers like to create situations in the classroom (using themselves or the students and their belongings) in which the language items for presentation are used realistically. Some props, such as books, pencils, clocks, and calendars, and the students' movements — going to the door, sitting, standing, writing, or drawing on the board — are used to clarify the new language item or concept, thus obviating the need for lengthy explanation in the native language.

The technique you use should depend on the age of your students, on their interests, on the feature or skill to be practiced, and on the length and major aims of your program. Each has merit. Many teachers today prefer the conversational approach, in which students hear, say, and study a short dialogue often to the point of memorization. They believe that the dialogue duplicates most closely the normal speech of native speakers. Whichever other technique you use to present any feature and whatever the needs of your students, provision should be made for giving them practice in using the language items in the normal forms of conversation (i.e., in listening to questions and answers, in making responses, and in participating in conversational exchanges of varying lengths).

You may prefer to vary your introductory technique depending on the bit of language or the subsidiary skill you are going to teach. With one, you may find it most desirable to start with a dialogue; with another, you may wish to start with a structure[1] in a situation you will devise and then (after you have practiced several examples) to incorporate it into a real conversation.

Certainly, within every unit of work which may contain two or more new sounds, structures, question types, etc., there should be provision for the study and dramatization of two or more dialogues of four to eight utterances. One dialogue could serve to introduce the new sounds, intonation, or structures (in combination, of course, with sounds, structures, and vocabulary which are familiar to the students). One could serve to reinforce the new language features *after* these have been taught. The "cultural setting" or situation of this second dialogue may be similar to the one in which the items were introduced. Another dialogue may give practice in the same language features but in a different socio-cultural situation.

As soon as wider reading is introduced, the context in which unfamiliar language items are found may — indeed should — be used to help motivate the need for their intensive study. It goes without saying that the reading content should also serve as the springboard for the reinforcement of new and familiar language features as well as for the development of the other communication skills.

## STAGES IN LANGUAGE GROWTH

Whatever the motivating technique (conversation, story, etc.), your teaching of any language item[2] should proceed in six sequential steps. These six steps, with variations depending on the learning level

---

[1] This technique is generally called the "monostructural approach."

[2] In this text, the terms "item," "structure," and "feature" will be used interchangeably. The item or structure may consist of a morpheme, a word, or a group of words (e.g., the preposition "to" is an item as is the verb phrase "may have gone"). In some textbooks, the term "structures" may be reserved for items of more than one word. Moreover, the terms "grammar" and "structure" may sometimes be used interchangeably in them. It is important that you read the author's explanations to determine his meaning.

of the students and on the feature or skill to be developed, are basic to the acquisition of linguistic competence and performance. (The integration of the discrete items within the broad communication skills will be discussed later in this text in Chapter IV.)

1. The pupils should be led to *understand* the new language material. This understanding may result from the fact that 1) the grammatical item or structure is similar to or contrasts with one in the students' native tongue; 2) the item is an extension or a deepening of knowledge about a related feature already acquired in the foreign language; or 3) the situation in which the item is presented is within the experience of the students. It is essential that students be helped to make a meaningful association between the sounds or sound arrangements in the new item and a familiar or clear, realistic concept.

The understanding may be brought about through association of sounds with real objects, sketches, or pictures; through paraphrases (sentences using familiar words to explain new words as, for example, "A butcher is a man who cuts meat"); through one or more dramatized situations in which the new item is clearly and realistically illustrated in actual use; through a brief explanation in the foreign language; or through the equivalent expression or a summary in the pupils' native language, when this is feasible.

2. They should be led to *repeat* the material after you say it as often as is necessary to acquire reasonable fluency in it. The first few repetitions should be in chorus by the entire group. Whole group repetition should be followed by smaller group repetition, again preceded by your model and then by individual student repetition, preceded by your model. It is generally desirable to have individual repetition done by the more able students first, so that the "poorer" students will have the opportunity to hear additional reasonably good imitations of your model.

There is no right number for the times an item or utterance has to be repeated. As soon as pupils repeat with reasonable fluency you should proceed to the generalization (see 3 below) or to other more challenging kinds of practice. Generally, the repetitions needed will depend on the number of new sounds or sound sequences in the material being repeated. If, for example, you had taught "Good Morning" in English or "Bonjour" in French, you could expect that the number of repetitions needed for "Good Evening" or "Bonsoir" would be fewer since some sounds and the intonation patterns would be familiar to the students.

3. The students should be helped through attention-pointing questions to *summarize* or to *give a generalization* of the salient, recurring, constant, *meaningful* features of the new language material presented to that point. (Some teachers like to consider this a medial summary

since it gives them insight into the fact that there has been perception and comprehension on the part of the students and that subsequent drill activities can be engaged in with reasonable success.) The generalization should pinpoint the *sounds, word form, position in the sentence, function,* and *meaning* of the item being learned. It should be a description in the students' words of what they actually say and do (their verbal behavior) as they use the new item.

4. They should be led to *practice* the material in as many ways as possible — the purely mechanical, rote practice giving way to more spontaneous, "freer" expression from the very first day, if possible. This will be discussed more fully below.

5. They should be led to *choose* the correct word, expression, or structure (in statements, responses, or questions) from several contrasting items in the foreign language.

When you attempt step 5 will depend on the age of your students, the length of the course, the degree of native language interference with the items being contrasted, and, especially, the students' grasp of the individual items in the foreign language (e.g., in French, the present versus the subjunctive after certain expressions, or masculine versus feminine "agreement" with nouns or past participles; in English, the simple present versus the "ing" present).

If you are quite certain that your students have reasonable facility with the two or more items to be contrasted, you should insert them in practice exercises and model several examples of the responses required in order to make sure your students understand what they are to do. With less able students, you may find it necessary to engage in repetition drills of utterances in which the contrasting features appear in random order, before asking them to select the appropriate form.

With some items, you may be able to engage in this step of "conscious" choice during the same lesson in which the second of the two items is presented and practiced. With other items, several lessons may have to elapse, during which students will be enabled through practice to gain greater understanding and control of the discrete items. This stage should not be rushed. Since language learning is a cumulative process, an incomplete or incorrect knowledge of any one item will produce poor learning (and frustration) in subsequent stages.

6. They should be helped to choose their responses freely and to *use the new material in any communication situation* where they can express ideas without worrying about inflection, word order, stress, or any other feature of the language system.

As was stated earlier, a foreign language program usually aims to develop the skills of understanding, speaking, reading, and writing while giving insight into the culture of which the language is a part. Within each of the skills, attention must be given to the phonology (the phonetic and phonemic system), to the grammar (the structure system), and to the vocabulary (the lexicon). Each of the language skills makes use of sounds (even reading, as will be seen), grammar, and vocabulary. We will therefore take these three major areas of language in turn and give some brief suggestions for teaching them. As we do so, we will make continuous reference to the "stages" listed above.

## TEACHING THE SOUND SYSTEM

The sound system is learned best through imitation of the teacher, a tape, or a record. It goes without saying that the teacher is to be preferred to any electronic or mechanical device for the presentation of the new material. The only situation in which the use of the tape or record before the teacher's live presentation is justified is one in which he feels that his command of the language is completely inadequate. Many teachers also prefer to introduce songs through recordings.

There is no question that tapes and records may be very effective in making possible the *additional sustained practice* which language learning requires, but where possible, however, these should be used only after the teacher's live presentation.

With older students, whose ingrained native language habits may seriously conflict with the production of the new language sounds, guided imitation of the teacher is usually not enough. Direct teaching of sounds and intonation patterns will be necessary. There is no magic age or cut-off point when imitation must be supplemented by direct teaching nor would all the students in the class reach that point at the same time. In teaching pronunciation as in teaching anything else, you, the teacher, can best judge when additional systematic help is desirable.

After identifying the sounds which cause the most difficulty to your students, you may use several techniques or a combination of techniques to teach them: 1) an oral or written description of the speech organs as the sound is being produced; 2) a diagram of the speech organs; 3) a comparison with the nearest sound in the student's native language;* or 4) a modification of a known foreign language sound. (This may be particularly good in teaching the voiced and voiceless pairs — b/p, f/v, s/z — and in teaching the vowels.)

Any description should be simple; e.g., for the /u/ in English: "The

---

* If a similar sound exists in the pupils' native tongue but in a different position, you should make the students aware that they do know and use the sound. You would then *isolate* it, *extract* it, and help them *use* it in the new position.

lips are rounded (show yours and/or draw a sketch on the board) and the tongue is back."

Any diagram should be uncluttered and clear. You should learn to sketch the lips, teeth, palate, and tongue on the board. Using dotted lines, indicate the position of the tongue or the movement of the tongue from one sound to the other.

A very effective device is to sketch a large profile on a cardboard, indicating the lips, teeth, palate, and bottom of the mouth. Omit the tongue. Cut out the cardboard to show the mouth cavity. Make a red mitten for your right hand. As you teach a sound, use your gloved hand in the open mouth cavity to simulate the tongue. Move it against or between the teeth, bunch it up in the back, curl it up to the palate, or indicate movement from one sound to another. Any student who is having particular difficulty in producing a sound may also be invited to put on the mitt and to illustrate the tongue position or movements. The kinesthetic effort may help in his perception of the articulation.

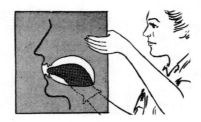

After you teach one sound alone (the sound of *th* in "thin," for example), you may teach a contrasting sound /d/or/t/or/ð/ in familiar words where possible, or in common unfamiliar words. If feasible, teach them in minimal pairs (that is, in words in which there is no difference except for the sound you are contrasting — for example: thin/tin; tin/din; beat/bit; Pete/pet; wine/vine; yellow/jello; zoo/sue; etc.).

With older students, you may find it desirable to give the meanings of the pairs in the native language to convince them that the phonemes do make a meaning difference. If you do give the native language equivalent, do it briefly and only once. Of course, pictures or quick sketches on the board would avoid the necessity of using the native language. You would eventually find it a profitable, time-saving device to prepare sets of pictures or a chart with pictures showing minimal pairs for those sounds in the foreign language which cause your students difficulty.

You may find it necessary, moreover, to give pronunciation practice which does not exist in your textbook if your students have difficulty producing certain sounds in high-frequency utterances, or even to change the textbook order of teaching the sounds.

It is unwise to give infrequently used words or archaic words merely for the sake of practicing a sound. It is preferable to use incomplete common words which exemplify a sound or a sound sequence.[1]

There are three essential steps in teaching your students to make sounds. They must be able to:

1) Hear the sound.
2) Identify it; that is, distinguish it from any other.
3) Produce it.

Following is a brief illustration of a procedure you may wish to use to ensure recognition and production of two contrasting sounds:

Let us assume the problem is the /g/ and /k/ in final position. Use simple pictures illustrating the words or the words themselves (which can be placed on the board in transcription,[2] print, or cursive writing).

| I | II |
|---|---|
| bag | back |
| hag | hack |
| rag | rack |
| sag | sack |
| tag | tack |
| wag | wack |

### Hearing

1. Say all the words in Column I (or Set I of the pictures) two or three times.
2. Say all the words in Column II two or three times.
3. Say the words across several times.

### Identifying

1. Give two words from either list and ask the students to indicate whether they are the "same" or "different," e.g., "bag/bag" — "Same." (Give ample practice in saying "same" or "different.") Do the first few examples together with your students. If there is confusion caused by students calling out the wrong response, give more practice and/or have only individual students respond for a few minutes.
2. Give three words from either list and ask the students to in-

---

[1] Most teachers prefer to give practice with words students can use immediately in communication situations. When incomplete words are used you should indicate the missing segment by a line, e.g., prob — (problem); — ferent (different); — ly (costly).

[2] The use of transcription is controversial. You will have to decide whether you wish to use IPA or other symbols, or whether you feel the intermediate step — sound, transcription, symbol — causes more problems. Why not experiment with both techniques in different classes?

dicate which two are the same (e.g., Say, "tag, tag, tack." The students in groups or individually say "one, one, two.").

3. Give a word from either list and have the students indicate on which list or set of pictures it appears by holding up one or two fingers.

### Producing

1. Say each word in Column I or in the first set of pictures. Have the students repeat each word.

2. Say each word in Column II. Have the students repeat.

3. Say the words across followed by student repetition (whole class, groups, or individuals).

4. Say the words across *starting from the right-hand column,* followed by student repetition.

5. Say a word in one column. Have *individuals* give you the same word or the contrasting word.

6. Have a *student* give one word and a fellow-student give the contrasting word *or* the same word.

7. *Use words from both columns in short utterances.* Have the students listen to and repeat each one in ways suggested above. The importance of inserting the isolated words into utterances cannot be stated often enough.

The "test," of course, is stage 6 in our language-learning process: Can students distinguish between sentences like "The sentence is long" and "The sentence is wrong," or "Would you get me the rag?" and "Would you get me the rack?," and can they produce the comprehensible sound in "free" communication situations? Can they hear and produce contrasting intonation patterns?

A word of caution is in order before proceeding to the other elements in the sound system: You may have to reteach the same sound or remind the students of the pronunciation of the same sound a hundred times or more. With older students particularly, habits of using the speech organs in one's native tongue are strong. Of the three major areas of language, the sound system is the most difficult to acquire.

Your major emphasis should be on teaching the *phonemes* of the foreign language (that is, the sounds causing the difference in meaning). Students should be helped to hear them, to identify them, and to produce them.

It goes without saying that, as quickly as feasible, much direct teaching and practice also must be given students to help them produce the variation of the phonemic sound which is most appropriate in the position in which it is found in a word or a sequence of words. For example, as noted above, in English an initial /p/ is pronounced with a small puff of air whereas final /p/ and medial /p/ are not. (These are allophones of the phoneme /p/.) While the meaning would be clear, the inappropriate allophone would cause the speech to sound unnatural or "foreign."

More advanced students should also be helped to recognize individual speech differences which are not phonemic. For example, many English speakers do not pronounce an "r" at the end of "sister," "brother," "father." Your pupils will gain in this recognition as they listen to other native speakers and to records and tapes spoken by others.

The same three steps — hearing, identifying, producing — are necessary in teaching intonation. Imitation and extensive repetition of many similar sentences are essential. We would recommend that you teach only the basic intonation patterns first: in English, the rise-fall intonation, and the intonation used in inverted questions (those usually requiring a "yes" or "no" answer).

It may be desirable to indicate intonation lines on the board, or numbers 1-4; to use an upward arm gesture to show rising intonation; to place up or down arrows ($\uparrow\downarrow$) at the end of the sentence; or to place curved arrows ($\searrow\nwarrow$) over the words having the highest or lowest pitch, or whatever helps *your* students. Any of the techniques for marking intonation will help; combinations of the techniques are even more helpful.

Phonemic stress (word accent) is taught by *contrast*. Hearing, identifying the difference, producing the difference, using the words in sentences which show meaning differences, and finally using the contrasting words in "real" speech situations are the steps needed to ensure a command of words in which stress is phonemic.

We would reserve for the intermediate or the advanced level* the placement of stress on different parts of the sentence to show varying emphasis. For example:

"₂Did you go to the movies yesterday?" (or your brother?)

"₂Did you go to the movies yesterday?" (or last week?)

"₂Did you go to the movies yesterday?" (or to the library?)

The typical rhythm of a language is learned by listening, by imitation, and by practice in saying increasingly longer sentences. One effective way is to use the words in the first sentence in longer sentences: in English, for example, May I have a book? May I have that big book? May I have that big history book? May I have those two big history books?

---

* If you are using a text in which sentence stress is used extensively as a device for teaching certain structures, you should teach it as needed, of course.

In general, your speech should not be slowed down or otherwise distorted, except temporarily. The normal rhythm of utterances should be maintained. If the students are having difficulties with one or more words, you may either use the backward build-up technique (see page 81) or you may 1) say the entire utterance twice in normal rhythm; 2) isolate the troublesome word and give repetitive practice in it; and 3) *reinsert the word in the utterance* and have it repeated after you several times.

With older students, you may also wish to teach the symbol /ə/, for example, and to write it over words which are "weakened" or reduced in speech; e.g., "Can /kən/ you go to the movies?" "Yes, I can." /kæn/. (Notice the full value of the vowel sound in the short answer.) You may also wish to teach some students the phonetic symbols as reminders of sounds.

Whether you do or not will depend on your experience in using them, the students' writing system, their ages, needs, interests, etc. If you prefer not to use transcription, you might want to prepare a list of short, common key words in which the more troublesome phonemes appear. Thus, you could point to the appropriate word(s) with which students are thoroughly familiar when they are having difficulty with a new word. Merely say "It's this sound" as you point to the key word.

It is unwise to strive for mastery of a sound or sound sequence too soon. Many students — either naturally or when "pushed" too hard or bored — may reach a plateau, that is, a temporary pause in their ability to show any improvement. It is preferable — when this stage is reached — to accept a reasonably good imitation of your speech or of a tape and to shape the students' production gradually. This shaping toward the desired terminal behavior will take place not only through repetitive practice but also through use of the sound or sounds in normal communication activities.

The emphasis in language learning today is on achieving understanding. It is recognized by most scholars that the complete elimination of a "foreign accent" in some secondary school students and adults is impossible without a tremendous expenditure of time and effort. This effort might better be given to acquiring greater fluency and more habitual control of structure. Of course, the practice of structure and of patterns will automatically contribute to more accurate sound production. You should strive for comprehensibility at all times during the lesson even during those segments of it when you are not giving concentrated practice on elements of the sound system.

## TEACHING THE GRAMMAR SYSTEM

A procedure you will find desirable in presenting the single word or more complex items which constitute the grammar of the language is outlined below:

1. *Motivate the new structure*; that is, indicate the need for it in communication. You may do this by dramatizing a situation* in which it is used realistically and clearly by reminding students of something heard or read, or by asking them how they would say something in their native tongue.

For example, after having taught the names of clothing you may wish to teach adjectives of color or material or expressions of size or cost. You could illustrate the functional use to which these new items can be put by dramatizing — through pictures perhaps — the purchase of an item of clothing.

After establishing the situation — shopping for clothing — you may say something like, "Listen to what this lady is saying to the clerk. 'May I have a (red) blouse?' or 'May I have a (silk) blouse?' or 'May I have this blouse in size 12?,' " or whatever you have planned to teach. "Listen now to the clerk's answer. 'Here's a (red) blouse' or 'Here's the blouse in size 12,' " or whatever.

You might even go back a step further. Before establishing the shopping situation, you may say something like, "We've learned the names of the clothing we are wearing. Suppose we wanted to buy a blouse (a suit, a pair of shoes, etc.). Would the name be enough? What else would we have to tell the clerk in the clothing store?" Elicit responses from the students in their native tongue or by touching appropriate pictures of colors, size, etc., to clarify your words. You could say in the foreign language that they would have to know the colors or expressions of size or material. After this introduction, you could display the shopping scene picture and simulate the conversation between the customer and the clerk.

2. *State the aim* of the lesson or — better still — help elicit the aim from the students: "What do you think we are going to learn to talk about today?" Elicit the aim in the target language when possible. At beginning levels — where students don't have a sufficient knowledge of structure or vocabulary — accept the aim in a brief statement in their native tongue (if you know the native language).

Give them the feeling that they are discovering your plans and that they are partners with you in the lesson development.

3. *Review briefly* the familiar language items in the foreign language, which you will need in order to present, clarify, or practice the new language item. For example, if you are going to teach adjectives, review appropriate content words; if you are going to teach the simple

---

* Examples of possible situations useful for presenting structures will be found in Appendix I, pp. 261-66.

present, you may wish to review expressions of time; if you are going to teach the present perfect, you may wish to review the verb *have,* expressions of time, and also the simple past (in order to contrast the two structures).

4. *Use the structure in a normal utterance.* Precede it by saying simply the equivalent of "Listen" or "Look-listen" (if a prop, picture, or action will accompany your modeling of the utterance). Make sure the students understand the utterance. Do this by dramatizing an action many times, by using a picture, by giving several sentences in the foreign language with familiar words which help explain the one you are teaching, or as a last resort, by giving them their native language equivalent.

If you give the native language equivalent, do it once only as follows: Say the foreign language sentence in a normal voice; then say the native language equivalent in a lower voice; then the foreign language again in a normal voice.

5. *Model the utterance several times.* The number of repetitions depends on the known sounds or sound sequences in the utterance. If you have a large class, walk to various parts of the room so that all students can see your mouth. Stand in one position, however, as you model the utterance.

6. *Have the utterance repeated in chorus* by the entire class several times. Give the model *before each repetition* you ask of the class. If the sentence is long (six or more syllables) or if the sound sequence is unfamiliar, you may wish to divide the sentence into smaller elements for practice. Divide it from the end. It is easier to keep the same intonation when you start from the end. Of course you may vary this occasionally by dividing a sentence from the beginning. Here is the procedure for breaking a sentence from the end. Let us assume you are teaching, "He's going to read now":

a) Say the entire sentence several times, so that students hear the normal intonation and rhythm.

b) Say "now." Class repeats: *now.*

c) Say "read." Class repeats: *read.*

d) Say "read now." Class repeats: *read now.*

e) Say "going to." Class repeats: *going to.*

f) Say "going to read now." Class repeats: *going to read now.*

g) Say "He's going to read now." Class repeats: *He's going to read now.*

7. *Engage in group repetition* of the same sentence (half a class, the right side, the left side, the front, each row, etc.). Indicate the group that is to repeat with a hand signal which you have devised and with which you have made your class familiar.

It is unwise to say things like "The front row," or "This half of

81

the class." You should learn to conserve your voice and energy for the modeling of sentences or for reading, dictation, and the other language activities which only you can guide.

Moreover, it becomes difficult for the students to remember the sound sequence they are to echo if other words come between your model and their repetition of it. Precious class repetition time is often wasted when routine directions which could be given by a brief signal are spoken.

A word of caution, however. In parts of the world where pointing is considered impolite, explain the reasons for pointing and gesturing to your students.

8. *Have individual students repeat* the same sentence. It is a good idea to start with your more able students. In that way, your less able students will have more time to listen to and repeat silently a reasonably correct sentence.

If there are errors in pronunciation, you should say the sentence again and engage the class in choral, group, or individual repetition. Merely say "Listen" and repeat the sentence.

9. *Using familiar vocabulary only, give several other sentences* which illustrate the point you are teaching and have the students repeat them. For example, if you are teaching the adjective of color after "be," say, *as you show each item*, "The pencil is red, The pen is red, The book is red, The notebook is red," etc.

Where gender and agreement of noun and adjective are factors in the foreign language you are teaching it is essential to group the items. For example, give a series of masculine (or feminine or neuter) items first, then a series of feminine, etc. Students will be helped by this systematic, sequential development to perceive the recurring, meaningful feature, to organize the material, and to formulate a "rule" in their own minds about agreement even before you guide them in doing so.

10. *Ask questions* which make your students *consciously aware of the sounds, the form, distribution* (position), *function*, and *meaning* of the structure you are teaching. In other words, help them to *generalize*.

a) Step 10 may be done after you place several sentences on the board in the form of a chart. Do not place the sentences on the board unless the students have heard them and can say them with reasonable accuracy and fluency. With younger students, you may prefer not to write sentences on the board at all.

b) The grammatical terms you use in helping your students "see" the form, distribution, and function of any new item will depend to a great extent on their knowledge of grammatical terms in their native tongue. Grammatical terms are not necessary, and neither are prescriptive rules of grammar. The "rule" elicited by your questions, if any, should be a description of what actually happens as the utterance is spoken (e.g., What sound did you hear after—? Where did we put the word—?, etc.).

c) Note a possible chart in English:

| The | Noun | "Be" | Color (or Adjective) |
|-----|------|------|----------------------|
| The | pencil | is | red. |
| The | pen | is | red. |

When for example, the plurals of nouns are taught, the charts may look like this:

| The | Noun | "Be" | Color |
|-----|------|------|-------|
| The | pencil | is | red. |
| The | pen | is | green. |

| The | Noun | "Be" | Color |
|-----|------|------|-------|
| The | pencils | *are* | red. |
| The | pens | *are* | green. |

You should use any device to help your students perceive or visualize the structure being emphasized. You may underline or circle the similarity or change in form or you may use different colors of chalk or crayon. You may use arrows to show changes in word order or to show elision. You may use "trees" and "branches" to show structural or sentence relationships.

11. *Encourage your students to describe the structure* (give the generalization) in behavioral terms. They should verbalize what they actually do as they use a structure. The verbalization should be stated briefly and simply first with relation to the *sounds*, then the *form* of the item or structure, its *position*, its *function* in the utterance, and its *meaning*.

12. *Engage the students in varied, controlled oral practice** of the new item using thoroughly familiar vocabulary. This practice — often termed "manipulative" — should lead the students in gradual steps to use the item habitually and correctly.

As noted above, on page 73, the practice you give should eventually include requiring the students to make a conscious choice between the newly presented item of structure and a familiar contrasting one. This step, however, will not be possible on the first day of presentation with many structures you present. In some instances, you will have realized that the new item has not been grasped well enough by your students.

---

* Practice activities are discussed on p. 73.

In other cases, you may be planning to teach another related facet of the structure during the next lesson and prefer to engage in the contrasting practice with multiple aspects of it. For example, you might wish to present two or more uses of the partitive in French or the present perfect in English before you include practice activities requiring the students to make a conscious choice.

13. *Help the students summarize* or verbalize again the distinctive features of the new structure indicating sound, form, position, function, and meaning. Stand at the blackboard or chart and point to the relevant facets as you elicit again the summary, "rule," or generalization.

14. *Prepare a paradigm* of the item and its form changes if one is appropriate and if you have taught enough of the form changes to warrant a paradigm. *Give the paradigm in complete utterances.* Place them on the blackboard or on a chart in an order and sequence which will enable students to internalize the "rules" and patterns of sound, form, or order characteristic of the language feature. For example, in English, students would find it useful to note that "I," "you," "we," "they" govern the same verb form (except for "be") and that the forms for "he" and "she" are inflected. At the appropriate time, a paradigm for personal pronouns in English may be: *I* need a book. Please give *me* a book. I have *my* book. This book is *mine*. I bought it *myself*. A similar paradigm for personal pronouns in French may be: *Je* voudrais un livre. Donnez-*moi* un livre. Il *me* donne un livre. J'ai *mon* livre. Ce livre-ci est *le mien*. (Ce livre-ci est à *moi*.) Je l'ai acheté *moi-même*.

15. *Give the students practice* in using the new items in gradually "freer," more spontaneous communication in which previously learned items are also included. (See pages 101-2 for suggestions.)

16. *Direct the students to copy* into their notebooks the model sentences, diagrams, paradigms, or anything else you have placed on the blackboard for further study at home. (It is unwise to interrupt the smooth flow of your lessons by having them copy during the lesson.)

### Some Cautions in Teaching Grammar

Before leaving this topic which many teachers will consider the heart of foreign language teaching, several additional comments should be made:

1. Whether or not the textbook you are using indicates an awareness of its importance, it is essential that you grade the structures carefully in presenting them. (The gradation of the practice activities will be discussed on pages 89-93.) For example, in teaching the partitive, we could start with the use of "some" with count nouns, e.g., "I'd like some apples"; then teach its use with mass nouns, e.g., "I'd like

84

some rice"; then proceed to the interrogative,* e.g., "Would you like some rice?" "Do you have any apples?"; then to the short answers, e.g., "Yes, I would (do)" / "No, I don't"; then present the negative, e.g., "I don't want any rice."

The gradation you decide upon would depend on the language you are teaching and the sub-elements within the features (e.g., in French *du, de la, de l', des, de, d'* in teaching the partitive). In general, however, it is desirable to start with one or two sub-elements in statements and to proceed to the interrogative of these same sub-elements. This would enable the students to practice questions and answers and other brief conversational exchanges quickly before you explore the entire topic.

2. The last remark leads into the second comment. The principle of the "spiral approach" should be kept in mind in planning any material to be presented. It is generally not feasible to teach every nuance of the subjunctive in French or of the omission of the definite article in English, let us say, even in one semester at the secondary school level. It is preferable to start with one function and to plan to teach the other functions in subsequent lessons, often interspersing other essential language items not necessarily related to the subjunctive or article or whatever.

When you present the second or third or fourth function, you should review the one or ones you had taught and help the students associate the new function with the familiar one. In this way, the students will be guided to perceive the internal organization of the language feature and to reconstruct it into a coherent whole.

We cannot underscore enough the importance of giving priority in teaching to an item or function needed by students to talk realistically about situations in their classroom or community. In situations where the foreign language being learned is to be used immediately for living in the community, the *past* may have to be taught before the *present*; the form *one of* may have to be taught before *some* or *any*.

3. Whenever there is any danger that students will make a false or incorrect analogy, it is desirable to indicate the limitations and restrictions of the structure you are teaching. To repeat a point made above: if in English, for example, you had taught verbs such as *know, like,* and *need* in the simple present, it would be necessary to make the students aware of the fact — when you are presenting the "ing" present — that those verbs are never used with "ing." If you are teaching the modals such as "I may go," "I should go," "I must go," etc., it is essential that you indicate through examples and through a generalization or "rule," that the modal *ought* is always followed by *to.*

---

* The interrogative form taught immediately after the positive allows for conversational exchange between pairs of students.

Needless to say, subsequent intensive practice involving "conscious" choice is needed so that students will establish the habit of using sounds or forms which are permitted to co-occur or which cannot co-occur in the system of the language you are teaching.

The approach and methods advocated above can be characterized as *eclectic* and *interdisciplinary*.

The suggestions outlined above do not subscribe to any one psychological theory. After establishing an appropriate frame of reference related to the learners' background or experience and after associating the new item with a *relevant* familiar one, the students are led *inductively* through examples to discover the essential features of the new item.

They then are helped to verbalize their behavior (what they actually did) when using the new feature and *deductively* they are engaged in practice of the new feature; that is, the varied practice is based on and stemmed from the "rule" or generalization they have given.

Consideration is given both to the operant conditioning theory in the tightly controlled drills leading to habit formation and to the cognitive code theory. Students are led to perceive the relationships of form and sound and to note the systematic recurrence of the distinctive feature. They are encouraged to verbalize what they have discovered and what they would have to do to create similar utterances. Both the stimulus-response-reward theory leading to habit formation and the cognitive code theory involving the higher mental processes of perception and cognition are brought into play.

The emphasis on the oral introduction or dramatization of the situation and the oral practice activities stems from the findings of linguistics on the nature of language. From the linguists, too, comes the attention to the problems of native language interference and the importance of contrasts in the presentation and practice of any item of grammar.

Psychological and linguistic theory are also at the base of the oral practice activities which will be discussed soon after we look at the third sub-system or area of language.

## TEACHING THE VOCABULARY SYSTEM

As noted in Chapter II, the lexicon or vocabulary of the language is divided into *function* words and *content* words. The function words are a closed class; we cannot add to the prepositions or auxiliaries or modals or any other structure word of the language. The content words, on the other hand, can be added to at any time as new scientific advances make new words and communication about new inventions necessary.

At the beginning level, it is essential that we emphasize the function words, following a logical gradation, of course, and paying attention to the spiral approach. Whenever we meet a function word, we should teach its use in that particular utterance or context, reminding students of any other function already learned. We would not, on the other hand, at any level of learning present and give practice in all the content words we meet in the listening and reading activities in which we will engage our students.

Another way of saying this is that not all of the words a student hears during any lesson need become a part of his "active" vocabulary during that lesson or even in later lessons. Some words in the new language (as is true in our native language) will remain "passive"; we understand them when we hear them or read them, but we may not use them ourselves in speaking or writing. The vocabulary for active use should be systematically presented and practiced, however.

In the pre-reading phase, we should concentrate on the more frequently used vocabulary items which are useful in giving practice in the basic structures and sounds of the language (e.g., What's this [that]?; Show us; Point to). We should also give precedence to the vocabulary which is intimately related to the environment and experiences of the pupils whether or not it is found in our textbooks or high up on a word-frequency list. If, for example, we are teaching in a rural area and our classroom looks out on a pasture with cows and sheep, we should teach those words first not only because the students can associate them with their environment but also because a logical, freer question such as "What do you see?" could elicit a response rooted in reality as pupils look out of the window or door.

It has become popular in the past two decades to minimize the importance of vocabulary teaching. While it is true that the learning of sounds, structures, and function words should take precedence in our teaching, it is nonetheless true that a store of content words of everyday life situations can make practice of the structures much more interesting to the students and can help them develop the ability to "perform" in real life conversations.

A question frequently asked is "How many new words can be taught in one lesson?" As is true of other questions related to teaching, there is no one answer. Children of eight or nine may learn four or five new words; children of ten or eleven may learn seven or eight; secondary school students may learn fifteen to twenty, while highly motivated university students may "absorb" thirty or more words.

In general, even with secondary school students, no more than about *eight* new words should be presented at one time. If your plan for a reading lesson, for example, requires that many more words be presented in one lesson, you may teach eight of them, engage in other related language activities and then teach another eight after about ten minutes. The context will often determine the number of words which students can be "encouraged" to learn.

Several additional premises and comments related to the teaching of vocabulary are offered for your consideration:

— Vocabulary should always be introduced in normal speech utterances. You may then isolate a word for intensive repetition but reinsert it in a normal utterance for further class, group, and individual repetition as soon as possible.

— New vocabulary items should always be introduced in known structures. The only time this is not possible is in the very first lesson of the beginning level.

— Whenever feasible, the vocabulary items should be centered about one topic. Words about food should be given in one lesson; words about clothing in another; words about weather in still another.

This makes a realistic conversation possible sooner. All the words around a "center of interest" (food, clothing, recreation, etc.) should *not* be taught at one time or at one level. Other words within the same "center" can always be added when they fit logically into the other socio-cultural topics being studied or when they are met in reading. (This concept, too, is in harmony with the *spiral approach* in teaching.)

The same situation or topic should always be used with a new word so that students will learn to associate the word with the situation in which it was learned. For example, "What mark did you get on that test?"; "The teacher gave me my mark."

— Content words should be presented and practiced with the words with which they generally co-occur. For example, a word of quantity or of measure is usually preceded by "a" and followed by "of" in English (e.g., a piece of bread, a head of lettuce, a pound of bananas).

— Whenever a familiar word is met in a new context or situation, it should be taught and practiced. A review or mention of the known meaning of a word should be made so that the students will understand that words may have a range of meanings depending on the situation. If possible, only one meaning — the one needed in the context being studied — should be taught at one time.

— Vocabulary items are taught in the same way we teach everything else. We give our students an understanding of the meaning in many ways: we dramatize; we illustrate using ourselves and our students; we show pictures or objects; we paraphrase; we give the equivalent if necessary; we use any appropriate technique.

— We practice vocabulary as we practice structures — in substitution drills, transformation drills, questions and answers, etc. (see page 93 ff.).

— We reintroduce the same vocabulary items many times with all the structures and in all the situations in which they can logically be used.

— In cases where the full understanding of the meaning of a word depends on knowledge of an item of culture, the overt facet of culture should be explained. For example, not only does *piso* in Spanish mean the floor in a building in which an apartment is located but it also means the floor of a room. In addition, *primer piso* (literally "first floor") is the equivalent of the second floor in American English.

## PRACTICING THE FEATURES OF LANGUAGE

We have seen that language acquisition, at the age level with which we are concerned, involves the formation of habits as well as a conscious understanding of the "rules" that underlie phrase structures of kernel sentences and the transformations of these permitted by the language system. Both habit formation and the establishment of "rule-governed" behavior are essential if the student is ever to be able to express his personal feelings or ideas and if he is to do so accurately, quickly, fluently, and spontaneously.

In order to achieve these learning goals, it is essential that students be given intensive practice to the point of over-learning. This practice will be tightly controlled by the teacher (or in the tapes when these are used) at whatever level any structure is first taught. The tight control will be relaxed gradually until the students can express themselves without the immediately preceding stimulus of the teacher or the tape.

The term "fading cues" has sometimes been used to describe the progression from tight teacher control with varied stimuli or cues to looser control without cues. (See page 98 for an illustration.)

The stage of tight control is generally called the stage of "manipulative" drill. The stage of "free" expression is generally labeled the stage of "communication." While the step of manipulation should always precede the step of communication, there is again no "best" length of time that students should be kept to manipulation. As quickly as possible — *from the very first day* of the program — students should be guided through appropriate questions, pictures, and other devices to engage in normal communication with you and especially with each other.

### Considerations and Criteria for Preparing and Engaging in Drills

One of the major responsibilities of the teacher is to select and grade drills which will lead to the students' habitual, correct production

89

of the items of language and to their internalization of the "rules" governing their use. The selection and gradation process must be applied not only to the drill *types* but also to the items or utterances *within* each of the drills as will be noted in our discussion.

Many drill types have been devised, some based on the tagmemic theory of linguistics (e.g., every slot in an utterance can be filled by a content word of the same class without altering the pattern of the utterance) and others on the transformational analysis theory. Some drills, as we shall see, are more appropriate for practicing certain language features than others.

Even at advanced levels of learning, all other drill types should be preceded by imitation, repetition, and single-slot substitution drills. You should engage in more complex substitution and transformation drills *only* when you hear that students are repeating after you with reasonable fluency and when they can make single substitutions in normal utterances with accuracy and without undue hesitation. In other words, they should have internalized the new structure and its "rhythm" before they are required to give probable "error-producing" responses.

Most drills, but substitution drills in particular, can be done with four kinds of cues: 1) You will *say* the word to be substituted or inserted and, where possible, you will indicate its referent (object or picture) at the same time. Notice that we again help students forge a closer bond between sounds and concept.

2) You will *say* the word to be substituted or inserted. 3) You will *point to* or *hold up* pictures, objects, or other props to stimulate the production of the utterance you are drilling. 4) You will *write* the cue words at the blackboard or on a chart or place them on flash or cue cards. Note that in steps 1 and 2 we do not require the students to recall the sounds of the word they are to substitute or insert in their utterances. In fact, in step 1 we again help students understand the concept by associating sounds and concept. Gradually we give less help. The same fading of cues is true for imitation and repetition practice.

In imitation drills which are always done first, your model or that of the tape *immediately precedes* the students' production. They are echoing you or the tape. In *repetition* drills, the students recall what they or their fellow students may have said. When, for example, you indicate that they are to repeat something twice, the first "production" is considered "imitation." The second is considered "repetition." The repetition may be of their own or their fellow-students' performance.

The cue word you give for question-answer and some other type drills should generally follow the question. You might say, for example, "At what time did you get up this morning?" — slight pause — "Seven." The student would then answer, "At seven" or "At seven o'clock" or "I got up at seven o'clock," depending upon your previous instructions.

What other criteria should we keep in mind as we prepare drills, over and above the imitation and repetition drills?

1. The items of grammar or vocabulary should have been *presented* prior to the practice with rigorous attention to stages 1 and 2 (see page 80).

2. *Separate drills* should be prepared for each new item of grammar or vocabulary.

3. The changes required should be *minimal*. In the beginning drills used with a new item, only one change should be required at one time. When the students are ready, the drills may be so structured that they will be forced to make more than one change. For example, a beginning drill of the pattern *Who is he?* may involve the substitution of *he* by *she, it, the boy*, etc. Later, *the men, they, Mr. and Mrs. X* will require a change from *is* to *are*. (Here we find ourselves at the stage of "conscious choice.")

4. The change required should be *consistent*. For example, in practicing frequency words, you might start with "always" and say, "Use 'always' in each of these sentences."

5. The *vocabulary* around which a pattern drill is built should *center around one topic* or one area alone (food, recreation, daily routines, etc.). It is desirable that even the rote drills be contextualized as far as possible. In this way the pattern drill practiced can lead to realistic conversation around one area of interest.

6. The drill sentences should be *short* so that students can concentrate on the change to be made without having to worry about keeping a long sentence in their minds, particularly in early drills.

7. The utterance elicited should be a *complete* one, not a segment of a sentence or utterance. We should remember, however, that in certain responses, a phrase or even a word would be considered a complete utterance. For example, a normal response to "Where did you go last night?" would be "To the (movies)." The normal response to "What did you do last night?" would have to be "I went to the movies." (You could have elicited *movies* by an oral word, a picture, etc.) On the other hand, an *oral* cue such as "I went — the store," eliciting the response "to" alone, would not be effective, even if you indicate the dash by clapping or some other gesture.

8. A minimum of *six to eight utterances* should be given for each drill type, since the first one or two are often said hesitantly without the characteristic rhythm and desirable fluency.

9. The drills should be *varied*. After the repetition and substitution drills, two or three additional drills of different types should be given. You will select, of course, from the drills below and any others you devise or find elsewhere those which will be most effective in making the particular structure or pattern clear and habitual.

91

10. The *directions* to the students,[1] emphasizing the changes to be made and the "behavior" required, should be brief and explicit. For example, in a *substitution* drill you could say, "Use the new word I will give you (or show you) in place of the word ———." In a *patterned response* drill, you might say "I will ask you some questions. Answer each one with 'Not at all,' " or whatever you are drilling. (See pages 93-101 for drill types.)

11. After giving the directions, *do several examples* (for each drill type) with your students. a) Say "Let's do a few sentences together." b) Give the model pattern. c) Have the students repeat it in chorus. d) Give the cue. e) Model the *new* sentence. f) Give another cue. g) Model the *new* sentence. h) Have the students repeat it. i) Say something like, "Now you will do them alone. Are you ready?"

12. The *cues* and *responses* should be *in the target language* except for the translation drill to be discussed below.

13. *All drill responses should be oral.* The drills done orally in class (or in the language laboratory) may later be assigned as written homework but they should be done orally first.

14. The drills should *reinforce* — as needed — any feature of the sound, grammar, or lexical systems normally used in listening, speaking, reading, or writing.

15. *The students should always be made aware* of the fact that they are being given practice in a particular structure having its own systematic sound, form, position, and function. You may say something like, "Now let's practice ———."

16. In order to avoid confusion, *all* drill responses, except substitution drills written on the board or in a text, should be given *by individual students.* Only imitation and repetition drills, where there is little or no possibility of error, should be done by the entire class or smaller groups. Nothing should prevent you, however, from having the entire group repeat together the response an individual has given. You may prefer to confirm his response before the entire class repeats it or you may have the class repeat directly if the response was reasonably good. Thus, possible steps may be:

— Model Sentence / / Cue / / Individual Response / / PAUSE[2] / / New cue.

or

— Model Sentence // Cue // Individual Response // (Nod and Slight Pause) // Teacher Confirmation // New cue.

---

[1] If all students speak one native language and if you know it, you may give the directions (for new drills only) in the native language the first few times, followed by directions in the target language.

[2] It is important to pause between a confirmation and the new cue to avoid a distorted sound sequence such as, "I have a new book pencil."

or

— Model Sentence // Cue // Individual Response // (Gesture for Group Repetition) / / Group Repetition / / PAUSE / / New cue.

17. *Questions and answers* can be practiced with the class divided into two groups. Say, "Listen to the question," e.g., " 'What would you like?' " Indicate the group to repeat. Say, "Listen to the answer, 'I'd like a ——.' " Indicate the other group. Practice questions and answers several times with the groups *before* reversing the roles. Precede each question with the word "question" and each answer with the word "answer," at the beginning. In later lessons indicate by cupping your hand over your ear that you want the question. Still later after sufficient practice has been given, you should be able to assume that students have developed the competence to recognize questions through the use of question words, question intonation, word order, etc.

18. The drills should be *graded* from simple to more complex. For example, an Expansion Drill (see pages 95-96) might start with cues which require no change in intonation and may proceed slowly through various steps, to those that require a change in intonation, in word order, in liaison, etc.

19. The help given students should be *diminished* gradually. For illustrations, see the Substitution Drill and Progressive Replacement. (See page 97.)

20. The type of *pupil participation* should be varied. (See page 187.)

### Basic Practice Activities*

Following are the commonly agreed-upon names and some examples of oral pattern practice activities which will help students grow in their control of the patterns and structures of the language. Please remember that in doing any drill, you should give two or three model sentences and show the students, by doing it yourself and having them imitate you, what you expect them to do.

*Substitution:* In this drill, students use another word *of the same class* in place of a word in a sentence slot. A noun is replaced by another noun; a verb by another verb; an adjective by another adjective; a determiner by another determiner; etc.

Let us assume you are teaching the present of "have" at the beginning level. Give students a sentence: "I have a pencil." Say (at the beginning, you may use their native tongue to make sure they under-

---

* These drills are often called by different names. Some specialists consider all drills except the substitution drill to be transformation drills. The name is not important. What is important is that students understand the changes to be made.

93

stand the direction), "Now, I'll give you another word. Put it (or use it) in the place of *pencil*."

1. Say "I have a pencil"; Have them repeat, etc. (see page 81). *Pause for a moment.* Show and say "ruler." The student called upon will say "I have a ruler." Pause. Show and say "notebook." The student will say "I have a notebook." Continue in this way, practicing about eight sentences. Then proceed to "You have," "We have," etc., using the same or similar vocabulary items.

2. Give the cue word without showing the object or picture.

3. Instead of giving the word, show an object or a picture. As above, say the pattern sentence; then show an object; *then* call on a student.

4. Instead of the word or object, show a picture or a chart of pictures. Give the pattern sentence, then point to one of the pictures — sometimes in sequence, sometimes at random. At times, have students come up and point to the pictures. They can then call on their classmates (individually, of course) to give the desired sentences; e.g., with pictures of fruit: "If I had had money, I'd have bought some (apples, pears, bananas, etc.)" or "This (pear) looks delicious. I think I'll have one (or eat one)."

5. Instead of the spoken word, object, or picture, you may use flashcards on which individual words are written or you may place (or have placed) a list of words on the board. (Use this fourth cue only after reading has been taught.)

6. The same procedure is used with any sentence (e.g., Substitute [car] : "If I had had the money, I'd have bought a [car].").

*Replacement:* The students will be expected to replace one class of word or expression by another; e.g., nouns or names by a pronoun (he, she, etc.).

1. Give a sentence; e.g., "John has a pencil." Individual students will be expected to say, "He has a pencil." Do not change the object (pencil) in any of the sentences in the drill. (In the drills described in this section [except for the Progressive Replacement Drill], only one element in the sentence is to be changed at one time.)

Use only *masculine* names at first; then give only a series of *feminine* names. When students can replace these with *he* or *she* — as the case may be — with some degree of facility, try giving the masculine and the feminine names in random order. (This becomes "conscious choice.")

2. Give sentences with *often,* for example. The students will give the same sentences with *many times a week* — e.g., "I *often* speak to him"; "I speak to him *many times a week.*"

3. Give sentences such as "I see the man." Students will say "I see

94

him." Notice here that, in English, a change both of stress and intonation will have to be made. In other languages, not only may the replacement necessitate a change of intonation but also a change of position and form. The context and vocabulary items of drills will have to be very carefully chosen so that students will not encounter too many difficulties at one time (e.g., in French, "J'aime *le garçon*," "Je *l'*aime," but "Je vois *le garçon*," "Je *le.*vois.").

4. One modal may be replaced by another modal. For example, "I *have to* go now." "I *must* go now." "I *ought to* go now." "I *should* go." In a drill of this type, change only the verb. Later change the subject pronoun and not the verb so that students will concentrate on the change *have to, must, ought to,* or *should,* for example.

*Transformation*\* (sometimes called conversion): The students will be given practice in changing from *singular* to *plural,* from *affirmative* to *negative* or *interrogative,* from *present* to *past* or *future,* from *active* to *passive,* etc. Give the model sentence and say, for example, "Now we're going to make questions from these sentences." Say, "He has a pencil." A student will say, "Does he have a pencil?" (or, "Has he a pencil?," depending on the book you are using or the form you use in your speech).

It is not necessary to use words like negative, past, etc. You can say instead, "Let's start each sentence with No," or "Let's use *not* in these sentences" (even though you may ask them to use the contracted form of *not*), or "Let's use *yesterday*," or "Let's use *going to*," etc. (Use the grammatical terms occasionally, however, if these are required in your school system.)

Question word (*Wh*) transformations are a necessary and rich source of practice. Notice possible practice with "have":

"Make a question with *Who*: '*Peter* has a cold.' "
"Make a question with *What*: 'He has a *cold*.' "
"Make a question with *When*: 'He had a cold *last week*.' "
"Make a question with *How long*: 'He's had a cold *for two weeks*.' "

While not wishing to belabor the point, it would be essential — before students could be expected to ask the *when* question with some accuracy and fluency — for them to have practiced *substitution drills.*

*Expansion:* The students will be given a word or expression to be inserted or added to a sentence you give them. Depending on the foreign language, the insertion or addition may require a change in word order, in agreement, or in verb mood. Notice some examples:

Say, "Let's add the word *too* to these sentences; Listen: 'The coffee is hot.' "

---

\* See pp. 54-56 for some of the other transformations which can be practiced at various learning levels.

95

Say, "Let's add the word *always* to these sentences; Listen: 'I have coffee at ten.' "

Say, "Let's add the word *intelligent* to these sentences; Listen: 'He's a student.' 'Mrs. X is a secretary.' " (Notice that *a* would have to be changed.)

Say, "Let's put *I'm sure (I know)* in front of these sentences; Listen: 'He'll come with us.' 'He went out.' "

Say, "Let's put *He said that* in front of these sentences; Listen: 'I'll come with you.' " (A student would say, "He said that he would come with me.")

Say, "Let's use *yesterday* in these sentences; Listen: 'I'm eating.' "

Say, "Let's put *The man asked me* in front of these sentences; Listen: 'How old are you?' " ("The man asked me how old I was.")

In some languages, the expression in the main clause will require the use of a subordinating conjunction and a subjunctive in the dependent clause. Unless the students are very able, a great amount of repetition and substitution practice should precede the expansion drills requiring multiple changes.

Expansions with tag questions present problems in English and should be carefully graded.

*Reduction:* This drill is a form of replacement drill because you "reduce" a sentence by changing an expression to a word. For example, "I have the pencil" to "I have it"; "I'm going to the library" to "I'm going there"; "Come to my house" to "Come here." Later you can practice *substitute expressions*: "I'd like one of the books in the window" to "I'd like one of those"; "I see all the people" to "I see everyone"; "I think it's raining" to "I think so."

In reduction drills, attention must be paid to changes in stress or intonation and to changes of position as well as to form changes.

*Integration:* Students are asked to combine two short sentences to make one sentence. For example, "I have a pencil. It's red" becomes "I have a red pencil"; "You saw the man yesterday. He is my professor" becomes "The man (whom) you saw yesterday is my professor."

*Restatement:* In this drill, students are given practice in expressing a concept in two different ways — e.g., Is this a new book? Is this book new?; Is this an urgent telegram? Is this telegram urgent?; This is my French book. I've got a French book.

*Paired Sentences:* In this drill, you will give a sentence and then ask a question. For example, you will say, "Mary likes to study." "And Jean?" or "What about Jean?" A student will say, "She likes to study too." This is a good drill for practicing verb forms or adjectives. For

96

example, "Joan is pretty." "And Helen?"; or "What about Helen?" — "Helen is pretty too."

Later, questions such as "What about you?" would force a change in verb form. When expressions such as *either* and *neither* are being drilled, your cue would be, "John doesn't like spinach. What about Harry?" "He doesn't like spinach either."

By varying the question to "and Harry" you would elicit, "Neither does Harry."

*Association:* The students will be given a basic structure (e.g., *I'd like*) to be used in all drill responses as well as words they will associate with their common co-occurring elements. For example: *water* (I'd like a glass of water); *pears* (I'd like a pound of pears).

*Progressive Replacement:*\* This drill needs much teacher help at the beginning, but students enjoy doing it after they've learned the technique. It is a *multiple* substitution drill. Whereas in the substitution drill, only one element was changed consistently each time (the noun or the adjective or the verb), in this drill a new element is changed in each sentence. The students *have to remember what was said in each preceding sentence* in order to form the new sentence. Notice:

| Teacher | Student |
|---------|---------|
| I have a red pencil. | I have a red pencil. |
| green | I have a green pencil. |
| He | He has a green pencil. |
| tie. | He has a green tie. |
| Mr. Jones | Mr. Jones has a green tie. |
| four | Mr. Jones has four green ties. |
| They | They have four green ties. |
| some | They have some green ties. |
| 'd like | They'd like some green ties. |
| bought | They bought some green ties. |

Until the students become accustomed to doing this drill, you might place the sentence on the board and point to the slot in which the substitution will be made. Later you might place five lines on the board representing the slots and point to the one for which you are giving the cue word. Later still, no visual help should be given. Students should know into which slot to insert the oral word you give them.

*Directed Practice:* This is an excellent drill for making the transition from "rigid" manipulation to "freer" communication. A student

---

\* This is sometimes called a Moving Slot Substitution Drill.

is directed (asked) to ask another student a question. The second student is directed to answer.* Similar step-by-step practice may include directions, such as "Ask me" or "Tell (me) (us) . . ." This drill also needs a lot of help from you at the beginning. It should be done in three stages until students are able to go to Step III directly.

— Step I — a) Teacher: "X ask Y, 'Do you have a pencil?'" (giving aloud the exact words to be said).
           b) Student X to Y, "Do you have a pencil?"
           c) Teacher: "Y tell X, 'I have a pencil'" or ("Yes, I do.").
           d) Student Y to X, "I have a pencil" or ("Yes, I do.").

— Step II — a) Teacher says, "X ask Y if he has a pencil."
           b) Teacher *whispers* to X, "Do you have a pencil?"
           c) X says *aloud* to Y, "Do you have a pencil?"
           d) Teacher to Y, "Y tell X that you have a pencil."
           e) He *whispers*: "Yes, I have a pencil."
           f) Y says *aloud*, "Yes, I have a pencil."

— Step III — You do not whisper the direct question (that is, you don't prompt the students). If the students don't know what to say, help them of course. If these drills are built up gradually over a long series of lessons, however, you will find that you have little or no prompting to do in Step III.

*Translation:* We have deliberately left this practice activity to the end of this series of drills for several reasons. First, there is controversy as to the advisability of doing translation. Only the teacher who knows the native language of his students can engage in this drill.

If translation is done at all, it should always be on a limited structure point, on one point only and *in a complete utterance*. The equivalent is always given; never, of course, a literal translation. Notice:

| Teacher | Student |
| --- | --- |
| (Native language) | I have a few pencils. |
| (Native language) | I have a few books. |
| (Native language) | I have a few notebooks. |
| or: | |
| (Native language) | I've been studying for an hour. |
| (Native language) | I've been waiting for an hour. |
| (Native language) | I've been resting for an hour. |

Ideally, the student should never say the native language, but we have found with some classes in some teaching situations that this hard and fast "rule" may have to be broken to provide an intermediate, simpler step in which the *teacher gives the target language* and the student gives his native language equivalent. Of course, as quickly as possible, this intermediate step should be eliminated.

In many countries in the world where a translation to or from the native language is an important part of the examination system, students must be helped to translate; that is, to render *the equivalent* of a passage of connected prose.

They will be able to do so only if they have been given systematic practice in giving the equivalent of one structure at a time. Gradually two or more may be combined in about six examples. At upper levels, paragraphs in the native language may be rendered in the target language or vice versa.

The translation or equivalent must always be at the complete utterance or sentence level since what is a verb in one language may be rendered as a function word or a noun in another. Students must be made consciously aware of these language differences through your guided questions and through emphasis on interlingual contrasts in the translations.

*Question-Answer Practice:* There are several basic types of question-answer drills. Moreover, each drill can be done in several ways: 1) You will ask all the students a question;[1] *one*[2] student will answer. 2) A student will ask you a question; you will answer. 3) A student will ask another student a question. 4) Pairs of students will face each other and practice. 5) Pairs of students will question each other in chain fashion. This, too, has several variations.

a) Student 1 asks Student 2 a question. Student 2 answers. Student 3 asks the same question of Student 4, who answers.

b) Student 1 asks Student 2 a question. Student 2 answers *and* asks the same question of Student 3, who answers and asks the question of Student 4.

c) Student 1 asks Student 2 a question; e.g., "Do you have a pencil?" Student 2 answers, "Yes, I do" or "Yes, I have a pencil." Student 3 asks Student 4, "Does he (or she) have a pencil?" referring to student 2. Student 4 answers. Student 5 starts a new chain with the same or a similar question.

Let us examine some basic question-answer drills which can be used effectively in teaching grammar and lexicon. (Questions which

---

[1] When picture series are used (see p. 166)., even more variety can be attained by using pictures in sequence first and then in random order.

[2] A choral answer may lead to confusion unless the teacher models both the question and the answer.

can be used in developing the skill of reading will be discussed later in Chapter IV.)

1. Notice the possible progression in the students' responses (at early levels particularly) with affirmatives and then with negatives:

Answer *Yes.* "Do you have a pencil?" or "Would you like a pencil?" Here listening comprehension alone is stressed.

Answer *Yes. Give a short answer.* "Do you have a pencil?" or "Would you like a pencil?" "Yes, I do" or "Yes, I would."

Answer *Yes. Give a long answer.* "Do you have a pencil?" "Yes, I have a pencil."; "Would you like a pencil?" "Yes, I'd like a pencil."

Answer *Yes. Give a short and a long answer.* "Do you have a pencil?" "Yes, I do. I have a pencil."; "Would you like a pencil?" "Yes, I would. I'd like a pencil."

Answer *No.* "Do you have a pencil?" "No."; "Do you want a pencil?" "No." ("Thank you" may be added, of course.)

Answer *No. Give a short answer.* "Do you have a pencil?" "No, I don't."

Answer *No. Give a short answer and a long answer.* "No, I don't. I don't have a pencil."

Answer *No. Tell what you have, want,* etc. (or *tell what it is*). "Do you have a pencil?" "No, I don't have a pencil. I have a pen."; "Is this a table?" "No, it's not (or it isn't) a table. It's a chair."

When an item is first introduced, you or an able student may give the cue which tells the students what to answer. For example, "Do you have a pencil?" You or the student say "pen" (or show the picture, object, or word *pen*), and a student will answer, for example, "No, I don't have a pencil. I have a pen." Later, students may give *any* appropriate answer.

2. *Choose one or the other.* "Do you have a pencil or a pen?" . . . "I have a (pen)." At the beginning level, make your second alternative the "correct" one so that the sounds the students are to produce are fresh in their minds.

3. *Patterned Response.* You will ask a question such as "Do you have a pencil?" or "May I borrow your pencil?" The student *always* answers with the utterance being practiced; for example, "Yes, here it is."; "Do you like salad (ice cream, swimming, etc.)?" "Yes, very much."

At more advanced levels, the patterned response drill can be used to practice changes in word order or substitute expressions. Notice:

I'm hungry . . . So am I.
I'm thirsty . . . So am I.
Do you think she's pretty? Yes, I think so.
Do you think it's going to rain? Yes, I think so.

or

100

Would you like a ham sandwich? Yes, thank you; or Yes, I would; or Yes, I'd like one; or No, thank you, not right now.

The drill can be made more interesting by adding an appropriate patterned clause to a reply (e.g., Will you play soccer this afternoon? Yes, I will if you'll play too; Will you study for the test? Yes, I will if you'll study too.).

4. *Question-word* (Wh) *Questions.*

> Who's in the first seat?
> Who's at the door? (John and Paul.)
> What do you need?
> Where's the baseball stadium?
> When will you see your friends?
> How long is the table?
> How many times have you been there?
> How far is the capital?
> Why are you so tired?

5. *Question-word questions and inverted questions* can be combined in realistic conversational exchanges. Notice:

— Have you seen X recently?
— Yes, I have.
— When did you see him?
— I saw him two days ago.

6. *Echo Response.* You or a student will ask a question and the student called upon will echo a segment of it before responding — e.g., "Where's your coat?" "My coat? It's in the closet."; "Where did you go last night?" "Last night? I went to the movies."

7. *Free Response.* Depending on the learning level and the items with which students are familiar, you might ask anything from "What do I have on my desk?" or "in my hand?" to "What did you bring to school today?" to "What new pictures do you see on the bulletin board?" to "What do you like to do on weekends?" or anything on which you wish to focus.

To help students with ideas, you or a student could again use cues — spoken words, pictures, objects, or written words — to elicit responses. Gradually, however, no cue should be used at all and you will find that none will be needed.

### Further Comments on Drills

• Some drills lend themselves better than others, of course, to the items we want to practice. For example, to practice adjectives, imitation, substitution, expansion, question-answer, and integration drills are especially suitable. Limited translations — with all the cautions we have expressed — could also be used effectively. To practice

101

verb phrases, imitation, substitution, replacement, question-answer, and transformation drills may be selected.

• It is important to vary the drill activities after about eight examples and to conduct the drills *briskly* in order to prevent boredom. You will find it desirable to place the cue words on a small card or on a slip of paper which you will keep in your hand and glance at if necessary in order to present them in a regular, smooth, brisk manner. Embarrassing pauses and uneven class rhythm produced by your having to think of the next cue deaden the enthusiasm of students and often undermine their confidence in you.

• As soon as interest in one type of drill flags, you should either 1) proceed to another type of drill; 2) change the order in which cues are given; 3) change the cue; or 4) vary the type of student participation involved, that is, proceed from choral repetition, to chain repetition, to your questioning students, to students questioning you, and then to their questioning each other.

• When you start a chain, break it after four or six people have spoken, and begin the chain again in another part of the room using the same sentences or, if you wish, changing some segment of the utterances but maintaining the same pattern.

• Even at the very beginning level, drills should be made natural and interesting. For example, when students are learning their names, a realistic drill may take the following form:

> You to Student 1: What's his name?
> Student 1: I don't know. (to Student 2) What's your name?
> Student 2: It's . . .
> Student 1 to you: His name is . . .

• Some drill types, including those requiring *sentence reconstruction* from several words, are best *seen* by the students and given orally. The written cue avoids students hearing something like John / buy / book / yesterday.

• Drills should lead gradually to the use and recombination of all language items learned in the social situations used by native speakers.

• Formulas of the language as well as rejoinders of all kinds (agreement, surprise, disagreement) will also require intensive practice in patterned responses as well as substitution and transformation drills. For example:

> "Does my smoking bother you?" "No, not at all."
> "Do you mind if I leave now?" "No, of course not."
> "Hello. We thought we'd come to visit you." "What a nice
>     surprise" or "What a pity. I was just about to leave."

• It is important to reaffirm that in planning drills, selection and

102

gradation are especially important. The drill types should be graded: the simpler, repetitive, no-error possibility drills giving way to those in which students may make errors because they will have to think of inflection, concord, word order, etc. Moreover, the drill types selected should be those which are especially effective for reinforcing the particular structure. The utterances within each drill type must also be carefully selected and graded 1) to produce only authentic utterances and 2) to enable the students to hear and practice together similar features of language, thus increasing their perception of the systematic "rule" which underlies the structure.

The principle of the 'spiral approach' should not be neglected in planning drill activities. After repetition and intensive pattern practice, new language material should always be practiced with familiar material. For example, when *ask* followed by an object is taught, we can introduce "having a pencil" — with sentences such as "He asked me if I had a pencil" or "I asked him if he had a pencil" or "Please ask him for his pencil," etc.*

Drills are essential at all levels of learning. When planned carefully and conducted efficiently, they contribute to the students' feeling of security and achievement; they help them internalize the features of language; they lead to habit formation; they consolidate the "rule" or concepts of the language's internal organization which the students had formulated; and they promote attentive listening, linguistic competence, and more fluent oral performance.

### Suggestions

— Select any language item for teaching at Level II. Indicate and exemplify five techniques you may use for introducing it.

— Select ten language items for teaching at Level I. Indicate ten possible situations you could use in introducing each of them.

— Using the same items, tell which items in the *foreign language* you should make sure the students know before presenting the new material.

— Select a language item for teaching at Level IV. Tell how you would introduce it and clarify its meaning.

— Select two vowels and two consonants in the target language. Indicate how you would present them.

— Construct a minimal pair word drill in the target language for five vowels and five consonants.

---

* For the sake of clarity and to illustrate the spiral approach, we have stayed closely within classroom vocabulary. The same drill types can be practiced with *any* vocabulary *at any level* of learning.

— Construct minimal pair utterances for two contrasting consonants; for two contrasting vowels.

— Prepare a chart of ten line drawings or pictures of common objects to present and drill two contrasting vowel sounds.

— List ten common words in the target language which contain a difficult sound. Use the ten words in ten authentic frequently used utterances.

— If your target language is a tone language, list five minimally contrasting words.

— Write five utterances of increasing length containing the same idea. How would you teach the rhythm of the sentences?

— Select ten language items for teaching. Indicate the level of your learners. Tell how you would bring about the step of association of sounds and concept.

— Using the same ten language items write the "generalization" or description which you would elicit from your students.

— List five language items in the target language. List five others with which each may contrast; e.g., he, she; present, past.

— Construct a drill for one of the contrasting features which will force the learners to choose consciously between them. Tell the directions you would give your students.

— Construct a single-slot substitution drill for any language item. Indicate the directions you would give your students.

— Construct a two-slot substitution drill in which concord, agreement, or some other type of interdependence requires a change in sound and/or form.

— Select one limited function of a feature of language. Tell which five oral drills (including repetition) would be most appropriate for practicing it.

— Write out in full five *sequential* oral drills which would be useful for reinforcing one feature of language. Indicate briefly the directions you would give your students for each drill. Justify the sequence you have chosen.

— From a textbook in the foreign language you are teaching, give an example of a poorly constructed drill. Indicate the changes needed with your reasons. Rewrite the drill.

— Make a list of several irregular but related verbs (the relationship may be in meaning or in form). Construct a drill for practicing these, so that the relationship among them will be perceived and internalized by the learners.

— Select five "classroom" words or expressions. Tell exactly how you would present them.

— Select five abstract words. Tell how you would present them at Level III or IV.

— Construct an eight-utterance translation drill on a limited structure from the target language to the students' native language.

— Construct a translation drill on a limited structure from the students' native language to the target language.

— List five errors that you assume your students will make by analogy with the native language. Suggest five drills for helping to extinguish each error.

— Construct three different single-slot substitution drills for *each* of the following sentences (give the student directions for each) : Joe went to the store. Let me have some ink. If I had had the time, I'd have bought a coat.

— Write detailed lesson plans for teaching a language item at Levels I, III, and IV.

### *Additional Reading*

BELASCO, S. *Anthology for Use with a Guide for Teachers in NDEA Institutes.* Boston: D. C. Heath, 1961.

BENNETT, W. A. *Aspects of Language and Language Teaching.* Cambridge, England: Cambridge U. Press, 1968.

BILLOWS, L. *The Techniques of Language Teaching.* London: Longmans Green, 1961.

BROOKS, N. *Language and Language Learning.* New York: Harcourt, Brace & World, 1964.

CORNELIUS, E. *Language Teaching.* New York: Thomas Crowell, 1953.

DACANAY, F. R. *Techniques and Procedures in Foreign Language Teaching.* Quezon City: Phoenix, 1963.

DODSON, C. J. *Language Teaching and the Bilingual Method.* London: Pitman & Sons, 1967.

HUEBENER, T. *How to Teach Foreign Languages Effectively.* (rev. ed.) New York: New York U. Press, 1965.

JERMAN, J., D. VAN ABBE, and B. DUTTON. *A Guide to Modern Language Teaching Methods.* London: Cassell & Co., 1965.

LADO, R. *Language Teaching: A Scientific Approach.* New York: McGraw-Hill, 1964.

MATHIEU, G. (ed.). *Advances in the Teaching of Modern Languages.* New York: Pergamon Press, 1967.

NIDA, E. *Toward a Science of Translation.* Leiden, The Netherlands: Brill, 1964.

RIVERS, W. *Teaching Foreign Language Skills.* Chicago: U. of Chicago Press, 1968.

# IV

# Developing
# the Communication Skills

## LISTENING — SPEAKING

While the drills we have discussed will undoubtedly contribute to the correct and even habitual production of sub-elements of utterances (e.g., to the accurate articulation of sounds or to the use of appropriate inflections or of co-occurring words), they will not automatically foster the listening comprehension and speaking abilities which may more properly be labeled "communication."

Let us look again at the subsidiary skills students need in order to listen with comprehension to connected discourse which may range from the understanding of several utterances spoken by others to listening to a speech on the radio where noise in the room or radio static may cause interference.

In *listening*, the learner must hear and identify (because they signal meaning):

1 — the *phonemic sounds* of the language and, eventually, the personal or dialectal variations of the phonemes as spoken by some native speakers;

2 — the *sequences of sounds* and their groupings; the lengths of the pauses; the patterns of stress and intonation;

3 — the *function words* and their required sound changes depending on their position before other words (e.g., English: *a* boy, *an* animal; the /ðə/ boy, the /ði/ apple, etc. — French: *le* garçon, *l'*homme; — Italian: *i* libri, *gli* sbagli; etc.);

4 — the *inflections* for plurality, tense, possession, etc.;

5 — the *sound changes* and function shifts (involving positional shift) brought about by *derivation* (e.g., just, unjust, justice, justly);

6 — the *structural groupings* (of verbals, of prepositional phrases, etc.);

7 — the *word-order clues* of function and meaning;

8 — the *meaning* of words depending on the context or on the situation

being discussed (e.g., the head of the statue, of the table, of lettuce) ;

9 — the *formulas, introductory words,* and *hesitation words* which occur in speech;

10 — the *cultural meaning* embedded in the message.

The understanding or decoding of any "message" or stream of speech will depend on the learner's familiarity with each of the elements above and on his *expectation* of them in a variety of situations, because he has heard them numerous times in different combinations and in situations in which they are appropriate. His rapid grasp of all the elements will hinge on two other factors of great importance: he must be aware of the elements of the language which are redundant (see page 10) so that he can gloss over the second (or third) redundant clue in order to concentrate on the elements which are high in information in the particular message he is hearing.

Essential, too, in listening is that the learner *remember* the important details of the first part of the message (an utterance or a series of utterances) while he continues to listen to the other parts.

These skills are developed over a long period of time in logical, incremental steps. We start with short sentences in one situation which students can retain easily; we proceed within the same situation to longer sentences, then to combinations of sentences first in the same and later in different situations. From emphasis on short-term retention, we proceed to give students practice in retaining material over a longer period of time — as, for example, in dramatizing a dialogue several days (or weeks) after its presentation; or in writing a paragraph on a film seen or a lecture heard one or two weeks before; or in taking a dictation in which the segment dictated is made increasingly longer.

To aid the students in retaining increasingly longer segments and later — as a corollary — in producing these longer segments, they should listen to the same material many times. As they hear the same stretch of speech the fourth or fifth time, they will anticipate or "supplement" the sounds and sound sequences they are about to hear. This phenomenon happens to us whenever we listen to our native language. The speaker whose speech style we are familiar with and the situation about which we are hearing or in which we are participating at the time as well as the lexical combinations which we have grown to expect, all make it possible for us to hear only fifty percent of what is being said and yet to "decode" or understand the "message."\*

In developing the learners' listening skill, it is essential that we

---

\* The importance of "supplementation" is discussed in the excellent study by Agard and Dunkel, *An Investigation of Second Language Teaching.*

do not slow down or distort speech in any way in the mistaken notion that it will help students to understand. Anything heard by the students should contain the rhythm, intonation, pauses, contractions, and elisions which are authentic and normal in the target language. (When a word, structure, or phrase is isolated for intensive practice, it should first be heard in a normally spoken utterance. After its intensive study, it should be reinserted immediately in the normal utterance or in a piece of connected speech, at normal, conversational speed.)

## Audio Activities

Among the experiences and activities which will enhance the students' listening ability are:
1. Listening to you as you:
   a) present sounds, sound sequences, intonation patterns, and utterances with contrasting stress and pauses;
   b) give directions related to classroom routines (e.g., taking attendance, assigning homework or other projects);
   c) give model sentences based on some grammatical or lexical feature of language;
   d) give cues or ask questions to stimulate appropriate responses in pattern practice activities;
   e) tell a story;
   f) read a passage, poem, or playlet orally;
   g) model a dialogue;
   h) tell about an incident that happened to you or someone else;
   i) establish the situation for a dialogue, a film, a radio broadcast, etc.;
   j) give a dictation (gradually increasing the number of syllables the students are to retain before they write) (see pages 133-34);
   k) give a listening comprehension exercise (see page 134);
   l) give a lecture on some aspect of culture;
   m) prepare them for writing a composition;
   n) greet visitors and engage them in conversation;
   o) give directions for tests;
   p) engage in directed practice activities (see pages 97-98).
2. Listening to other pupils give directions, ask questions, give summaries, recount incidents (e.g., what they saw or what happened on their way to school).
3. Engaging in a dialogue dramatization.
4. Listening to outside speakers or to other school personnel.
5. Listening to the *same* phonograph records of language lessons, songs, plays, poems, speeches, *many times*.

6. Listening to tape recordings of pronunciation, structure, or vocabulary drills; dictations; comprehension exercises; poems; speeches; songs; lectures; or plays, *often enough* so that they can anticipate or "supplement" what they are about to hear.

7. Listening to sound films *several times* — those especially prepared for language learners or short clips of longer, general ones — and selected radio and television programs.

8. Engaging in telephone conversations.

9. Interviewing people.

10. Attending lectures, conferences, and foreign language club meetings.

11. Participating in discussion groups and panel discussions.

12. Going to the movies and to the theater.

13. Playing language games.

14. Participating in a spontaneous, unprepared role-playing activity in which they are forced to listen attentively in order to make an appropriate response to a statement or question spoken by their partner. ("Let's pretend you are an employer and X has come to you for an after-school job." Since the first speaker may say anything from "How old are you?" to "Have you had any experience?" to "What makes you think you can do this job?," the second speaker must have been trained to seize the important element in the first speaker's utterance and to retrieve a suitable response from his stock of those learned.)

Since two people are always involved in them, the mention of telephone conversations or "role-playing activities" brings us to a consideration of the speaking skill. Listening and speaking are interdependent to a great extent. Generally, but not necessarily, improvement in listening comprehension may bring with it an improvement in the ability to speak. However, a person may speak with a certain degree of fluency and speed — in giving a summary, for example — without a correlative degree of facility in understanding the normal stream of speech of a native speaker. In the give-and-take of conversation, and especially in listening to a telephone conversation or to a radio broadcast, listening may lag far behind speaking. While we can control what we say, we cannot control what others will say.

This is true although speaking is a more complex skill than listening for, in addition to knowing the sound, structure, and vocabulary systems of the language, the speaker must think of the idea he wishes to express, either initiating the monologue or conversation or responding to a previous speaker; he must change the position of tongue and jaw in order to articulate the appropriate sounds; he must be consciously aware of the grammatical, lexical, and cultural features needed to express his idea; he must be sensitive to any change in the "register" or style necessitated by the person(s) to whom he is speaking and the situation in which the conversation is taking place. All of these interrelated acts — mental and physical — must take place simultaneously.

The spontaneous, creative use of language may take years of learning depending upon the age of the learner, his motivation, his aptitude, and, above all, on the quality of instruction. It is brought about gradually — nearly imperceptibly sometimes — by the enthusiastic, creative teacher using special techniques and specially designed materials.

It is brought about by the teacher and the curriculum writer, recognizing that the skill of speaking must be developed in two parallel streams. In order to engender interest and encourage communication, simple authentic conversations should be engaged in from the very first day; songs should be taught; stories with repetitive refrains should be heard to which students respond; questions such as "What would you say" should be asked to which students will respond in the target language. For example, after teaching greetings, you might say, on the very first day, *in the students' native tongue,* "You are walking to school and you meet Mr. X. What would you say?" (As quickly as possible the question "What would you say?" should be asked in the foreign language.)

At the same time, however, each item of language and each grammatical operation possible should be taught in a systematic, logical progression so that the appropriate features of sound, arrangement, and word form are eventually used habitually and automatically, and so that the stream of speech becomes increasingly more sustained and more complex. It is essential, too, for us to teach students the range of experiences and situations in which certain patterns of speech are permissible. For example, in English, we say "How do you do" only when we are introduced to someone. We say "Good-bye" only when we are taking leave of someone at any time during the day or night. The dimension of experiences in which an expression or segment of speech may be used should be taught along with the sounds, meaning, and position of the expression.

There are numerous activities in addition to the pattern practices (see pages 93-99) which will gradually foster the innovative, stimulus-free speaking behavior which is one of the primary objectives of foreign language instruction. Some of those listed below are best done at beginning levels; some must be left for upper intermediate and advanced levels. Only you, the teacher, can select and grade the activities which are most suitable for your students at any particular time.

## Speaking Activities

In addition to engaging in pattern practice drills, students may be asked to:

1. Respond to directions given by you or by another pupil.
2. Formulate directions for other pupils (for example: "Show me [Show us] the . . ." "Point to the —." "Walk to the door and open it." "Ask X how old he is." "Ask X if he thinks he will continue his studies.").
3. Prepare "original" sentences based on language patterns or vocabulary being learned.
4. Answer questions based on any class or out-of-class experience (clubs, TV programs, movies, work).
5. Frame questions to ask you or other pupils, based on reading or on a shared experience.
6. Tell what appears in a picture or on a chart.
7. Tell a favorite tale or experience in their own words. If necessary, key words may be suggested by you.
8. Give a report on a prepared topic and be prepared to answer questions on it.
9. Summarize a paragraph, an article, or a book.
10. Set up stores, a library, a post office, and other appropriate community resources and simulate realistic conversations for each. (These can be made increasingly longer and more complex as learners grow in language ability.)
11. Play language games.
12. Conduct a discussion, a forum, or some other oral group activity based on research (e.g., a cultural topic).
13. Make tape recordings or records.
14. Engage in telephone conversations and role-playing activities.
15. Read a book in the native language and give a report on it in the foreign language.
16. Dramatize a dialogue, a situation, or a play.

Several other activities as well as the use of dialogues mentioned in 16 above are so effective in developing the students' speaking ability that we should examine them in greater detail.

## The Use of Dialogues

Dialogues in which individuals listen to a speaker and react, either by speaking themselves or by performing some action, are especially well suited for practicing language in realistic communication situations. The time spoken about and reacted to may be the present, the past, or the future. The reaction or response to initial statements, questions, or formulas (expressions such as "Would you mind?" or

111

"How do you feel?") may include: answering questions; asking questions; making statements; making a rejoinder; expressing agreement, disagreement or some other emotion; performing some action; using another formula. Dialogues permit the students to practice whole statements, questions, or formulas of the language rather than items or bits of language which, by themselves, do not duplicate the real communication or interaction which goes on among individuals. The study and dramatization of dialogues helps students gain insight into the various cultural aspects of the foreign community. A dialogue in English about having a date with a girl would signal to Spanish learners, for example, that dating customs differ in their country from those of many English-speaking countries.

Hearing models which they learn to imitate and studying variants of the dialogue utterances, as will be suggested below, should guide the students toward an understanding of sentences they may never have met before and toward the creation of sentences they may never have spoken before.

Dialogues, as noted above (see page 71), may be used effectively as an approach or introduction to the learning of aspects of grammar, vocabulary, or pronunciation. After a dialogue is learned, you may, in presenting a language feature for intensive study, help the students recall that they can already understand it and have learned to say it.

On the other hand, you may prefer to use the dialogue as a "culminating" activity, that is, as a learning experience which recombines in a normal, conversational exchange many of the language features that had been presented and practiced in individual utterances and in drill activities.

It may be important at this point to add that it is not necessary for the students to have an active grasp of each structural or vocabulary feature of a dialogue. Some items included in a dialogue may not be taught intensively either when it is initially presented or, indeed, for several weeks or months after that.

Dialogues should be prepared for each unit of work in your text (if none are included) and for each large socio-cultural category such as Identification (names, addresses), School, and People and Places in the Community. Dialogue themes may be further subdivided — where relevant and essential — into such topics as Shopping for Food, Clothing, and Travel. As is obvious, many of the dialogues could be placed under different headings, since they could include vocabulary common to several possible situations.

Within each category, three types of dialogues* should be practiced:

---

* Examples of the three types of dialogues will be found in the Appendix.

1. *Conversational exchanges of two single utterances.*

2. *Sustained dialogues.* These are of two kinds:
   a) In the first, the speakers make *more than one utterance* each time they speak.
      Here is an example:
      — Gosh! That's a good-looking jacket. When did you buy it? (formula; statement; question)
      — Do you really like it? I bought it a week ago. It was a graduation present from my parents. (question; statement; statement)
   b) In the second type, there is an *extended exchange of utterances* between two speakers. The utterances may be single or multiple. Here is an example:
      — Where did you go last night?
      — To the movies.
      — What did you see?
      — "The Windmill."
      — Oh! I saw it. Did you (enjoy) it? (multiple utterances)
      — Yes. Very much.

   In most instances, it will be possible to practice a dialogue such as the one above in logical sub-divisions. You will note, for example, that the first two sets of lines constitute normal two-utterance dialogues.

3. *Spiral dialogue.* This is a series of dialogues dealing *with one theme* which grow progressively more complex. The language items used in the first dialogue are repeated in the second, third, or fourth of the series but they are expanded or combined with other items in numerous ways — phrases, clauses, adjectives in pre-noun position may be added, for example, for use at more advanced levels of language learning.

## Presenting and Practicing a Dialogue

To help students *understand*\* the dialogue or the segment of a sustained dialogue you are teaching, you may use any one or a combination of these procedures:

1. Give the situation of the entire dialogue simply and briefly in the foreign language, pointing to objects or pictures and *pointing to each of the figures* (stick figures drawn on the blackboard, draw-

---

\* Students' books should be closed during the "understand" and "say" segments of your lesson.

ings, flannel board cutouts, etc. [see pages 171-72]) as you tell what each one is saying. Students must be helped to relate the utterances to the appropriate speaker.

2. Teach new words and expressions through association with pictures, real objects, pantomime, or gestures before saying the dialogue.

3. Give the native language *equivalent,* not word-for-word translations, of each utterance. (This is practicable only when all students have the same native language background and if you know their native language.)

4. Explain the situation briefly in the native language.

To help students *say* the dialogue with reasonable fluency, you may wish to follow this procedure:

1. Have the students listen to the short dialogue or to a short portion of a longer one,* three or four times. The first two times stand at the board and *point to each figure as he or she speaks.* After that, particularly if the group is large, you may wish to stand in various parts of the room so that students can see your mouth and your gestures.

2. Say each utterance three or four times and engage the entire group in choral repetition. Model the utterance each time before you ask the group to repeat it.

3. Divide the group in half. Help each half of the group take one role in the dialogue.

4. Reverse the roles. (Repeat this procedure several times.)

5. Ask a more able student to come to the front of the room to take one role of the dialogue. You will take the other. Help him by standing behind him or next to him and whispering the utterance he has to produce.

6. Follow this procedure with several individual students, depending on the complexity of the dialogue.

7. Help two students dramatize the utterances or ask one student to take one role *while the rest of the class takes the other.*

8. Help the students learn the dialogue by writing it on the chalkboard; gradually erasing more and more words from each utterance; and encouraging the students to reconstruct it.

In the case of long utterances, you should divide them into short logical segments for ease in repetition. (See page 81 for a suggested procedure.)

---

*Some teachers like to say the entire dialogue through once even when they are planning to teach only a short segment of it intensively during that lesson.

# Extending and Reinforcing Language Skills through Dialogue Study

As noted earlier, dialogues may be used as "points of departure" for the intensive study of sound, structure, vocabulary, or culture. They may also be used to place linguistic features which have been studied in isolation into situational and cultural contexts in which they are generally found. They can also help to give students insight into the numerous ways in which newly learned linguistic items can be combined with familiar ones.

Dialogues serve many additional purposes, however, any of which will contribute to the growing ability of students to understand, speak, and, later, to read and write while learning something of the customs and values of the foreign speakers. For example, you may ask that:

1. The dialogue itself be *read, copied, summarized,* or *adapted* (to indicate different speakers, a different time, or a different point of view), preceding and following such activity by dramatization and oral reading.

2. *Students answer questions* about it or that they *formulate questions* which their fellow students will answer.
   The questions are generally of three kinds:
   a) Those which are based directly on the utterances, people, and situations in the dialogue being studied (often called Dialogue Variation);
   b) Those in which the dialogue situation is related to the lives and experiences of the students. If, for example, the dialogue is about listening to records, the questions could elicit the likes and dislikes of the students, their listening habits, etc. (called Dialogue Personalization);
   c) Those which require the students to make inferences. ("How do we know?" "Why do you think ...?")

3. *Students change the dialogues.* More able students at the early levels or all students at intermediate or advanced levels may be asked under your guidance to suggest *alternative whole utterances* which could be substituted for a given utterance in the dialogue, without changing the situation. For example, a first sentence such as "Let's study together tomorrow" may be changed to "Would you like to study with me tomorrow?"

4. *Students create a dialogue.* As the students build up a repertoire of utterances from dialogues they have learned and as they gain insight into the conversational situations into which the utterances fit, they should be able to recombine these and to create their own dialogues. For example, the two dialogue utterances:
   — Where did you go yesterday?
   — I went shopping for a (dress).

may be formed from two previously learned dialogues such as:

I $\begin{cases} - \text{I went shopping for a dress yesterday.} \\ - \text{Did you buy one?} \end{cases}$

II $\begin{cases} - \text{Where did you go yesterday? I didn't see you.} \\ - \text{I had to go to the (library).} \end{cases}$

Students should also be guided to "create" dialogues within *different* socio-cultural situations. For example, if they have learned to use the structure "How much" with relation to shopping for food, they should be guided to create utterances or entire dialogues using "How much" in buying a plane ticket or buying clothing. A dialogue about a visit to the doctor should lead to the preparation of another about a visit to the dentist. To illustrate further, a dialogue in which the ending of a business letter is discussed should lead them to write a dialogue about informal letters.

Activities such as these are particularly important if we wish to avoid the shock that language learners experience in speaking to native speakers when their stimulus sentence is not followed by the response they had been led to expect. This often happens, when a dialogue has been memorized without further study or creative recombination.

You may notice that we have not mentioned "memorizing" the dialogue. If a dialogue is memorized at all, it should be only by dint of its repetition, dramatization, and adaptation, and not because students have been asked to go home and memorize it. More important than memorizing a dialogue is to "exploit" it by adapting and varying it in ways suggested above.

5. *Students write narrative paragraphs* from the dialogue.
   The dialogues and the many learning activities which they should suggest to you can be used to update traditional textbooks in which few or any dialogues are found or to supplement the dialogues which may already exist in the texts you are using, with others closer to the lives and interests of your students. There is no doubt that their study in the ways suggested and in the ways which your imagination and spirit of creativity will devise, will not only help students grow toward a firm control of separate language skills but, more importantly, will give them the models and the topics they need in order to communicate — the primary goal of language learning.

### Other Techniques for Stimulating Conversation

In addition to their use in sustained dialogue (see page 113), multiple responses should be practiced as soon as the students are able to make them. Whereas at the beginning level the stimulus statement can be "That's a nice tie" and the response "Thank you," the second time the response may be "Thank you. I'm glad you like it," or "Thank you. It's new," or "Thank you. It's a gift from my parents," or anything else you have practiced previously in pattern practice drills.

With more advanced classes you may devise a code or a format for stimulating normal conversational exchanges, which students can eventually follow with little or no prompting on your part. The following (or even a longer list) may be placed on a chart for permanent, easy reference during many parts of the foreign language lesson (the warm-up, summary, "free" conversation period, etc.).

| S (Stimulus)* | R (Response)* |
|---|---|
| Q (Question) | St (Statement) |
| Q and St | Q |
| Q and St and St | St and St |
| St and St and Q | St and St and Q |

The cues in both columns are purely arbitrary. For example, we could have started with a statement which might have elicited a question as a response. You will enjoy making your own chart depending on what you have taught, what your students enjoy, etc.

Your advanced students can use any of the above combinations to prepare increasingly longer conversational exchanges within the list of cultural situations given in Chapter II and the others on pages 266-69. You may wish to prepare another easily accessible chart with a list of twenty or more topics of particular interest to your students in your community. Thus, students can select a topic and be guided to speak about it utilizing the cues in the chart above to practice the normal forms of conversation of native speakers. Following is a simple illustration of this technique using the above format:

## Topic: *A SUIT*

1. Is that a new suit?
2. Yes, it is.

1. Is that a new suit? It looks very good on you.
2. Do you really like it?

1. Is your suit new? I've never seen it before. It looks very good on you.
2. Yes, it is new. It's the first time I've worn it.

---

* The words "Stimulus" and "Response" should not be placed on the chart. They are for your use only.

1. I've never seen that suit. Brown is a good color for you. When did you buy it?
2. I bought it last week. Brown is my favorite color. Do you really like the suit?

It is essential that, as soon as feasible, students also be given practice in recognizing and using the polite forms and appropriate responses of the language. For example, in a situation related to eating:

— Would you pass the salt, please?
— Won't you have a (cup of tea)?
                             — Yes, thank you.
— Won't you have another (sandwich)?
                             — Yes, thank you very much.
                             — No, thank you. I can't now.
— May I get you a (cup of coffee)?
                             — Yes, thank you. I'd like one.
— I'd be very grateful if you got me (a cup of tea).
                             — Of course. I'll be glad to.

etc., etc.

Other items which give the language its authentic "ring" are words like (English): *So, Well, Then, Of Course, As a matter of fact,* which many native speakers use to begin their utterances. Systematic practice should be given in these as they arise in the texts you are using. You should make provision to teach them, however, whether or not they appear in the formal instructional materials.

One other technique you may wish to use is the following: Give the students some sentences about situations and then ask: "What would you say?" or sometimes: "What would you do?" For example, say: "You meet someone in the street who invites you to a party at his home. You've never been to his home. What would you say? What would you ask?" ("Thank you. I'd like to come. Where do you live?"; or "Is it a special occasion?"; or "I'm sorry. I'll be away," or any appropriate response which has been practiced and which, thanks to the situational cues, the students are encouraged to retrieve from their memory store.)

The development of reading and writing abilities to which we will now turn will also contribute to the consolidation of the listening-speaking abilities. Far from devoting less time to listening and speaking as reading and writing activities are engaged in, the reading and writing should serve as a "jumping off" point for oral questions and answers, discussions, summaries, word study activities, or recital of personal, related experiences. The reading and writing activities will provide or add to the content of what the students can talk about.

# READING

The third skill we help our students acquire is that of reading — of bringing meaning to and getting meaning from printed or written material. In addition to helping students comprehend the written material in the texts we are using, we should give them the knowledge and the ability to be able to read other material out of class and later in their lives with ease and enjoyment. With guidance, they should be able to turn to books freely and with a feeling of pleasure and eventually, perhaps, to read the literature of the foreign country in the original.

Before proceeding to the stages or techniques in reading, we would like to make several comments which result from observation and experimentation:

1. Reading is a language-related process. Students should be helped to respond to the visual symbols which represent the same auditory signals to which they had responded previously.

2. Listening and speaking should always precede reading. It is only after students can say material with reasonable fluency that they should be permitted to see it.

The length of time the teaching of reading should be deferred has been a matter of some controversy among language specialists. Again, it has been our experience that there is no one answer which will suit every situation. Before being asked to teach a language television program for children of ten and eleven, one of the authors had considered it desirable to defer the teaching of reading to children for one or two years. The letters the television viewers sent indicated that they tried to write what they had heard using their own "native" language spellings. The spelling was completely distorted, of course.

In a study completed at the University of Chicago by Dunkel and Pillet,* one of the findings indicated that pupils who can read in their native tongue want a textbook. They are used to textbooks in other subjects; the text permits them to reinforce at home what had been learned in class; it gives the study of foreign languages the status and respectability of other subjects in the curriculum.

Certainly language learners should hear any material *many* times and be able to repeat it with reasonable accuracy before they see it, but the number of class hours which should elapse between hearing, saying, and reading must be flexible and should depend on several factors. In addition to the age of the students, their literacy in their native tongue, the length of the course, the examination requirements, and the other factors within the students which must always be con-

---

* Dunkel, H. and R. Pillet, *French in the Elementary School: Five Years' Experience.*

119

sidered in presenting and practicing any feature or skill, the similarity or divergence between the graphemes (the written symbols) of the native language and those of the foreign language must also be taken into account. In some languages, the "fit" is good; that is, there is a one-to-one correspondence or nearly so between the sound and the grapheme. This is true, for example, in Spanish and Italian. It is not true in English or in French. In English, for instance the /i/ may be written as *i* (machine), *ie* (piece), *ea* (peace), *ee* (see), etc. The same written letters may have different sounds in other combinations. Note p*ie* /paɪ/, t*ear* /tɛ:r/, b*een* /bɪn/.

The chart below is *not* designed to provide the definitive answer to this knotty question but to help you arrive at your own conclusions.

| Age | Duration of Program | Principal Aims | Length of Time of *Possible* Deferment of Reading |
|---|---|---|---|
| 11-14 | 5 years | The four skills | 1 or 2 months or less |
| 14-18 | 2 years | | 2-4 weeks⎫ or less |
| | 3 years | The four skills | 4-6 weeks⎭ |
| 18 and | 1 year | Reading | 1 week or less |
| over | 2 years | The four skills | 2-4 weeks |
| | More than 2 | The four skills | 2-4 weeks |

With highly motivated students,* the reading of basic utterances taught may be engaged in during the very first lesson. After students hear and say "Good morning," for example, twenty or more times, you might place "Good morning" on the board and say "Look, listen." Then you would say "Good morning" exactly as you had been saying it during oral practice, sweeping your hand over the entire expression.

3. In reading (and this happens in reading our native tongue, too), we make sounds in our throat. We read faster, if we know how to say and group the sounds and if we don't stumble over them. It is essential, therefore, that any difficulty in sounds, sound sequence, intonation, or pauses be clarified *before* students are asked to read silently or orally.

You should always read aloud for the students any material you are going to assign them. Since many languages are not written the way they sound, it is important that you read aloud so that: a) students don't reinforce incorrect sounds in their silent speech; b) they will comprehend words they meet in their reading which they have heard spoken and vice versa. If you are not convinced, pause for just

---

* See the article by G. Lipton, "To Read or Not to Read" in *ACTFL*, Vol. 3, No. 2, Dec. 1969.

a moment and say the following English words ending in *ough:* enough, through, though, bough, dough, hiccough.

In addition to the rapid identification of sound-symbol correspondence and of words, students must be helped to read *word groups* which have meaning over and above the meaning of each word. Look at the sentence: "He went in spite of the rain." Unless "in spite of" is read as a group, the meaning of the sentence is not clear. Students may give two other meanings, "He went in" and "He went in spite," depending on the pause.

In reading, as in listening and speaking, *meaning* is a composite of pronunciation, grammar, lexicon, and culture.

"Free" reading is a complex skill. In order to read with comprehension, ease, and enjoyment, students must know all the elements of the sound system of the language, its syntax and structures, and its vocabulary.

In addition, they must be familiar with the situation which is under discussion and with any allusion to an aspect of culture. This is as true in reading one's native language as it is in reading a second language.

What are your responsibilities in developing reading skills? There are six principal ones:

1. You may have to *extend* the experiences of the pupils so that they will understand the situations and the cultural allusions;
2. You will have to *teach* the *sounds* and *meanings* of new words;
3. You will have to teach the *sound-symbol correspondences;*
4. You will have to help them *understand the structures* ("included sentences" are usually not easy for language learners) ;
5. You will have to teach them the *comprehension skills;*
6. You will have to help them *increase their speed* in reading.

In order to keep the students' motivation at a high level, your teaching should proceed in *two parallel streams:* You will help the students read interesting, meaningful material as quickly as feasible. At the same time, you will systematically teach them the sound-symbol correspondences they will need to know and respond to habitually in order to read independently. Proportionately more time should be spent on the actual reading of material at the students' maturity and interest levels than on the systematic development of the correspondences. The reasons are obvious.

### Developing the Subsidiary Skills

How do you help students develop the skills they need in reading? In several ways:

1. You help them *enrich their vocabularies* by giving them (or

helping them discover) cognates (if their native language is one with similar word roots), paraphrases, antonyms, synonyms, and words of the same family (e.g., bed, bedspread, bedclothes, or jewels, jewelry, jeweler, jewelry store). You help them "see" little words in bigger words (able, unable, inability). You help them recognize prefixes (unkind, unable, unaccustomed; or retell, redo) and suffixes (childish, mannish, or quietly, slowly, kingly). You help them guess meanings of words from the surrounding words, or in other words, you help them use "contextual clues." You sometimes give the meaning of abstract words in the native language of the students if you know the language. (You should ask a native speaker of the foreign language the term for important abstract words which cannot be pictured and either say them yourself or have a native speaking teacher or student assistant say them.) You teach the students to use a suitable dictionary.

2. You help students grasp the meaning of structures in any of the ways mentioned above and you give limited practice in their use. During the reading lesson, the presentation or practice of a new structure should be brief and confined only to its function in the reading materials. *The important thing is to get to the reading.* Naturally, nothing will prevent you from giving a more detailed presentation and more extensive practice in the structure when logical and feasible. Indeed, an excellent device for motivating the teaching of a structure is to remind the students that they had met it in a reading passage.

3. As simply as possible in the foreign language and with the help of pantomime, pictures, clocks, calendars, or any other appropriate device, you give the pupils a knowledge of the situation in the reading passage and insight into the cultural allusions. If you can, and if you consider it necessary, you may give a brief explanation of the situation in the students' native tongue.

4. Using high-frequency words with which students are familiar, you will teach the graphemes, the written symbols which correspond to each sound of the language. This knowledge is built up systematically but gradually from the simpler to the more complex. For example, in English we might proceed from the spelling of the sound [æ] in one-syllable words to the variant spellings of the sound [e] to the spelling of words with "silent" letters as in *know* and *gnaw*.

5. You ensure comprehension in various ways. We will mention only a few:
   — You ask many different kinds of questions on the same sentence. (This procedure is often labeled "saturation" practice and is especially recommended at the first two levels.)
   For example, with "John is an American," you can ask:
   a) an inverted question: "Is John an American?"

b) alternate questions: "Is John an American or an English-man?"

c) question-word questions with "Who," "What," etc.: "Who is an American? What is John?"

d) In later stages, you will ask "Why" questions and inferential questions on the reading material: "What do you think ...?" or "How do you think ...?"

— You will ask questions, the answers to which the students can find verbatim (word by word) in the material being read.

— You will give sentences in the passage out of sequence and ask the students to place them in the proper order.

— You will ask for a summary of a paragraph. The summary should include the important ideas in the sequence in which they appeared in the paragraph.

— You will ask for the main idea of the paragraph.

— You will ask the students to find the words or sentences which describe a person or a process, which show that the person talked about was in a hurry or angry, or whatever the passage is about.

— You will ask students to give the key words in each sentence. (This will enable them to take notes later on [see page 133].)

6. How do you increase the students' speed?:

a) You read the material aloud for them.

b) When you have them read silently, you time the reading.

c) You keep decreasing the time judiciously throughout the year.

d) You discourage lip movements.

e) You give them a definite purpose for reading. They must find the answer to some questions, or some words, or an idea, or a title, or the central thought, etc.

## The Stages in Reading Growth

We have talked about the process of reading. Let us talk now about the stages in the teaching and learning of reading. There are several stages which should be followed wherever possible.

## Stage I

Students read the material they have learned to say very well or material they may have memorized. This may be a dialogue, a song, a series of action sentences, a simple story of an experience the class members have had and which they have discussed, model sentences containing some of the structures taught, etc.

In this stage, as in the next one, students must be helped to

123

develop increasingly automatic visual responses to the graphic shapes they will see in print. They must be made consciously aware that the written words represent sounds.

You will have the students say the known material without looking at it. Then you will read the material aloud as the students look at it in their textbooks or workbooks, or on the blackboard.

They can then read it in chorus after you. Next, groups and individuals may be asked to read it.

At beginning levels, individual words or related groups of words from the reading may be placed on flash cards or cue cards. One student may be asked to read a card; another student may be asked to match the word(s) on the card with those on the board. This is particularly useful when the graphemes are not similar to those of their native tongue and when the "fit" is poor.

To give practice in instant recognition, you may place familiar directions on flash cards to which students are to respond instantly (e.g., Raise your right hand; Stand; Face each other).

## Stage II

You and/or a group of foreign language teachers in the school or community combine the known words and structures into a different dialogue or paragraph. The students are helped to read this newly organized material in which all the elements are familiar to them.

## Stage III

The students start to read material in which some of the words and structures are unfamiliar to them. A committee of teachers can write this type of material, or existing texts with a low vocabulary and structure level, but at an interest level in harmony with the age of the students, may be used. Informal experimentation has shown that students experience little or no difficulty when one new word is interspersed among about thirty familiar words. Often grammar texts contain paragraphs and selections which are suitable for reading at this level. Below you will find a detailed technique for teaching reading at Stage III.

## Stage IV

Some reading specialists recommend the use of simplified literary texts or magazines. There are others who object to the use of simplified texts on the ground that they do not convey the style or the spirit of the author. There exist excellent simplified books on the commercial market, however, which can be used to great advantage with students who are still not advanced enough to read the originals and who may never, unfortunately, reach the stage of doing so. The technique used for teaching this simplified or adapted material will be the same as the one outlined for Stage III.

## Stage V

Unlimited material. The whole world of books should be open to your students.

When do learners attain the skills required for Stage V? Some may never attain them as they would not in their native language. Some may do so after a six-year program in the junior and senior high school; some after one or two years of university training. All the factors in learning which we have stated several times must be considered in discussing the "mastery" of this skill as of any other.

### *A Procedure:*

When Stage III reading is introduced, the reading lesson should be done intensively; that is, the students' attention should be drawn to nearly every sound, every grammatical structure, word or cultural fact contained in it. A number of questions should be asked about each utterance in the material. This procedure is outlined under Technique A below. After about a month of intensive reading practice,* you might introduce the procedure for extensive reading (Technique B). When students have developed reasonable ability in using both techniques, you might vary the procedures, depending on the difficulty of the material, its interest to the students, or the number of pages you are required to cover in one semester. You could do all the reading intensively for one week or two weeks and extensively for another week or you can do both types of reading in one lesson as outlined here.

In teaching reading at Stages III and IV, you will find it desirable to:

1. *Divide the reading* for that day into two or three sections so that you can vary your techniques and break up the vocabulary load.

2. *Motivate the reading. Relate it to the pupil's own experiences,* or, if the reading is part of a long story, relate it to the longer story by *eliciting a summary* of the material already read. Follow this by asking a challenging question or questions to interest the students in the reading and to ready them for the part to come.

---

* Of course, other language activities and other skills are also developed during this time. See the chapter on "Planning a Balanced Program."

3. *State the purpose of the reading.* "What do you think will happen? . . . Let's find out," or "Let's read more about . . ."

4. *Explain any difficulties* in the first portion. Place (or have placed) the new words on the board, not more than eight if possible. Say them; have the students say them after you. Explain them in the ways we have mentioned. You may even wish to give a short summary of the reading portion weaving in the words on the board. The difficulties may be in the sounds or sound sequences (elisions, contractions), the structures or syntax, the vocabulary, or the cultural allusions.

5. *Read the passage.*

After the difficulties have been clarified, you may do several things: You may use Technique A (below) for the three portions of the day's reading; or you may use Technique B for the three portions; or use ABA or BAB. (When you first start Stage III reading with your students, it is desirable to use A for most of the reading as noted above.)

## Technique A

Read *each* line aloud,* in logical normal thought groups. Ask simple questions on each line. Make sure the answer is on the printed page so that students will feel free to refer to it. (The use of the exact words in the text will minimize the possibility of errors.) At the end of the paragraph, ask for a summary, with several students contributing one idea each. If the summary causes problems, ask questions to help elicit the summary. It is essential that the summary be sequential as a preparation for other oral and written activities.

## Technique B

Read the entire portion aloud; then ask the students to read it silently. *(Time the reading.)* After they have read, ask them questions; or have them complete sentences which you have placed on the board; or ask them if statements you make are True or False (if they are false, they are to give the true answer) ; or ask for a summary.

6. *Elicit a complete summary* of the day's reading.

---

* The question of "book opened" or "closed" is also controversial. Some teachers advocate closed books. Some prefer that students' books be open. If time permits, you may have students close their books while you read the first time and have the books opened during your second *oral* reading which will be followed by questions.

We should remember, however, that reading means looking at a page of writing. Classroom activities should distinguish between "listening comprehension" — where students will not see any written material — and "reading comprehension."

*Vary your techniques* according to your program, the time available, your students, etc.

7. *Engage the class in related activities.*

   a) Distribute four or five sequential questions you have pre-pared on the reading material. Have one student read a question; another answer it orally; another place the an-swer on the board. When all the answers are on the board, correct any mistakes with class cooperation and then read the answers. The students can read them in chorus after you. The sequential answers will constitute another sum-mary of the material.

   b) Read the selection, one sentence at a time, and have the class read in chorus after you.

   c) Have the new words (see step 4) used in other appropriate sentences.

   d) Do word study drills with your students (e.g., "Find the synonym of ............... in line 4." "Make a noun from the word ............... in line 3." "Use the word ............... in a sen-tence." "Explain the word ................" "Give a paraphrase of the expression ................").

   e) Have the students formulate questions (inverted or *Wh*) on the story which they will ask their classmates to answer. Place question words — who, what, when, where, how, how much, how long, why, etc. — on the board or on a chart for easy reference to help them in the formulation.

   f) Have them retell the story using the key words you will supply.

   g) With books open, have them give the key words in each sentence.

   h) Have them give sentences similar to selected ones in the text.

8. *Assign the same reading passage for home or laboratory study.* Assign appropriate related oral and written activities like those above or others you will devise.

• A few other words should be said about reading. You may wish at the intermediate or advanced level to assign supplementary reading in the foreign language to your more able students. Suggest modern books in their area of interest; give them sufficient time to read a book. (You may wish to assign different parts of the same book, or books with different points of view, to several students.) Create the opportunity for them to tell you and their classmates what they have read. Make the supplementary reading the stimulus for discussion and "free" communication.

• The use of "bilingual" texts is also controversial. By a bilingual text we refer to one in which the native language and the foreign language equivalents are given on two facing pages. Such texts can be used profitably, as can any other instructional material, with careful teacher guidance.

Assuming that the equivalents have been well rendered, the bilingual text forces the students to perceive language on a sentence level rather than on a word-by-word level. The nature of language and the different inherent systems of language will become increasingly clear to them as they see, for example, on the English side, "He has just gone out" and on the French side, "Il vient de sortir" — or on the Spanish, "Acaba de salir." The equivalent expressions will be reinforced as they are read aloud or silently, discussed, or used in other oral activities.

The occasional and judicious use of a bilingual text eliminates the students' "thumbing through" the dictionary all the time and often coming up with the incorrect equivalent. We strongly believe that students should be taught to use the dictionary, but that skill, too, should be guided by the teacher who can point out the contextual clues which make one dictionary meaning more logical or appropriate than another one.

If bilingual texts (with facing pages) are available you may wish to use them occasionally as an aid in reading or translating. With an inexpensive opaque projector, the two pages can be flashed easily on the screen or on a wall and can serve to motivate a host of language activities.

• It is generally unwise to ask students whose oral reading is poor to read aloud for the entire class. Neither the student nor his fellow students will profit from the oral reading. On the contrary, poor pronunciation may be reinforced or you will have to make numerous corrections. The student should be asked to read to you alone at your desk (so that you may help bring him up to class level) at times when the rest of the class is occupied with other meaningful work which you have assigned.

• Many other reading-related activities are preferable to having individual students stand and read one or two sentences of the narrative reading passage. Individual oral reading (except for dialogues and special poems) should generally be engaged in on a limited basis — perhaps five minutes of any reading period. (This is not a hard and fast rule, however. You, the teacher, are the best judge of the amount of time to be spent on individual oral reading.)

• Occasionally, but judiciously, you might ask for the translation of one or more expressions or sentences. In general, however, reading and translation should be separate classroom activities.

128

# WRITING

The fourth and last of the communication skills to be discussed is that of writing. When we say "writing," we mean primarily the carefully guided marks on paper that we assist our students in making unless we are teaching a course in creative writing or advanced composition.

We guide our pupils through several stages over a long period of time — the length depending, as usual, on their ages, interests, capacities, needs — to a freer stage where they are able to write a "composition" or "essay" on a topic of interest to them with few or no errors.

Specialists in the field of second language teaching and learning usually recommend that in the secondary schools, this "freer" type composition be deferred until the middle of the third year. At the university level, it may well come in the middle of the second year.

Naturally, the type of writing system (alphabet, picture) which exists in the native language is an important factor in determining the ease or speed with which our students will learn to write (that is, to put down on paper the conventional symbols [the graphemes] for the sounds they have learned to say). Some students may have to learn an entirely new writing system.

## General Considerations

Before discussing several types of activities which will give students practice in writing and which may help lead to creativity, let us mention a few general considerations.

— Little or no writing should be practiced in class. Class time should be devoted to listening and speaking activities which the students cannot do by themselves outside of class. (It goes without saying that with students who are not accustomed to writing the graphic symbols of the target language, some class time may be devoted to holding paper, pen, and pencil, and to putting down the graphic shapes. This need be done only when writing is introduced, however.)

— In order not to interrupt the normal, oral flow of your lesson, any copying of model sentences, paradigms, dialogues, vocabulary items, etc., should be done at a specific time toward the very end of the lesson.

— Dictation and aural comprehension exercises, however, should be done in class. (Procedures for giving these will be explained below.) We generally give dictation of six to ten lines about once a week.

— Writing should reinforce the structural and lexical items which have been taught, as well as the listening, speaking, and reading skills.

— Progressively, and in small steps, you should teach students:

1) The sound-spelling correspondences
2) The mechanics of writing (punctuation, capitalization, spelling)
3) Letter writing, formal and informal (greetings, endings, other mechanics)
4) Practical, functional writing needed for note-taking, outlining, summarizing
5) The organization and expression of an idea which will convey its desired meaning and permit the reader to understand the message
6) The differences (where such exist) between speaking and writing, between informal and more formal styles of writing, and between "modes of discourse"

    In English, for example, we generally contract and elide sounds in speech but we do not necessarily do so in writing. The vocabulary we use may differ depending on the message we are attempting to convey and the person(s) to whom we are addressing the message. (These variations have been termed "registers," as you know.)

There are two major types of writing, both overlapping: practical and creative. Practical writing is found in letters as well as in outlines, summaries, or a series of notes; creative writing, in literature. Many of your students will never write "creatively" as they would not in their native tongue, but creativity, where observed or suspected, should be encouraged and carefully nurtured. *All* students can be taught to express their ideas clearly and correctly.

Students should be helped to recognize and to use different "modes" of discourse. The mode may be narrative, expository, critical, or a combination of these. Any of these "modes" may be found in letters, dialogues, poems, essays, or plays.

— Writing has been characterized as written thinking. Students should be encouraged to express their ideas, experiences, thoughts, and feelings. Any free or creative writing they are required to do should have a content in harmony with their evolving interests.

The ideas may be suggested by you directly, but, better still, they should result from many experiences and oral discussions which you will provide. When this is feasible, students should listen to recordings of music, plays, or speeches. They should look at and discuss works of art; they should examine pictures for details of color, shape, and form; they should view films, slides, and filmstrips; they should read material in many fields of interest; they should listen to talks and lectures by guest speakers.

# Guided Writing Activities

What are some of the guided writing activities which lead to correctness and ease in writing? Students may:

1. *Copy* model sentences, dialogues, or anything that has been spoken or read.

2. *Write out in full* the pattern practice sentences they have practiced orally. Say, for example: "Use the words in the list to write sentences like sentence 1."

> I went to the store.
> to the library, etc.

3. *Write out in full* a number of pattern sentences (using elements from each group previously practiced orally). Say: "Write ten sentences using any word from each column." (It is important to choose words carefully so that the combinations will be logical.)

| I | bought | a | pen. |
| John | wanted | a | pencil. |
| Mr. Jones | found | a | notebook. |
| The boy | paid for | a | ruler. |

4. *Change* the sentences in a known dialogue, short paragraph, or series of action sentences in any one of the following ways:

a) Change the subject and verb to the plural
b) Change the subject (the name of the person or pronoun)
c) If the subject and verb are in the plural, change them to the singular
d) Change by adding *yesterday, later,* or *tomorrow*
e) Change the point of view of the paragraph (e.g., "I went to the movies. I liked the film. The hero was excellent" to: "I went to the movies. I didn't like the film. The hero was terrible," etc.).

5. *Add to* a known dialogue using newly learned structures and vocabulary when these are appropriate. (See pages 115-16.)

6. *Answer* a series of specific questions on any activity or on a reading passage. Wherever possible, the questions should be in logical sequence so that the answers will constitute a well-formed passage. In beginning stages, the questions on the reading passage should be simple inverted questions but should be so worded that the answer will require more than "Yes" or "No" (e.g., Is Harry tired or isn't he [is he not]? Did he study for three hours or didn't he [did he not]?).*

---

* In French, for example, you may prefer to start questions with "Est-ce que" and present inverted questions at a second stage.

7. *Complete* a series of related sentences. The completed sentences will constitute a short "composition." For example:

I went ............................. the other evening.

.............................. went with me.

The music was ........................... .

We heard ........................... .

After the concert we went to a ........................... .

We had ........................ and ........................... .

8. *Write a summary* of material which has been read.

9. *Write an outline* of material which has been read.

10. *Write a letter* (after the appropriate form has been taught and practiced) in which they expand the ideas given by you. For example: "Write a letter to your friend. Tell him the subjects you are studying; the ones you enjoy; your plans for the future. Ask him about his plans."

11. *Write a short paragraph* for each picture in a series (three or four at the most) related to one theme.

12. *Write an original ending* to a story which they have read.

13. *Write an ending* to a story they have *not yet* completed reading or hearing.

14. *Write a simple dialogue* using (or recombining) known structures.

15. *Complete a dialogue* when the first few lines have been given.

16. *Prepare a narrative paragraph* from a dialogue. This activity, as will the next, will require much teacher guidance and patience. (Many similar sentences should be changed to indirect discourse and should be linked together with appropriate connectors over a long period of time in preparation for this activity.)

17. *Prepare a dialogue from a narrative paragraph*.

18. *Reconstruct a dialogue* from one or two words given in each utterance.

Other writing activities — many of them combined with listening, speaking, and reading activities — will also be found effective in preparing students for the "freer" expressional writing which we hope many of our language learners will be able to engage in. You may find one or more of the suggestions below helpful to your students.

Ask the entire class, small groups or individuals as the need arises to:

1. *Combine clauses or sentences* using connectors such as *and, but, although, unless*. (Two sentences only should be combined at first, then three, then four, etc.) Needless to say, extensive practice should

have been given with each connector before students are asked to choose among them.

2. *Use connectors between sentences or paragraphs,* such as *on the other hand, nevertheless, however, furthermore, similarly,* etc.

3. *Transform kernel sentences,* as on pages 54-57, to note the different stylistic effects possible through various transformation rules.

4. *Proofread paragraphs* you will compose containing some mechanical errors, inappropriate vocabulary items, or incorrect structures, etc. (These may be flashed on a wall or screen or they may be duplicated for distribution.)

5. *Take a dictation.* (A procedure will be suggested below.)

6. *Take notes* on a reading passage. Learners will need extensive help in determining what the key words are.

7. *Take a listening comprehension* exercise in which the answers are to be written. (A procedure is outlined below.)

8. *Add an explanation* or appropriate details to a statement that has been given.

9. *Place a series of sentences* in a logical sequence. This may follow reading and oral discussion.

10. *Study a model paragraph* several times in order to note the central thought, the connecting words, the transitional sentences, the details explaining the topic sentences, or the sequence of steps.

11. *Supply* the missing words in a model paragraph which has been studied.

12. *Paraphrase a model paragraph,* substituting not only individual words but structures and phrases. (These words may be supplied by you, or the students may be expected to recall them from previous learning activities.)

13. *Write a paragraph* based on a model but on a different topic (suggested by you but using the same organization and structures).

14. *Memorize carefully* chosen sentences or brief paragraphs.

15. *Reconstruct* a paragraph using key words you will supply.

16. *Rewrite* a paragraph using a different register or style (more formal or colloquial, etc.).

### Giving a Dictation and a Listening Comprehension Exercise

*Dictation:*

In the early stages of learning, the material should be familiar. Its source may be: a short poem or paragraph that has been used for choral reading; a simple song that is sung in class, in the assembly, or in the community; a dialogue that has been dramatized; a paragraph from the reading.

In the intermediate and later stages you may use any selection of about ten lines, such as an anecdote, a short poem, a passage from a reader, or an original passage prepared by you to illustrate a structural item or some cultural concept. The material should be slightly more difficult than that which has been used in the early stages.

The following procedure is recommended at *all* stages of learning (except with isolated words given for spelling or pronunciation practice) :

1. *Motivate* the dictation by relating the material to an experience with which the pupils are familiar — a trip they have taken, a story they have read, a picture they have seen, or a song they have sung.

2. *Give a short summary* of the material to be dictated.

3. *Explain any difficulties* in sounds, vocabulary, concepts, structure, or punctuation* which may appear in the passage. (You may wish to keep some of the "new" words on the blackboard during the dictation.)

It is also desirable in the early dictations to review all the terms used for punctuation marks which students will need for the day's exercise.

4. *Read* the passage at normal speed. (The pupils listen attentively but *do not* write during the first reading.)

5. *Read* the passage again in thought groups, including punctuation. The pupils, at their seats, will write what you dictate. If you plan to correct the dictation in class immediately after giving it (always a good idea), one student may write the dictation on the blackboard during this step.

6. *Read* the passage at normal speed, at which time pupils insert words or punctuation marks they may have missed during the second reading. (Pupils should be trained to leave a space for words they have not understood during the second reading. There should be *no* repetition of words or punctuation for individual students at any time during the three readings.)

7. *The material is corrected* (see page 189 for a procedure).

In step 5 above, the minimal thought group should be dictated in the beginning stages. Later, the thought groups should become increasingly longer to help stretch the memory span of the learners.

There are, of course, variations possible in the procedure. For

---

* Some teachers feel that punctuation marks should be obvious to pupils because of context (people speaking, for example) and intonation. We find that students prefer being told where and how to punctuate.

example, again at beginning levels, in step 5 you may read a thought group and ask the students to repeat it after you *before* they write it; you may read the passage several times before reading it in thought groups; or you may, if you consider it necessary, read a thought group twice before the students are asked to write it. On the other hand, at advanced levels you might wish to train your students to take dictation as they would be required to take it in real life (that is, the material is dictated in thought groups and written down immediately without a preliminary or third reading).

If you have time and appropriate facilities, you may wish to prepare copies of paragraphs for dictation, leaving blank spaces in various places. In this type of "spot" dictation, students (at the second reading) will write *on their separate answer paper* only the words that are missing. You may vary the techniques for giving a spot dictation also as suggested above.

*Aural Comprehension:*

These also provide excellent practice in listening, understanding, and writing. The paragraph chosen for this activity should be short and, if possible, should constitute a complete idea about which you can ask four or five questions, the answers to which can be taken word for word (or nearly so) from the paragraph.

The procedure for conducting an aural comprehension activity is as follows:

a) Motivate the passage by giving a brief summary.
b) Clear up any difficulties.
c) State your aim and the procedure you will follow.
d) Read the paragraph through *twice* at normal speed.
e) Read a question *twice*. Give the students the opportunity to write the answer. (One or two students may write on the board).
f) Continue until you have given all the questions.
g) Read the paragraph again at normal speed.
h) Read the questions again at normal speed.
i) Give the students one or two minutes to check their own work.
j) Correct the material (see page 189).

It goes without saying that 1) *after* step c, many variations are possible, and 2) that the responses to the *Wh* questions should have been built up gradually over a long period of time.

### "Freer," More Creative Writing

Let us examine a procedure which has been found useful in teaching foreign language classes to write several paragraphs, usually labeled "composition."

1. Based on reading that has been done in class — a current event, picture study, something of interest in the environment of the students, or any cultural topic which is timely — the class members select a possible topic with teacher guidance. The title of the theme is placed in the center on the blackboard. *The board is divided into thirds.*

2. We engage in oral discussion of the topic. Students suggest any idea which might be included. The ideas are placed *on the first board* by a more able student or by the teacher in the order in which they are given.

3. The students now discuss the logical sequence of the ideas on the board. What should come at the beginning, in the middle, at the end? The ideas are now listed *in sequence* on the second section of the blackboard. This is also done by an able student (or by the teacher).

4. On the third section, the teacher writes next to each idea the structure and vocabulary items needed to develop it. Some items can be suggested by the students; others are supplied by the teacher. The new items are pronounced by the students based on the teacher's model. The teacher gives several examples of each structure and of each word in sentences related to the composition theme. If time permits, we engage in one or two very brief pattern practice exercises with the new structures, because here as in the reading, the important thing is to get to the writing.

5. Individual students are asked to express one or two sentences under each idea using the language items on the board.

6. Students begin writing the first paragraph. As they do so, the teacher moves about the room suggesting a word, noting errors, looking for a well-written paragraph, etc.

7. After several minutes, two students who have written effective introductory paragraphs are called upon to read them to the group.

8. The class members (or group members if the composition writing has not been a class-wide activity) are asked to copy the material from the board into their notebooks. They are asked to complete the composition at home and to return it after the weekend or a reasonable period of time.

We generally assign one composition every three weeks so that there will be ample opportunity for correction* and for rewriting if it is necessary.

Most important, the intervening time is spent on other listening,

---

\* A procedure for correcting compositions will be found on p. 190.

speaking, reading, and writing activities, all of which contribute in some way to the development of skills for effective writing.

To sum up, "creative" or "freer" writing will evolve from numerous oral language activities. Its content will have been triggered by many sensory experiences and oral discussions. Its surface expression will have been shaped gradually over a long period of time through a multitude of guided, sequential writing activities. As someone noted recently, perhaps only one second language learner in a million will use the second language for "imaginative self-revelation" or for "reflective speculation," but all second language learners *can* be helped to communicate in writing.

Teachers need to ask themselves continuously: What kinds of writing should be given priority at this stage? Has the students' previous instruction in their native tongue and in the foreign language prepared them for this kind of writing? How can they enrich their ideas and their vocabulary? How can they be guided in small, sequential steps to use writing as another means of communication?

These considerations are as valid in teaching writing as in teaching any other facet of the language arts — indeed in teaching anything. The request "Go home and write" should never be made unless you are reasonably certain that the students have been adequately prepared. Only thus can there be any assurance that the learners' efforts will be met with a feeling of achievement and success.

## Some Concluding Remarks

Although the development of each of the language arts has been treated separately, it is essential to reaffirm that each one reinforces all the others and that all of them are integrated in the actual communication of literate, native speakers. We learn to speak, for example, primarily by speaking, but also by listening and by reading.

Our most important task is to help students build a repertoire of utterances which are introduced and emphasized over and over again in appropriate socio-cultural situations so that they will learn to expect them and even to anticipate them as they are listening to a stream of speech or as they are reading.

The knowledge about and the experience of developing each of the skills is attained as students are given extensive practice — from tightly controlled to gradually decontrolled practice in the same wide range of utterances. Gradually, they must be led to understand the utterances as they listen to and read them and to retrieve the appropriate ones from their memory store in speaking and writing in increasingly longer sustained discourse.

No skill is developed without continuous and intensive practice. No skill can be maintained unless it is used frequently. The planning for continuous and intensive practice in which the material which has been taught is constantly reintroduced and consolidated with known material is one of the major responsibilities of the teacher of any foreign language.

## *Suggestions*

— Select a short passage for a listening comprehension exercise for Levels II or III. Write a detailed plan for its presentation.

— Select a short paragraph for a dictation exercise for Level IV. Write a detailed plan for its presentation.

— Using the same paragraph, prepare a spot dictation. Tell the exact words you would use in giving directions to your students for taking the dictation.

— Choose an everyday communication situation.

1) Write four dialogues of four to six lines around the topic for each learning level;
2) Tell how you would make each succeeding dialogue more complex;
3) Give the exact words (and visual materials) you would use in clarifying the situation for your students.

— Prepare a dialogue of six lines for Level I around a common theme. Tell:

1) what questions you would ask about it;
2) how you would help the students vary it;
3) what personal questions based on the theme you would ask.

— Prepare a dialogue of eight lines for Level IV. Tell how you would help relate it to your students' experiences.

— Choose a reading passage from a textbook. Show how you might adapt it to make it simpler; to make it more complex.

— Using the same passage, indicate by vertical lines how you would read it in thought groups.

— Using the same passage again, prepare a series of "saturation" questions on each line.

— Select two brief paragraphs. Copy them. Recombine them.

— Select two dialogues. Copy them. Recombine them.

— Write a detailed plan for teaching twenty selected lines of reading *intensively* to a Level II class.

— Write a detailed plan for teaching twenty lines of reading *extensively* to a Level III class.

— Choose two pages of reading. Tell how you would combine intensive and extensive reading techniques in teaching them. Justify your procedure.

— Using the same reading passage, discuss ten oral activities which would be used in conjunction with it.

— Discuss five ways of "exploiting" a reading passage.

— Prepare five *sequential* exercises which you can use in carefully guided writing.

— Prepare brief drills you could prepare to teach your Level I students the important sound-spelling correspondences in your target language.

— Select a paragraph of twenty lines. Paraphrase it.

— Choose any theme. Prepare a detailed lesson plan for helping your students write a composition about it.

### *Additional Reading*

FRIES, C. *Linguistics and Reading.* New York: Holt, Rinehart & Winston, 1963.

LADO, R. *Language Teaching: A Scientific Approach.* New York: McGraw-Hill, 1964.

LEFEVRE, C. *Linguistics and the Teaching of Reading.* New York: McGraw-Hill, 1963.

O'CONNOR, P. *Pre-Reading Instruction: Modern Foreign Languages in High School.* Washington, D.C.: USOE, 1960.

RIVERS, W. *Teaching Foreign Language Skills.* Chicago: U. of Chicago Press, 1968.

WEST, M. *Learning to Read a Foreign Language.* London: Longmans Green, 1926.

# V

# Providing Cultural Insights

## A DEFINITION

If we define culture from the anthropological point of view as the totality of the ways of life of a language community and if we view language not only as the central feature of culture but also as the basic medium for its expression, the teaching of culture should be a relatively simple task. As we teach the language, we would automatically teach culture. The forms of address, greetings, formulas, and other utterances found in the dialogues or models our students hear and the allusions to aspects of culture found in the reading represent cultural knowledge. Gestures, body movements, and distances maintained by speakers should foster cultural insight.

The range of cultural topics to be taught in the foreign language, however, will include many which, while expressed through language, enter into the realm of art, science, and social studies (economics, politics, government, geography, history, etc.) and may not be found in the usual text dialogues and reading passages.

You will, therefore, have to select and present cultural topics for intensive study. The topics selected for emphasis should serve two major purposes:

1. They should contribute to the intellectual, social, moral, civic, and emotional development of individual students.

2. They should provide the students with insight into another way of life, not only as a means of neutralizing possible prejudices through understanding and appreciation but also as a way of developing a fuller, more complete knowledge of their own culture.

There is consensus among educators that the secondary schools should develop in students the skills, knowledge, information, attitudes, and habits leading to *self-realization,* a sense of *civic responsibility,* an awareness of the importance of *the world of work,* and an insight into the complexity of *human relations.* The linguistic-cultural or purely cultural aspect of language study is ideally suited to fostering the attainment of these objectives.

As students learn that there exists another mode of expression to talk about feelings, wants, needs, and thoughts, and as they read the literature of the foreign country or study its art forms, for example, their intellectual curiosity is aroused and satisfied. They may well be motivated to pursue numerous interests which will contribute to their feeling of self-realization. As they learn about other governments and other attitudes toward the rights and responsibilities of citizens, for example, they are helped to develop a sense of civic responsibility. And so, with the other major secondary school objectives.

Under your guidance, the study of another civilization should produce more enlightened citizens of your own country and young people anxious and eager to comprehend another civilization and predisposed to the sympathetic study of other cultures in later life.

If we accomplish nothing beyond making students aware of the basic oneness of human existence, we will have accomplished a great deal. If, moreover, we underscore the facts that 1) man's interaction with the physical features of nature and 2) historical events over which a society may have had little or no control have produced differences in overt cultural behavior, students will grow in their awareness that such differences do not indicate more innate capacity for creativity or higher forms of intelligence.

In order to inculcate this view in our students, we should ourselves have the conviction that in the basics of life, people everywhere share similar values, concerns, and habits. You will recall* that a study (see page 59) done several years ago at Yale University found that all human beings possessed *seventy-five* traits in common. It is this concept leading to self-illumination which should be transmitted to our students.

Having talked briefly about the "why" of teaching culture, let us take a quick look at the questions "When do we develop cultural insights?" and "How may it be done effectively?"

The development of cultural insights should be both "incidental" and "systematic." As a facet of culture is met in any listening, speaking, "viewing," or reading experience it should be explained. The depth of the explanation will depend on several factors. For example:

1) What is the overall importance of the feature as a clue to the values the people hold dear or to a custom of which one must be aware, either when visiting the foreign country or when meeting or conversing with a native speaker of the target language?

2) Do you plan to teach that particular facet of culture later in the semester more systematically?

3) If there exists a curriculum guide in your school, at which learning level has the facet of culture been placed for more intensive systematic study?

---

* Carroll, J. B., *Language and Thought.*

We have found the "spiral" approach preferable. Instead of teaching a feature of culture intensively at any one time or even at any one level, it is often more interesting to the students to return to it and integrate their new knowledge with a piece of information they have already acquired or an experience they have had.

Incidental, too, would be considered the discussion of holidays of the foreign country as they arise, or of current events as reported by newspapers and magazines or radio and television. Correspondence with a "pen pal" in the foreign land and a student's reporting of some item in a letter received would also be an excellent motivation for the acquisition of some information about the culture of the foreign country. Has the pen pal visited an art exhibit? Has he gone to a concert? Will he spend his vacation working? A brief discussion of art, music, work customs, and family relationships may well arise from an item casually mentioned in correspondence.

Many of the topics listed in Chapter II should be presented systematically. You should choose first those which are modern and contemporary and thus closer to the students' lives. Ideally the selection and gradation of topics should coincide with the evolving interests of young people at their age level. If this principle of "evolving interests" is not written into the curriculum, it may be desirable to indicate on a record card provided by the school the titles of the topics you have covered with a particular class. Reinforcement of the same topic by the next foreign language teacher would not be deleterious but, for the students' sake, coverage of the topics required in examinations they will be expected to take is an important part of your professional responsibilities.

Some teachers prefer to spend about thirty minutes a week on a cultural topic; others spend an hour every two weeks. Your systematic teaching of culture will depend on numerous other factors. For example, does your school have a laboratory and a film-borrowing program? If so, is there provision for the frequent viewing of foreign language films or for listening to plays in the language laboratory which could serve as introductions to the topics you have chosen or as a culminating activity for the topic? Do you have a well-stocked library of books on the foreign culture which can be assigned to individual students who will later give a "book report" on the material read?

## DEVELOPING CULTURAL INSIGHTS

And now, what are some of the ways in which cultural insights can be provided? Any one of the techniques noted below, and preferably a combination of them, should be used. These are listed in no particular order. Some are possible at every learning level. Some, such as the reading of literary masterpieces, will only be possible at the fourth or fifth level, if at all.

1. The classroom should reflect the foreign culture. (This is possible, we realize, only when one or more rooms in the school are set aside for foreign language instruction.)

a) At the beginning levels, parts of the room may be labeled in the foreign language.

b) Maps and posters of the foreign country should be attractively displayed.

c) A bulletin board should include newspaper or magazine clippings of current events in the foreign country, taken either from foreign language or native language sources, advertisements, comic strips, proverbs, pictures, songs, and music.

d) A windowed closet or a table may contain objects related to the foreign culture such as a collection of dolls, money, stamps, menus, costumes, and other artifacts.

e) A library corner should contain books and magazines *in the foreign language* at the reading and interest levels of the students. Books in the curriculum areas used in the foreign schools are of particular interest to students. There should also be books about the foreign country written in the students' native language. Wherever possible, a piece of literature in the foreign language and its equivalent in the students' native language should be provided.

It is also informative to have books written by foreign speakers about our country. What is their view of us? Why? If it is unfavorable, could it be changed? How?

Newspapers, where possible, can be a source of study for format, style, point of view, attitude toward others, etc.

The magazines should be on sports, adventure, science, love, and anything else that is of interest to the students and which will motivate them to learn the language while developing cultural awareness.

f) A record player and records of contemporary music or folk songs should be available for frequent use.

2. Individuals and groups of students should carry out projects related to the foreign culture which will then serve for class reporting and discussion. The projects may include the preparation of:

a) Maps — physical, economic, geographic — showing the relation of the foreign country to the one in which you are teaching, the location of important cities, monuments and places of interest, regions where natural resources are found or certain foods produced, areas which are the setting for well-known literary masterpieces.

b) Itineraries — for actual trips to pertinent places of interest in the community or for trips to the foreign land.

c) Floor plans of houses and other buildings — with appropriate labels.

d) Menus of food eaten on special occasions.

e) Calendars indicating special holidays.

f) "Information Please" or quiz programs.

g) Word study materials (foreign words and expressions in the native tongue; native words and expressions in the foreign tongue; common word origins [where feasible, of course]).

h) A foreign language newspaper.

i) A scrapbook (current events, art, science, etc.).

j) Filmstrips or picture series.

k) A play reading.

l) The preparation of an original skit or playlet.

m) A book fair.

n) Forms, documents, and other pertinent materials related to commerce and industry in and trade between your country and the foreign country.

3. The foreign culture may be learned and/or experienced in:

a) An assembly program (songs, dances, backdrops, talks).

b) A festival to which community members are invited.

c) Hearing and learning songs and dances of the country.

4. The showing of visual materials and the language laboratory should be used as vehicles for:

a) Listening to recitals or readings by contemporary authors.

b) Viewing filmstrips and films on any aspect of the foreign culture.

c) Listening to spoken descriptions of museum materials as students view works of art or artifacts.

d) Seeing short films of interviews with people in the news.

5. Masterpieces of literature should be read and studied (adapted when necessary), since a real work of literature reflects, as perhaps no other art form or material, the character of the people, the situations in which people interact, the historical or geographical rationale for their behavior, the values to which people are attached; in short, the entire gamut of the values, customs, and beliefs included in the term "culture."

Moreover, the study of a literary masterpiece permits discussion of linguistic style and aesthetics and perhaps of language registers, dialects, and idiolects which no other art form can exemplify as well.

Although this is a controversial issue, we are convinced that a good translation of a masterpiece is better than not exposing the students to the literature of the country at all.

6. The possibility of correlation with other areas in the curriculum should be explored continuously. For example, the relationship between the study of the native tongue and the foreign language can be emphasized through study of plays, stories, and films which are translated and shown in your country.

The music department in your school, if one exists, will be delighted to cooperate with you and your students as they learn about any outstanding composers and their works or as they learn the songs and dances of the foreign land. The social studies department will welcome your support in discussions of the interrelationships between governments in economic production, imports, exports, etc. The impact of geography and history on the culture of any society would be a fruitful field of correlation between the two departments (social studies and foreign language).

7. Resource people should be invited to speak to the class on cultural topics. If the talk is in the foreign language, it would be desirable to ask the speaker to explain important words or to show visual materials to clarify his topic. His delivery (gestures, distance maintained, facial expressions, use of certain expressions, intonation) will still be helpful to the students whether or not they understand everything.

If the visit is preceded by a letter of invitation and followed by a letter of thanks, the authentic formulas used in letter writing (including the writing of dates, numbers, salutations, closing remarks, etc.) will be another example of cultural knowledge the students will acquire.

8. A "pen pal" project should be initiated very soon after the students learn to write. The first letter need not be elaborate but may simply indicate: "My name is so and so. I'm sending you a picture. I go to X school. Please write to me . . ." — with an appropriate heading and closing of course. (Sources of "pen pals" will be found on page 301.)

9. Teachers of art, science, and social studies may give brief lectures in the native language. You can then engage the class in oral activities in the foreign language related to the topic.

10. Last, but most essential, you can give a twenty-minute illustrated lecture in the foreign language on any cultural topic, followed by questions and a summary.

The cementing of good relationships leading to world brotherhood and peace based on reciprocal understanding and respect should be the primary concern of all educators. Teachers of foreign language — by tradition, by training, and by interest — are in the most favorable

145

position in the schools to contribute toward the realization of these concepts upon which our future and the future of all mankind may depend.

## Suggestions

— Assuming that one foreign language is taught in one room, draw a room plan indicating what you would include to create the appropriate cultural atmosphere.

— Indicate fifteen possible themes for a foreign language bulletin board in the classroom or corridor.

— Choose one cultural theme and tell what materials you might include to illustrate it.

— Select from your textbooks a dialogue or reading passage for Levels I, II, III, IV.

    1) Tell which cultural insights are found in them.

    2) Indicate the explanations you would give your students about each of them.

— Choose any cultural topic. Write a detailed lesson plan for a twenty-minute oral presentation by you. Indicate the materials you would use to vitalize the presentation.

— Select another cultural topic. Indicate how you could divide it among four groups of students for presentation and discussion. Justify your divisions not only with relation to the topic division but also with relation to the students' interests and abilities.

— Write a detailed lesson plan for a student composition on a topic related to the foreign culture.

## Additional Reading

BROOKS, N. *Language and Language Learning*. New York: Harcourt, Brace & World, 1964.

BROWN, R. et al. "Developing Cultural Understanding through Foreign Language Study" in *PMLA* 48, No. 5. New York: MLA, 1953.

FRIES, C. *Teaching and Learning English as a Foreign Language*. Ann Arbor, Mich.: U. of Michigan Press, 1948.

JOHNSTON, M. "How Can Modern Language Teaching Promote International Understanding?," in *Foreign Language Teaching*, J. Michel (ed.). New York: Macmillan, 1966.

NOSTRAND, H. "A Second Culture: New Imperatives for American Education," in *Foreign Language Teaching*, J. Michel (ed.). New York: Macmillan, 1967.

SEELYE, N. "Analyzing and Teaching of the Cross-Cultural Context" in *The Britannica Review of Foreign Language Education*, E. Birkmaier (ed.). Chicago: Encyclopedia Britannica, Inc., 1968.

# VI

# Planning a
# Balanced Program

In order to devote sufficient time to the development of all four skills, and to provide variety and maintain interest at a high level, it is essential to organize the students' learning experiences with great attention to detail.

After the principal aims and emphases of the program have been determined, it is still essential to ask some fundamental questions. For example:

1. How much emphasis should be given to each skill at each level of language learning?

2. How might a "unit" of work as found in a textbook be divided most effectively? (See pages 161-62 for an example.)

3. How might each teaching period be varied?

4. How might a teaching week be divided?

A happy balance should be struck which will make provision for systematic, orderly development as well as for variety, fun, and surprise. Students should know whether to take their readers to school or their "verb" books or any other necessary material on a clearly pre-established day. They should know, too, when their compositions are due; when they will have a quiz; when homework will be corrected each period. Such routine classroom procedure gives them a feeling of security and helps to relieve some of the tension that a haphazard arrangement might engender.

On the other hand, the activities within the warm-up period discussed below, the mode of introducing a grammatical item, the varied use of vivid instructional materials, the "intuitive" grasp by the teacher that enough practice has been given, albeit temporarily, on a dialogue or structure or whatever, can spell the difference between a plodding, pedestrian lesson and one enjoyed by teacher and pupils alike.

Below are indicated some suggested proportions of time for the teaching of features of language and for the development of skills which seem to work best for us and for many of our colleagues. These are not to be considered inflexible, inviolable time schedules. All the factors in the teaching-learning situation which have been discussed must be taken into account in planning for balance and variety. "Balance for whom" and "to achieve what end" must be two of the questions in our minds as we plan the techniques and materials we will need for any particular lesson.

## A POSSIBLE DAILY SCHEDULE

Assuming a forty-five minute session, you may wish to experiment with the following division of your time. *Use only the activities within each segment appropriate to your teaching level.*\*

*Warm-up* review of thoroughly familiar materials: the day; date; weather; questions on activities or on materials covered in any previous session; a language game; a song; the dramatization of known dialogues; oral conversation on any appropriate topic designed to limber up the students' tongues; or a brief monologue by you on a topic of current interest, designed to immerse the students in the sounds of the foreign language. (This may be followed by oral questions, of course.) — 5 minutes.

*Homework correction* (if homework was assigned); short, previously announced *test* — 7 minutes.

*Pronunciation drill* (including intonation, rhythm, stress) — 3 minutes.

*Readiness (motivation) for new material* by review, by related experience, by comparison or contrast with known material — 5 minutes.

*Statement of aim of the new lesson.*

*Presentation of new material* (dialogue, structures, cultural topic, reading, writing) — 5 to 10 minutes.

*Oral practice activities:* pattern practice, "free" conversation, oral reading, oral composition, etc. — 15 minutes.

*Summary of lesson* — 2 minutes.

*Overview of homework assignment and/or review of conversations, summary of reading* — 3 to 5 minutes.

*Looking ahead to the next lesson.* (Give your students a reason for wanting to come back.)

---

\* The activities below will be explained in greater detail in Chapters VII and IX.

## A POSSIBLE WEEKLY SCHEDULE
(assuming a five-hour program)

| Activity | Level I | Level II |
|---|---|---|
| Learning of pronunciation | ½ hr. | ½ hr. |
| Learning of dialogues | 1½ hrs. | ½ hr. |
| Study of grammar | 1½ hrs. | 1½ hrs. |
| Reading | 1 hr. | 1½ hrs. |
| Writing | ¼ hr. | ½ hr. |
| Gaining cultural insight | ¼ hr. | ½ hr. |

### Levels III & IV

Study of grammar — 1½ hours
Reading (intensive and/or extensive) — 1½ hours
Preparation for writing — 1 hour
Cultural material — 1 hour

### Level V

Study of grammar — 1 hour
Reading (intensive and extensive) — 2 hours
Preparation for writing — 1 hour
Cultural material — 1 hour

It goes without saying that the study of grammar is accompanied by oral practice activities including dialogue study; that reading, writing, and cultural study are preceded and followed by oral discussion or questions.

When five hours are not available (and this is true in too many school systems) or when a teacher meets his class on Monday and Tuesday only, for example, modifications will have to be made. Furthermore, additional time will have to be spent in the warm-up period to compensate for the fact that students have had five days to forget what they had learned.

### Suggested Proportions of Time for Skill Development

| Skills | Levels | | | | |
|---|---|---|---|---|---|
| | 1 | 2 | 3 | 4 | 5 |
| Listening | 40% | 30% | 45% | 45% | 30% |
| Speaking | 40 | 30 | | | |
| Reading | 15 | 30 | 40 | 40 | 50 |
| Writing | 5 | 10 | 15 | 15 | 20 |

There will be much overlapping, of course. For example, *reading and writing* activities should always be preceded and followed by oral explanations, discussion, questions, or summaries.

149

## Providing for Group Instruction

You may, in some teaching situations, have to provide for teaching two quite different groups* within the same class hour, different either because their previous foreign language instruction (duration or quality, for example) has placed them on varying points on the continua of the listening, speaking, reading, or writing skills; or because of wide divergences in aptitude; or because they have come from another school system; or because of a number of cogent reasons. If this is the case, your schedule may look like this:

| *Activity* | Mon. | Tues. | Wed. | Thurs. | Fri. |
|---|---|---|---|---|---|
| Warm-up | Entire group | ⟶ | | | |
| Pronunciation | Entire group | ⟶ | | | |
| Differentiated Activities | You will devote most of your time to | | | | Entire group: Culture Dictations, Songs, Poetry |
| | Group I | II | I | II | |
| Summary and Overview of Homework | Entire group | ⟶ | | | |

## WRITING THE LESSON PLAN

Whether or not the school or department head has special requirements for the submission of a written plan or for the form the plan should take, all teachers should prepare a step-by-step procedure of their lesson before entering any classroom. You may find it desirable to prepare a plan for each of your classes a week in advance so that you can apportion the time for each activity with a longer time span in mind. You may prefer, on the other hand, to prepare all the lessons within a unit which may be of more or less than one week's duration.

The length and complexity of the plan will depend on your years of teaching experience, on your familiarity with the text, and on the type of lesson you are planning to teach. A grammar lesson, for example, would require you to think about and jot down 1) the situation you will use to introduce the material and to bring about its understanding; 2) your model sentences; 3) the types of pattern drills you will use and the cue words within each; 4) the audio-visual materials you will need. To illustrate further, a reading lesson would require you to think of the motivation, the words and concepts to be clarified, some of the pivotal questions you would ask to ensure understanding, and whether you intend to treat the reading intensively or extensively.

---

* This problem is discussed in some detail on pp. 224-26.

In addition, the homework to be assigned should be clearly written out, particularly if you plan to have a student place it on the board.

Generally, the overall written plan may take one of two shapes. Some teachers, with the approval of the school head, prepare a weekly plan such as the following:

| | Period: 1 | 2 | 3 | 4 | 5 |
|---|---|---|---|---|---|
| First day | | | | | |
| Second day | | | | | |
| Third day | | | | | |
| Fourth day | | | | | |
| Fifth day | | | | | |

The plan above has the advantage of letting you see at a glance what went on the day before and how today will be linked with tomorrow, enabling you to make reference to yesterday and tomorrow as you are teaching today's lesson.

Another type of written plan is one in which a full page in a notebook is devoted to each day. (Beginning teachers may find it helpful to use the full-page format which permits more extensive notation.)

Whichever format you use, the following minimal information should be immediately apparent to you:

*The date*

*The class*

*Aims* (e.g., Review the sounds b/v; teach the present perfect with *since;* "The Necklace" [the name of the story to be read]; composition preparation; etc.)

*Motivation* (Situation or Approach, as it is called by some teachers)

*Oral presentation* (This will depend on the type of lesson as noted above.)

*Drills, Activities, and Experiences* (With drills, cue words needed should be listed; with reading lessons, all items to be clarified.)

*Audio-visual aids* to be used in conjunction with the presentation and practice.

*Homework:* Study, say, read, write, etc.

151

# An Overview of Some Lesson Types*

*Preliminary activities*: Warm-up; Pronunciation practice; Homework correction and/or Quiz.

| New Lesson | Dialogue | Grammar | Reading | Composition Writing | Culture |
|---|---|---|---|---|---|
| Motivation | | | | | |
| Statement of Aim | | | | | |
| Teacher's Oral Activities | Explaining situation Clarifying difficulties Dramatization Questions Variation of utterances Study and "Exploitation" | Creating situation Reviewing related material Giving models Eliciting generalization Engaging students in drills Providing "communication" activities | Clarifying difficulties Oral reading Questioning Word study and related activities | Eliciting ideas Supplying lexicon and structures Helping to put ideas in sequence | Clarifying difficulties Giving an oral presentation with audio-visual aids Asking questions Helping with individual projects |
| Students' Oral Activities | Repetition Dramatization Answering questions Responding to drills Engaging in related activities | Repetition Generalization Engaging in drills Engaging in "freer" conversation | Answering questions Formulating questions Giving medial summaries Engaging in word study, etc. Reading aloud | Expressing ideas Suggesting vocabulary and structures Giving related sentences Preparing an introduction | Working on group or individual projects Answering questions Discussing (comparing or contrasting) aspects of culture |
| Summary and Evaluation | | | | | |
| Looking Ahead | | | | | |

* For details of presentation, see appropriate sections in the text.

Two additional comments are pertinent:

1. You should devise some notation for yourself to indicate that you did not complete a lesson or perhaps that it was not learned to your complete satisfaction.

2. You should make every effort to *learn the steps of your lesson by heart* so that you don't have to consult your plan book every few minutes. You should also prepare a small card (which you keep in one hand) containing the essential information you will need to allow the lesson to proceed smoothly.

The lines of the dialogue, the sequence of drills, the cue words needed under each, model sentences for grammar instruction, a dictation, vocabulary to be clarified in the reading, and questions to be asked in the reading should all be indicated on your card. Most helpful too is to indicate on the card in red, or in another color, next to the activity, the audial or visual material to be used in conjunction with it (e.g., BB [blackboard], PC [pocket chart], Pic series, Pix, etc.). (See pages 165-70.)

To facilitate your teaching and planning, it is desirable to keep a cumulative vocabulary list (with lessons in which the items were introduced), test items asked, and homework slips or cards for each lesson. These should be kept from year to year but modified, as necessary.

### Suggestions

— Make an inventory for each level of learning of the possible warm-up topics you might use from the very first week.

— Write, giving the actual words, twenty transitional or introductory statements that you would use in going from one learning activity to another within a class period, devoted to various types of language lessons.

— Assuming a lesson with a new dialogue as the *main* focus of attention, indicate all the activities of your lesson, including the greetings.

— Assuming a lesson with a grammatical item as the *main* focus of attention, indicate all the activities of your lesson.

— Assuming a lesson with a cultural emphasis, indicate all the activities of your lesson.

— An unexpected happening prevents you from completing your lesson. What five things should you do, *in addition to not panicking?*

— Take a unit from a textbook in use in your country. Indicate how you would divide it into one or more teaching days. Justify your sequence of presentation.

— Assuming you have two learning groups in your classroom,

indicate some types of *integrative* activities you would prepare; indicate some differentiated activities.

— Prepare a weekly plan for a two-group classroom, scheduling the integrative and differentiated activities and indicating how you would divide your time between the two groups.

— Draw a similar weekly schedule for three groups.

— Assume that you have been given a bilingual teacher aide (a paraprofessional). List ten ways in which you might use her talents to make learning more effective.

## Additional Reading

BROOKS, N. *Language and Language Learning.* New York: Harcourt, Brace & World, 1964.
HUEBENER, T. *How to Teach Foreign Languages Effectively.* New York: New York U. Press, 1964.

# VII

# Making Effective Use of Materials and Techniques of Instruction

We shall begin this chapter on teaching aids by reaffirming our unwavering belief that the teacher is the most important single factor in the teaching-learning process. There can be no question that given students with some interest in language learning, it is what we as teachers do to promote a friendly environment in the classroom, to create and organize materials, to overcome shortcomings in our textbooks, to stimulate and maintain interest through varied practice activities, to emphasize the enjoyable aspects of language learning, and to give students necessary feelings of success which will determine their growth toward communication.

In many instances, the desire to learn a new mode of communication can be fostered even in students who do not have a strong initial interest in language study. By the same token, alas, many students who approach the study of a foreign language with enthusiasm are often deflected by teachers who follow the textbook slavishly or who follow, in a mechanical manner, some of the learning steps outlined in our discussion.

There are so many devices and techniques which can supplement the textbook and often even the teacher's voice that it seems a pity for the alert teacher not to make use of them. In this section, therefore, we will indicate or reinforce some of the materials and techniques which may help bring enthusiasm into the language-learning classroom. Let us start with *people* and *materials*.

## USING THE CLASSROOM AND MATERIALS OF INSTRUCTION EFFECTIVELY

### The Teacher, His Students, and the Classroom

While language laboratories, films, and other audio-visual equipment may all be desirable, the teacher can learn to make effective use

155

of *himself, his students,* and *his classroom,* no matter where he is teaching.

**You can,** for example:*

1. Indicate the kind of pupil participation you would like at any particular moment by:
— making an encircling gesture with both arms if the entire class is to respond or repeat;
— making a smaller encompassing gesture when a smaller group is to repeat;
— raising your right arm with the palm turned away from you when you wish the students at the right side of the room to repeat, and doing the same with your left arm for the left side of the class;
— pointing to individual students. (The effectiveness of pointing as a device should be explained to students in those parts of the world where such a gesture would be considered impolite.)

2. Signal the responses you desire (at the beginning language-learning levels) by pointing to your mouth when you want the students to "say" or to "repeat"; or by cupping your hand over your ear when you would like the students to "answer."

3. Use a downward movement of your right arm for falling intonation and an upward movement for rising intonation.

4. Demonstrate the relationship of the tongue and teeth in producing sounds. For example, by holding your left hand so that fingers represent the upper teeth and putting your outstretched right hand directly beneath and beyond it, you can show the position of tongue and teeth when producing the "th" in "thank you."

5. Show, by the shape of your mouth (rounded or stretched), the position of your jaw (lowered or raised), or the placement of your tongue, the production of sounds or sound sequences.

6. Tap out with your fingers or with a pencil the stresses of two or three syllable words and the rhythm of utterances or sentences.

7. Point to yourself, items of clothing you are wearing, or things you may be carrying in teaching language patterns, ranging from "This is a suit (blouse, etc.)" to "I'm a teacher" to "I'm writing on the blackboard now" to "I haven't any money. If I had money, I'd buy some fruit on my way home."

Gestures must be thoroughly understood by your students. Hand signals, for example, are recommended not only to clarify directions or the position of vocal organs for pronunciation, but also to permit

---

* Adapted from an article by one of the authors for the American Book Company.

an immediate response by the class without any intervening and possibly distracting request from the teacher such as "And now this half of the class."

If you are using your own clothing to illustrate the meaning of a word, you should then point to a similar garment worn by students or as displayed in pictures. To avoid any confusion, it is necessary to illustrate a number of examples for a single type of clothing. Otherwise, students may think that "shoe," for example, means a certain style of shoe. Or, in teaching "shirt," if your hand happens to touch or point to only a part of the shirt, the class may make further errors of conceptualization. They might confuse "shirt" with "collar," "seam," or "shoulder." In addition to numerous examples, it is important to sweep your hand over *the entire item* so that the part will not be mistaken for the whole.

Many speech patterns can be taught by drawing attention to parts of the room or the furniture in it: "What's this?"; "What's that?"; "Is this a . . .?"; "Yes, it is"; "No, it's not"; "Walk to the . . ."; "What's on the wall?"; "There's a book on the desk"; "How many . . . are there?"; "Point to the . . ."; "I can't reach the ceiling."

The seating arrangements also facilitate the teaching of such patterns as, "Who's sitting next to . . .?"; "Where's . . . sitting?"; "Count the people in the front row, the second row"; "Who's first?"; "Point to the first seat"; etc.

## Visual Aids

### Using the Blackboard

The teacher's most widely used and most valuable tool, however, is the blackboard. Among its major uses, let us cite the following:

1. When introducing a dialogue, you can sketch stick figures on the board and point to whoever is speaking, thus clarifying the roles of characters in the conversation. After the dialogue has been practiced orally, it can be written on the blackboard, then read, and later referred to as needed when being dramatized by you, individuals, or the class.

2. In teaching such expressions as "He's happy, ill," etc., or "I'm unhappy," you can draw an upward-downward curving mouth; then, pointing to it, ask for the appropriate statement or response from the students.

3. Removal of a stick figure (previously drawn on the board as a picture story is told), will assist you in teaching responses to questions such as, "Who was here?"; "How many were here?"; "Is the man still here?"; etc.

157

4. Expressions such as "Good morning (afternoon, evening)" may be taught in conjunction with a drawing of a clock or a listing of hours which are appropriate to each greeting.

5. In the case of younger children, weather may be represented by drawings of an umbrella or the sun.

6. Arithmetic examples may be "read."

7. Direction is often grasped more firmly if illustrated in diagrammatic form on the blackboard. A square can represent a park and lines can be drawn to demonstrate the meaning of "around," "through," "across," "near," etc.

8. Line drawings can clarify "bigger than," "longer than," "shorter than," where a purely verbal explanation would often be less successful, and where using the students to compare size, weight, etc., might prove embarrassing.

9. Aspects of time may also be presented and referred to during practice activities in this manner:

|  |  | Today |  |  |
|  |  | Now |  |  |
| Past | Yesterday | | Tomorrow | Future |
|  |  | Later |  |  |

A cross (x) on one of the lines would indicate a *single* occurrence of an event; a bracket (‿⁀), an event which has lasted or will last over a period of time.

10. The blackboard is also an excellent tool for teaching grammatical structure. You will find it useful to place utterances in frames so that the recurring features and the slots of the pattern become immediately apparent:

One

| I'd | like | a | book. |
| I'd | like | an | egg. |

More than one

| I'd | like | some | books. |
| I'd | like | some | eggs. |

11. Simple substitution drills can also be practiced from the blackboard through a scheme such as this (the drill should have been practiced orally first):

Let's take a | walk.
            | swim.
            | drive.

12. Similarly, more complex drills for extended oral practice, written on the board, enable the students to read sentences across and then to make other logical combinations with the words. Note, for example:*

| Harry | is playing | the guitar. |
| Paul | | piano. |
| The boys | are playing | horn. |
| Those men | | saxophone. |

13. In progressive substitution drills, you might write the model sentence on the board and draw lines under it representing the slots into which the learners will be asked to substitute other words. As you give successive word cues, you can point to the line indicating the slot (e.g., subject, verb, object, complement into which the cue words are to be fitted).

John went to the store to buy a book.

This visual help should be eliminated as soon as pupils can engage in the drill with reasonable accuracy and fluency.

14. You might also find it useful to draw the shape of the lips and the position of the jaw on the board when teaching certain elements of pronunciation. In addition, rising and falling intonations are easily and simply indicated by either lines, numbers, or arrows, in this way:

$_2$The boy is $^3$speaking.      The boy is speaking. ↓

$_2$Is the boy $^3$speaking?      Is the boy speaking? ↑

15. In teaching reading, the blackboard is indispensable. New vocabulary words together with their equivalents or meanings should be written on the board as well as questions, multiple-choice items, matching expressions, and summaries to ensure comprehension.

16. When guiding students' writing, you may write out model sentences or paragraphs for the class to copy, sentences that are to be joined by means of connecting words, or transitional sentences (those linking paragraphs). Similarly, key words and concepts within one theme which students could use as guidelines for writing compositions can also be placed on the board.

---

* See French, F. G. *English in Tables*, London: Oxford U. Press, 1960, for numerous examples of drills of this type. Any of them might be adapted for drilling in your target language.

159

It is apparent that the blackboard (or chalkboard, as it is often called) is an invaluable tool. It can be used also, for example, to indicate the next lesson's assignment, to have some students write out their completed homework for class correction, or to write out test items.

While many of the above suggestions could be handled in other ways, we have emphasized the blackboard because it is widely available and not generally subject to mechanical breakdowns.

## Using the Textbook

The ideal textbook[1] for every situation will never be published, but the conscientious teacher can use and breathe life into *any* textbook. It is a question of studying it carefully, deciding what its "good" points are, and noting its weaknesses in meeting your aims with your students, in your community. Some of the material in the textbook can be added to, deleted, combined with other material, taught out of sequence, etc. In the case of "traditional" textbooks, dialogues and oral practice activities could be prepared. Any translation exercise could be modified. (See page 98.)

In examining or using any book, it is good to remember, moreover, that the author may not necessarily intend the book to be used at a specific level or for a specific period of time.

The author's introductory remarks should always be studied carefully since he does not usually expect a teacher to follow the items within each unit or lesson exactly as they are written. For example, a textbook may start with a conversation or reading passage containing new vocabulary; then give five grammar points for intensive study; then indicate ten exercises; and then list the vocabulary. It is not generally intended that in presenting the units, the teacher will do all the conversation or reading first; then all the grammar; then all the exercises. For example, the new vocabulary should be clarified and practiced when it is needed; that is, before the conversations are learned or before the exercises are done.

Beginning teachers will find it desirable to study the entire text if possible but certainly each unit of work (or "lesson")[2] carefully when preparing to teach it. All the new material in the lesson should be listed and then placed under several categories: 1) pronunciation problems; 2) new structures; 3) vocabulary and culture; 4) practice activities, including reading and writing; and 5) homework.

---

[1] A checklist for use in selecting texts will be found in the Appendix, pp. 256-59.

[2] By "lesson," we mean here the unit of work which must then be divided into several teaching lessons. The number of lessons will depend on the students' aptitude and level as well as on other relevant factors.

You should then study the items of *new* material in order to decide: 1) the number of teaching lessons you will need to treat all of it; 2) the review needed to relate the new work to familiar work; 3) the gradation of the material in a logical sequence.

You will ask yourself: Which pronunciation items should be introduced first? Which new structures will be presented and practiced first? Which sentences within each of the activities or drill exercises will be used with which new structures? When will the new vocabulary items be taught? How will the material be introduced — through a conversation, a story, a related structure? What homework can be assigned? What audio-visual materials will be needed?

It goes without saying that the material within a teaching unit has to be carefully ordered, and that we should constantly keep in mind the psychological "laws" of learning mentioned in our previous discussions: build on what our students know; go from the simple to the more difficult; do *not* present more than one new point at a time; give intensive practice; relate the new material to other known material in actual speech (and later reading) in order to give our students the feeling that this new building block occupies an important place in our "communication building."

Following is an example of a possible division of a unit which emphasizes the teaching of a dialogue and grammar and which would be particularly appropriate for teaching at Levels I and II. Only "new" items are mentioned. For warm-up, pronunciation teaching, and other preliminary and closing activities which should always be included, see the *Possible Daily Schedule* (page 148).

The sections on *Reading* (pages 119-28) and *Writing* (pages 129-38) will suggest possible divisions within lessons devoted to them.


## A Suggested Unit "Breakdown":

SESSION I

> Introduction of the dialogue
> Learning of four or more sentences of the dialogue through listening, repeating, and dramatizing
> Questions and answers based on the dialogue itself and dialogue personalization (where feasible)
> A language item (repetition and substitution drills)

SESSION II

> Learning four or more sentences of the dialogue
> Questions and answers based on the new dialogue segment
> A language item, structure, or pattern with repetition and substitution drills

Pattern practice and freer conversation on the language item taught the previous session

A game which embodies the new language items

## SESSION III

Language items or patterns — one or more depending upon their relationship to previously taught patterns or to the students' native language

Repetition and substitution exercises of the new items

One or more pattern practices

Some dialogue sentences

A related game, questions, and answers on the dialogue and dramatization

## SESSION IV

Language items or patterns — one or more

Repetition and substitution exercises of the new items

One or more pattern practices of items taught during sessions I-III

Dramatization of the new dialogue and of other related ones

## SESSION V

"Free" conversation exercises in which new items are combined with others previously taught

Introduction of the reading selection (motivation and clarification of difficulties of the first segment)

Oral reading and intensive study of the reading selection

## SESSION VI

Performance of the dialogue

More difficult practice drills, such as the progressive replacement drill

Review of the reading selection (e.g., student-formulated questions), word study exercises, practice on note-taking

Short dictation (either on the reading selection or on material prepared by you to consolidate grammar learnings)

Examination

## Other Visual Aids

Among the many other visual aids which may stimulate the imagination and encourage fuller student participation are the following types. Of course, one must bear in mind that not all are equally suitable for all age groups.

162

## Real Objects

Students understand and retain the meaning of a word better when they have been shown or have touched some object associated with it. For this reason, all teachers should make a collection of everyday objects, including such things as newspapers, tickets, menus, flags, bottles, cans, containers, toys (for children), magazines, dishes, bits of cloth, etc.

A collection of this sort will facilitate the presentation and practice of many language items. To illustrate — at beginning levels, the names of articles may be practiced first within categories and later at random. Students may be asked to name them, put them somewhere, give them to someone, etc. At a later date, they may be placed on a table and you or a student may remove one of the objects. Another student may be asked to name the article which is no longer there using the verb in the past (e.g., Was it the . . . . . ?). Many language games are possible, of course. A student may be asked to leave the room or to close his eyes and then guess what is missing from the collection on the table. He will ask questions of his classmates (limited to their level of language learning) such as, "Is it round (square, etc.) ?," "Is it food?," "Is it green?," etc.

In other lessons, you may exhibit a train ticket and map and begin a dialogue about traveling. Restaurant menus also form an excellent introduction to students for words for different kinds of food and for expressions related to meals. Students may pretend they are ordering a meal or that some piece of the china or silver service in a restaurant is dirty or missing from the table. Negatives can be practiced by having the students tell what foods they dislike. An activity using real objects which students of all ages enjoy is the setting up of a food or clothing store. All sorts of greetings and courtesy formulas, as well as concepts of sizes, brands, weights, measures, and prices may thus be practiced in a true-to-life situation.

## Using Real Objects in Games and Play-Acting

Closely related to the collection and use of everyday items is the question of when games can and should be used in the classroom. Much depends upon the age group, the learning level, and the presentation methods employed. Younger learners may enjoy playing at housekeeping or moving about the rooms to hide or to find things. For older students, telephoning, role-playing, and acting in short plays have been found successful. Most of them enjoy playing word games. They like doing crossword puzzles or playing scrabble.

Games* provide an excellent opportunity for practicing grammar

---

\* See Bibliography for collections of games.

163

and vocabulary. The game, unless it is a general review exercise, should be guided toward the use of specific language items. At beginning learning levels, students may be asked to take prearranged objects out of a box and practice such expressions as "What's in the box?," "What do I have in my hand?," "Give him (her) the . . ." Pieces of various materials may be used to practice requests: "Make a house." "Now give the house to . . ."; "Make a suit." "What else do you need?"

Play-acting can also be very effective. Students acting out the roles may speak in the present tense, as, "I'm John and I'm working in an office." (A toy telephone, papers, and other office props will be needed.) Then you may ask questions such as, "What's his name?" and "What's he doing?" Later you may, by asking "What was John doing?," elicit the verb form "John was working in an office."

There are any number of variations upon this theme. The life of a person during the day may be enacted, enabling the class to practice both time of day and verb tenses or aspects (e.g., "What did John [the doctor, the secretary, etc.] do in the morning?," "What did he eat for lunch?," "What has he done all day?"). A large cardboard clock with movable hands is most helpful in this type of activity.

Something should be added about puppetry. Hand puppets are an excellent vehicle for language practice and are invaluable in classrooms containing only boys or girls where articles of clothing are being described, for example. Moreover, their manipulation behind an improvised stage (an old wooden or cardboard crate will do) may provide the necessary anonymity for the more timid students who are too shy to stand before the class and recite.

## The Picture File

Every classroom should contain a file of pictures which can be used to give interesting, meaningful practice in the sounds, structures, and vocabulary of the foreign language. Only pictures used in developing language items will be treated here. A file of up-to-date pictures reflecting authentic aspects of culture is also essential.

The file should contain three kinds of pictures: 1) pictures of individual persons and of individual objects*; 2) pictures of situations in which persons are "doing something" with objects and in which the relationship of objects and/or people can be seen; 3) a series of pictures (six to ten) on one chart. You may wish to create several of these charts: for instance, one for count nouns (the objects or furniture in the classroom, for example); one for mass nouns (foods, for example); one for count and mass nouns placed at random; one for words

---

* A suggested list of pictures will be found in the Appendix, pp. 272-74.

illustrating difficult consonant clusters without regard to "count" and "mass"; one for work activities; sports; etc. Below are some examples:

Count Nouns Chart

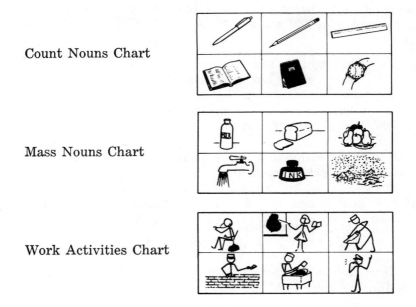

Mass Nouns Chart

Work Activities Chart

The file should contain *more than one picture* of individuals and of objects. This is necessary if students are not to assume that your finger touching the fender of a car, for example, indicates that "car" (the word you are teaching) and "fender" are synonyms. Many pictures of different kinds or sizes of cars, or pens, or boys, or women, or whatever you are teaching and, in addition, a sweeping movement of your hand over the *entire* picture will ensure the proper association of word and object or person.

What criteria should guide us in choosing or drawing pictures? Pictures should be large enough to be seen by all students. The pictures of individual objects or people should be as simple as possible. Some of them should contain color for later use in teaching adjectives of color or in writing dialogues or compositions. The pictures should contain *no captions** of any kind since you will thus be able to use them in later stages to have students recall the association of word and object. Situational pictures should not contain captions either since you may want the same scene to serve as the basis for various oral discussions.

* A caption, title, or brief description for your own use on the back of the picture is helpful.

## Using the Picture File

The pictures can be pressed into service in numerous ways. Individual pictures may be used, of course, to introduce, to practice, and to test language items. Individual pictures can be used in pairs — e.g., pictures of a boy and a bicycle can be used to teach structures such as:

> The boy goes to school by bicycle.
> How does the boy go to school?
> The boy is riding a bicycle.
> Does the boy go to school by bus?
> No. He goes by bicycle.

To give more varied practice, pictures* of boys, girls, men, and women can be stacked one behind the other, and pictures of means of transportation can also be stacked. With a student assistant who will help you flip the pictures, double substitutions can be made — e.g.:

> The girl goes (went, will go) by bus, (train, bicycle).
> The woman goes (went, will go) by train.

Three individual pictures (or stacked individual pictures) can be used in the same fashion — e.g.:

> The boy went to the library by bus.
> The girl went to the hospital by car.
> The man went to the capital by plane.
> How did he go to the capital?

The further use of individual pictures for testing purposes will be discussed in the chapter on testing.

The situational pictures recommended are for eliciting "real" language. "What do you see?"; "What are they doing?"; "Are they sad?"; "Would you like to do that?," and any other structure (of age, weather, clothing, action) to which the picture lends itself can be practiced. If possible, situational pictures should be used to stimulate ideas for the "freer" compositions discussed above.

Another very good use of situational pictures which you would have to create (very simple line drawings are all that is needed) would be to practice complex sentences with *before, after,* etc., or words such as *first, then, later.*

---

* The stacked pictures — people, places, means of transportation, for example — may be attached to a piece of cardboard by means of rings. By flipping the pictures over the rings, making visible only those which are needed, the practice of many sentence combinations can be facilitated.

Pictures like those above could show individuals doing something (eating, dressing, going to school or work, etc.). Each should contain a *clock* with an hour clearly marked. You can then practice patterns such as:

> (He) (always) (eats) before (he goes out).*
> (He) (ate) before (he) (went out).
> Did (he) (go out) after (he ate)?
> What did (he) do after (he ate)?
> What did (he) do first?

To practice expressions with "while" and the appropriate aspect of the verb, you would need to use situational pictures.

> (He) was (working) while (she) was (sewing).
> What was (she) doing while (he) was (working)?

The *series of pictures on a chart** will be found extremely helpful in giving extensive practice in numerous structures with a limited *known* vocabulary. You may add variety to the "sameness" of the chart by pointing to the pictures in the order in which they appear; by pointing to them at random; or by having a student point to them in sequence or at random and call on a classmate to make a statement or to respond appropriately.

Let us take as an example a chart containing pictures of a pencil, a pen, a book, a notebook, a ruler, a box. Notice some of the possible patterns which can be practiced using the same chart at any level of language learning. (Please remember that you always give the pattern sentence several times first.)

> What's this? It's a ...................
> This is a ................................. (if the students are touching the pictures)
>
> That's a .....................................
> Is this a ...............................? Yes, it is.
> No, it isn't. It's a ...........................

---

* In giving the pattern sentence, make sure *all* words (for the pictures) can fit logically into it.

What do you (have)*?

(I) (have) a .............................

(Do) (you) have a ................? Yes, I do.

No, I don't.

I have a ........................, a ........................, and a ........................

Show us the ........................ That's the ........................

May I have the ........................?

Where's the ........................?

Where are the ........................?

I'd like a ........................

How much is a ........................? It's ........................ cents.

I have a (new) ........................

My ........................ is (new).

The ........................ is (on) the (desk).

The (girls) have a ........................

There('s) a ........................ (on) the table.

I'm going to (buy) a ........................

Please give (me) the ........................

I'm buying a ........................ now.

I (always) use a ........................

Do you have any ........................?

I have (some) ........................

I (bought) a ........................

(He) gave (her) a ........................

(This) ........................ is (mine).

Did you (buy) a ........................?

Let's not (buy) a ........................

Don't (buy) a ........................

The ........................ is (new), isn't it?

The ........................ isn't (new), is it?

I can (buy) a ........................, can't I?

I'm sure the ........................ is (new).

If I had a ........................, I'd ........................

If I had had a ........................, I could have ........................

I'd like to (buy) a ........................

I'd rather use a ........................ than a ........................

Thank you for (bringing) the ........................

I wish I could have (bought) a ........................

He asked me if I knew where to buy a ........................

I'm going out to buy a ........................ later unless it starts raining.

And we could continue! Surprisingly enough, the students do not get bored with the same vocabulary. If the pace is brisk, if the pro-

---

* Parentheses indicate that other words can be substituted.

cedures are varied, if they're saying the new structures you are teaching correctly, they will find pleasure and comfort in the familiar words. The series of pictures on sports can elicit such pattern sentences as "He's swimming," "I'd like to go swimming," "January isn't a good month for swimming," "When can you go swimming with me?"

Many other uses of pictures can be cited. They can be used to teach pronunciation contrasts, grammar, vocabulary. They can be used to play games and to illustrate stories. Above all, carefully selected pictures can clarify aspects of culture which could not be visualized through verbalization alone.

## Charts

Simple charts which can be kept permanently displayed in the classroom, which can be taken out of the closet as needed or carried under your arm from room to room, will be found extremely valuable. Among those we have found most effective are the following:

1. The Viëtor Triangle (see page 46) for clarifying or reinforcing pronunciation. (After students learn all the vowel sounds, we use it frequently during the warm-up period to "limber up" tongues and lips.)

2. The cross section of the vocal organs (see page 43).

3. The principal question words. Students can be encouraged to formulate questions with one or more of the words for their fellow-students to answer during various phases of the lesson.

4. Prefixes and suffixes.

5. A list of twenty socio-cultural topics. (See pages 143-45 for a possible procedure for its use.)

6. A stimulus-response format for engaging in increasingly more sustained "free" conversation (see page 117).

7. A time aspect chart similar to the one recommended for the blackboard (see page 158). This chart will be in constant use.

## Flash Cards, Word Cards, Number Cards

Cards with individual words (either printed or in manuscript) can be prepared and filed within the same categories and in the same order as the individual pictures. The cards should be about twelve inches long and four inches wide.

Beginners can be asked to match cards and pictures as soon as they can read. They can also match the cards with words written at the blackboard or on a large cardboard.

The individual cards can serve as word cues in the oral substitution drills outlined in Chapter III. They can be used for review purposes ("Make your own sentences using this word") or in playing games (associations, synonyms, antonyms, word families).

Commands written on the cards can help students gain instant recognition of the written symbols, if they are asked to carry out the command as soon as the card is flashed. Practice of this type is helpful in the beginning stages.

Cards on which low numbers have been written can be used to practice such expressions as "How many?," "Do (you) (have) (six) of them?," and "No, (I) (have) only (four)." High numbered cards will enable you to call on students by number instead of by name, thus reinforcing listening comprehension. Later, the students themselves can call on their classmates, using the number cards.

Small cards are invaluable in pairing your students for realistic, paired practice. Two students turn in their seats, face each other, and, using the cue cards as a stimulus, engage in a conversation.

## The Pocket Chart

This simple teaching tool is an excellent device for dramatizing word order and for teaching beginning reading. It is easily made by taking a piece of cardboard or hard paper (about two feet in length by about one foot in height) and pinning (stapling or gluing) to it two narrow pockets about two inches high.

The pocket chart can be used, for example, to teach negatives, interrogatives, and relative clauses. In a base sentence such as "Peter is here," pushing apart the words *is* and *here* and inserting *not* or adding a particle meaning *not* dramatizes the formation and position of the negative in English.

Placing a card with *Don't* before a request illustrates the simplicity of negative requests. The word order in expanded sentences becomes immediately clear as cards are moved to other positions before the eyes of the students.

Younger learners particularly will enjoy going to the pocket chart themselves and making questions from statements, placing *not* or *don't* in sentences, or later changing questions to indirect questions or statements. In fact, it may be desirable to have younger students make small individual pocket charts so that they can "manipulate" sentences at their seats as you or a student do so at the large pocket chart in front of the room.

Basic words (forms of *be*, *do*, and *have*), frequency words, pronouns, names, punctuation marks, etc., can be kept on individual cards in clearly marked envelopes for easy reference and quick changes.

Sound-symbol relationships and beginning reading material such as dialogues or a Gouin Series (see page 275) will be learned more pleasurably and efficiently through the pocket chart.

## The Flannel or Felt Board

Another widely used visual device is the flannel board. This inexpensive device is an excellent way of presenting and practicing structures and vocabulary and of clarifying the socio-cultural situations in which language is used. In the case of younger students, it can also provide an effective medium for dramatizing stories.

It consists of a piece of low-cost flannel, pinned to, glued on, or simply laid over a board — even a blackboard. On it can be placed pictures of paper (backed with flannel or sandpaper to make them stick to the flannel) or flannel cloth cutouts of various items. (Flannel adheres easily to flannel.)

The board may be used as a device for demonstration when you are telling a fairy tale, or for showing role changes in a dialogue. It is very useful, too, in illustrating various structures and vocabulary items.

For example, you may prepare several pictures of silverware and table china. Students may then be asked to find the items and place them on the board. This might be followed with questions such as, "Where's the spoon?," eliciting the answer, "To the right of the plate." Not only would an experience of this kind be useful in teaching agency and directional prepositions and other vocabulary items, but it also affords an opportunity to talk about differences and similarities in table settings, meals, the use of hands, and so on.

A large letter X and a question mark made of flannel will enable you to teach *Wh* questions (*Who, Where,* etc.), inverted questions, and negative words. For example, a cutout of a girl and a stove (the stove symbolizing the kitchen) may afford practice in "Alice is in the kitchen." By adding a question mark above the two cutouts, students will practice "Is Alice in the kitchen?" or "Where did Alice go?" By placing a large X on the stove, you can elicit "Alice isn't (or is not) in the kitchen" or "She didn't go into the kitchen." By quickly having a student place a bed, tree, couch, etc., on the board, students can continue with "She's in the bedroom" or "She went into the bedroom." You can devise other symbols to which you and your students will attach the same meaning; e.g., → (is going to or went) ; ← (came back) ; ⋀ (a place).

A use of the flannel board which has been popular in many coun-

171

tries is one in which we cut out the figure of a person from another piece of flannel: the head, ears, nose, mouth, eyes, neck, arms, body, legs. We've named it *"Poor Jim."* *Poor Jim* serves to practice the names of parts of the body, words like *right and left,* and names of illnesses. (When a student points to various parts of Jim's body, for example, a classmate would say, "Jim has a stomach ache," or "Jim had a sore foot yesterday," or "He would have gone to the party, but he had a sore throat," or whatever you are teaching.)

Fairy tales are more enjoyable to young students as some of the characters are placed dramatically on the flannel board and moved around as need be. (Try doing this with "Goldilocks and the Three Bears" someday, even with adult students.)

Another amusing way in which the flannel board can be used is as follows: Make a cutout of a house or a room or anything which lends itself to this game. Let us assume you have made a house. Two students go to the flannel board. One removes the window and says, "This is a funny (peculiar) house. It doesn't have a window." The next student quickly places the window back, removes the roof, and says, "Oh, yes, it has a window, but it doesn't have a roof," etc. Two or three pairs of students may play this game during a class period.

## The Magnetic Board

This can be used in much the same way as the flannel board. Small magnets are needed to keep the materials in place. It is not as easily available, however. The initial cost is greater, and the language teacher without a room he can call his own will balk at carrying it, dramatic though it may be.

## The Opaque Projector

This is a comparatively inexpensive, simple to operate machine which enables you to project — on a white wall or screen — anything printed, drawn, written, or painted. Such flat materials as sheets of paper on which is written material to be proofread (see page 133), pages still bound in a book, pictures, photographs, small maps, graphs, or stamps can be effectively shown to a large class by means of the machine. (With machines currently in use, the room should be darkened.)

## The Overhead Projector and Transparencies

The overhead projector is gaining in popularity for several reasons: It permits the teacher to face the class in a fully lighted room while writing or making quick line drawings on the transparencies used with the machine. The teacher may write with a grease pencil or water-soluble marking pen, both of which are erasable.

By utilizing overlays* (transparencies which are either attached to the sides of the master transparency or superimposed on it), you can gradually build up stories, longer sentences, or paragraphs. By removing or folding an overlay back, phrases or words from a paragraph or picture can be removed, thus requiring students to recall them. Overlays can also be prepared for use with dialogues or drills of various kinds to illustrate that alternative utterances or single words may be substituted in slots or for whole utterances.

## Kodachrome Slides

These are especially suitable for giving students cultural insights and appreciation. Colorful slides permit students to get the full impact of some aspect of the foreign country directly, without any need to hear an explanation in their native tongue or to translate inwardly. The slides can be held as long as needed. The language used to discuss them can be as simple or as complex as feasible. The students themselves can be asked to tell what they see, always at their ability level.

## Filmstrips

Filmstrips (slides which are arranged in sequence and which can be projected by a filmstrip projector on a wall or on a screen) can be used effectively to practice vocabulary and structures while taking the pupils out of the confines of the classroom. Filmstrips need not have been prepared specifically for foreign language teaching. Any strip illustrating a fairy or folk tale or illustrating some aspect of the foreign country can be used.

The filmstrip — like slides — has several advantages. It can be stopped at each frame for as long as you desire. It can be turned back or pushed forward to any frame. Since it contains no sound, you and later the students can create appropriate utterances for each frame within the ability of the students. In harmony with the "spiral" approach, the same filmstrip or slide can be shown many times throughout the program, each time with more complex structures.

## Miscellaneous Materials

1. A cardboard clock with movable hands.
2. A puppet stage (made from an old crate or box).

---

* The vendors of these machines generally supply all the materials and a Manual for teachers.

3. Puppets (paper or rag).
4. Calendars (large ones showing days of the week for an entire month or for the year).
5. A large thermometer with a movable black or red strip to indicate the rise and fall of the mercury.
6. Books and magazines (from the foreign country whenever possible).
7. Maps (your neighborhood, your city and country, the foreign country, the world, with an indication of the places where the foreign language is spoken).
8. Newspapers.
9. Scrapbooks.
10. Stamp collections.
11. Bulletin boards (containing announcements in the foreign language, postcards and photos, news items, student-made drawings of places of interest).
12. Toy telephones.
13. A spirit duplicating machine with master sheets on which anything can be drawn, typed, or written by hand (invaluable for providing individual worksheets, material for games, dictation, proofreading exercises, etc.).
14. A Polaroid camera.
15. Film and tape splicers.
16. A screen.

## Audio Aids

### The Record Player

Songs, stories, plays, operas, poems, dances, and speeches, as well as the voices of people in a market place (all of which are available on records), are invaluable in teaching the foreign language and should be used at whichever step in the lesson they would be most appropriate. Language learning can be combined with recreation or aesthetic appreciation for a change of pace in the classroom to enhance motivation.

### The Tape Recorder

Where tape recorders exist, the teacher should make every attempt to use them extensively. If tapes have been made of the textbook lessons, they will be invaluable in giving the *additional* practice needed to reinforce the work taught in the classroom.

Tapes have the advantage of maintaining the same intonation, repeating endlessly without tiring, providing a uniform length of pause for student repetition, etc. These characteristics may not always be true of the teacher who teaches many different classes a day.

Many kinds of supplementary materials can be placed on tape: pronunciation drills where contrasts are featured; sentences of varying lengths to teach rhythm; sentences illustrating basic intonation patterns; dialogues and stories for listening and repeating; oral practice activities where students "manipulate" a sentence to create a new one; dictations; aural comprehension exercises; and even tests.

In addition to tapes of the textbook lessons themselves, the teacher can use commercially taped stories, plays, dialogues, or drills to enrich the material he is teaching.

The tape recorder will also be found effective in demonstrating to pupils the progress they are making in learning the new language. Intermediate students may be asked, at the beginning of the semester, to record a small passage. At the end of the semester they can be asked to record the same passage again.

For easy identification, each student should give his name before he starts to read. The number on the tape counter should be noted in a book. Enough tape should be left after each student's reading to permit him to re-record next to his original performance. In this way, the progress (or sometimes, unfortunately, the lack of it) will easily be apparent.

A single tape recorder in the center of the classroom can be heard easily by a class of about forty students. Tapes of drills with model sentences and pauses for student repetition can be prepared. Pattern practice drills in which model sentences are followed by a cue and a pause for student response can be done effectively with one tape recorder. You can indicate by gestures the type of pupil participation you desire. The fact that you can direct students to respond (according to need and ability) and that you are able to monitor all the student responses directly often makes the single tape recorder more effective than the language laboratory in beginning language work.

Stories, dialogues, poems, speeches, and songs are particularly appropriate for group listening. Dictations and listening comprehension exercises can be placed on tapes for more advanced students.

An output jack with six to eight earphones attached to a single tape recorder makes small group instruction feasible. Any language learning material appropriate for listening alone or for 1) *listening,* 2) *thinking of the answer or change in the form* in the case of drills, and 3) *hearing the correct answer* can be placed on the tape.

*Passive listening* should be discouraged. When students are not engaged in a dictation or aural comprehension exercise, they should be asked to repeat silently, to mark items on a sheet of paper or in their notebooks, or to study related pictures.

A final, important note on the tape recorder: Students at the beginning levels particularly should never be asked to listen to anything which has not been presented live by you first. The shape of the mouth, gestures, and the warmth of the teacher cannot be captured on tape.

## The Radio

The *radio* is good as an additional means of immersing your students in sound, but, for beginning students, general programs have disadvantages. Several programs especially prepared for language learners are now available in many countries. In addition, you may find it desirable to transcribe a radio program (speeches, news broadcasts, ceremonies, songs) on tape for later repeated use in your classes.

## The Language Laboratory

Many excellent books* have been written about language laboratories so that we will not duplicate here what has been said so eloquently elsewhere. We would like to underscore a few items of principles or procedures, however.

1. A language laboratory need not be an elaborate installation of twenty or more sound booths. One tape recorder, when properly used, may be considered a "laboratory."

2. It is not absolutely necessary to make provision for student playback. Recent experimentation and observation indicate that listening to a good model and repeating a correct response are generally more effective than listening to oneself. This is especially true at the beginning level when students cannot distinguish sounds or discriminate between them.

3. The directions on the tape (if teacher-made) may be in the language of the students followed immediately by the foreign language equivalent, unless the teacher has clarified the directions in class or is present to clarify them. Gradually, the directions in the native language may be omitted. When native language directions are given, they should be spoken in a low voice followed immediately by the foreign language spoken at a normal volume.

4. In general, unless the teacher feels that his control of the foreign language is not at all adequate, *the initial presentation* of the teaching material should be done by the teacher. The tape recorder can give more intensive and extensive practice, but it cannot answer

---

* See the "Additional Reading" section at the end of this chapter.

questions, indicate relationships, emphasize, underline, and detect problems by looking at the learners' faces.

Where the teacher is not a native speaker and feels that the tape recorder is necessary for the first presentation of new material, he should, of course, not hesitate to make use of it. He and the students can listen to and repeat the dialogue or the conversation together. It is more desirable, however, for him to listen to the tape as soon as possible before coming to class and to present the material in it "live" first. We cannot emphasize this point strongly enough.

5. When students use the laboratory outside of class time, the teacher should give them the opportunity to display their greater accuracy or fluency when they return to the classroom.

6. Whether the laboratory is part of the classroom, whether it is used by the entire class at one time under teacher guidance, or whether it is used as a library by individual students, the materials studied in the laboratory should have been presented in class first.

7. The ideal tapes are those which are prepared by the classroom teacher who is thoroughly familiar with his students' learning style, strengths, or weaknesses. There are, however, many excellent tapes on the commercial market, some of which are designed to accompany specific textbooks. Others give practice in basic items of structure or contain dialogues, plays, songs, or any other material which can be recorded.

8. The tapescripts* must be prepared in minute detail.

9. Voices other than that of the teacher should appear on the tape.

10. Male, female, and children's voices should be built into the dialogues or playlets. For more advanced levels, different registers, dialects, and idiolects may also be recorded.

11. In pattern drills, at least eight practice sentences should be given for each drill type or language item.

12. In addition to crystal-clear directions, two model sentences, illustrating the base sentence, the cue, and the desired response should be included.

13. *Listen and repeat* drills are effective for such material as dialogues or reading selections.

14. Pattern practice should be done in *three-phase* or *four-phase* *drills*. In the *three-phase* drill, the students 1) listen to the cue; 2) make the desired response; 3) listen to the correct response (the confirmation). In the *four-phase* drill, the students are given the opportunity, during the appropriate pause on the tape, to repeat the correct response as the fourth step.

---

* See pp. 181-83 for illustrations.

15. When putting dialogues on tape for student repetition or recall, it is desirable that, after a reasonable number of listen-repeat phrases, the pauses permit the students to take first the role of the listener and then the role of the speaker who initiates the conversation.

16. As with the single tape recorder, the students must be active participants. They should not be asked merely to listen.

Following is a list of Dos and Don'ts related to the laboratory, prepared by the tireless Modern Language Association of America.

## PLANNING AND OPERATING
## A LANGUAGE LAB OR AN ELECTRONIC CLASSROOM

("Lab," as used here, may refer to any installation of foreign language teaching equipment)

### A Dozen Dos and Don'ts:

1. DO hire a consultant (not employed by a lab equipment manufacturer), to help you plan, evaluate bids, do the final checking of installed equipment.

2. DO define your teaching objectives first and then choose equipment that will implement them.

3. DO see at least three different types of successful installations in operation before you decide on your equipment.

4. DO follow the instructions and guidelines (pages 26-28 and 263-87) in the Council of Chief State School Officers' *Purchase Guide* (Ginn and Co., 1959) and its *Supplement* (Ginn and Co., 1961).

5. DO arrange your seating and equipment with provision for viewing as well as hearing and speaking.

6. DO write exact specifications into your contract and accept delivery as completed only when the equipment tests up to specifications and functions smoothly for a full month and when there are adequate provisions for servicing.

7. DO build an expandable and flexible lab to handle future increases in demand and new improvements in equipment and methods.

8. DO provide for regular preventive maintenance, with an annual budget of 3% to 5% of your total initial cost.

9. DO plan for short lab sessions; 20 minutes of active daily use is the ideal.

10. DO insist that the lab work be an integral part of the foreign language course.

11. DO urge each teacher who is to use the lab to study the growing literature on the subject and take a workshop course.

12. DO cut in half the teaching load of the lab directors and allow released time for all teachers who prepare lab materials.

178

1. DON'T try to do it yourself; planning a lab requires as much knowledge as planning a school *and* a radio station.

2. DON'T leave the planning entirely to administrators or A-V specialists, who may know little about foreign language teaching.

3. DON'T plan a lab for use by everyone (foreign languages, English, shorthand, speech); this will result in confusion and frustration.

4. DON'T forget that a lab is no stronger than its weakest component, mechanical or human.

5. DON'T accept inferior sound; it should be free of extraneous noise, and as natural and full-ranged as a live voice.

6. DON'T forget Murphy's Law of Electronics: Anything that *can* go wrong *will*.

7. DON'T overlook the alternative of electronic equipment in each foreign language classroom instead of a single lab.

8. DON'T forget to budget for tapes, discs, and other expendable equipment.

9. DON'T expect *all* your equipment to function all the time; provide 10% to 20% spare parts or use only 80% to 90% of capacity.

10. DON'T impose the lab program on unwilling or unprepared foreign language teachers; start with one beginning course taught by an enthusiast, make it a success, then add other courses one at a time.

11. DON'T expect the foreign language teacher to teach and operate the lab at the same time; hire a technician to assist him.

12. DON'T expect the lab to reduce the teacher's work; it will increase it, redistribute it, reorient it, and make it more effective.

## Preparing Tapescripts

If you should want to or have to make your own tapes, the following general criteria, some already noted in this Guide, and samples of tape directions may be helpful:

1. The material on the tape* should have been presented "live" in the classroom.

2. There should be constant reminders to the students on the tape that this practice or piece of material will reinforce something already done in class.

3. The tape should duplicate a "slice" of the classroom lesson as closely as possible: There should be a *motivation*, a *statement of aim*, *crystal-clear directions*, *different kinds of cues*, a *variety of practice activities*, *confirmation of responses*, and *transitional statements* between one practice activity and the next.

---

* While many of the suggestions are made primarily for tapes to be used in the language laboratory, they are equally pertinent for the single tape recorder in the classroom.

4. Moreover, since you cannot always be available in the language laboratory situation, you should occasionally make some comments on the tape which will encourage students and make them feel that you are actually talking to them — something like, "That was fun, wasn't it?," or "We'll do more of these next week," or "Let's take a break for a minute or two and listen to a song (a joke, a poem, etc.)".

5. Listening should never be passive. It should be accompanied by other purposeful activity. For example, they might be asked to look at a text, to study some visual material, to write some answers, to copy something, to select an answer from a number of possibilities, or to guess something and check (on a prepared answer sheet) the letter or number they have guessed.

6. The tape should contain authentic language.

7. More than one voice should be recorded. This is particularly true for dialogues, unless you are a wonderful mimic.

8. The tape should be no more than twenty minutes in length.

9. The material on the tape should be divided into logical segments.

10. About six to eight utterances should be supplied for each drill.

11. In giving dialogue practice, provision should be made for students to take both roles.

12. The pauses for student response or repetition should be long enough for the students to be able to think and speak, but not so long that they start dawdling or thinking of the native language equivalent.

13. Provision should be made for students to receive immediate confirmation of the correctness of their response when the tape is heard in the laboratory away from the classroom and your immediate supervision.

This confirmation can be written into the tapes, or it can be provided on a checklist on the back of the students' answer sheets. A correct dictation, for example, could be placed on a chart or could be flashed on a screen by means of an opaque projector.

14. Students should be encouraged to display their greater fluency or knowledge in the next classroom period during many phases of the lesson.

15. The material on the tape should be referred to whenever feasible during the regular classroom lesson before the laboratory session.

16. Provision should be made for the continuous integration of the taped material with the subsequent classroom lessons.

17. You should always prepare a detailed written script. It is difficult to improvise in front of a microphone. Include an identification

number, a title, and other useful information which will not only be spoken on the tape but also placed on the outside of the box in which the tape will be kept and on another form for immediate, easy cross-reference.

18. You should make every effort to eliminate background noises (unless you are recording a street scene in which background noise would give the tape a ring of authenticity). If your room is not sound-proofed, you might try placing the tape recorder about four feet from a wall, under an overturned chair which has been covered by a blanket or a coat.

19. When speaking into the microphone you should turn your head slightly away, so that the puffs of air we generally make with certain sounds are not picked up.

20. If at all possible, it would be desirable to make the preparation of the tapescript and tape a "team" project (e.g., other teacher, community resource person, someone from a neighboring school, etc.).

21. If you can press native speakers of the target language into service, all well and good. But you should not hesitate to record your own voice. After all, your students hear it in class.

22. Whether or not you explain the dialogue situation and give the directions in the native language of the students will depend upon your students' learning level, the language in which you generally clarify situations and directions in class, etc. Naturally, as quickly as possible, all material on the tape should be spoken in the target language.

### Some Examples of Beginning Tapescripts

*Dialogue Practice:*

*Listening and Repetition*
• "The dialogue you will hear is about the first day of the school year. John has gone to Peter's home. The boys are going to walk to school together." (Give as much of the situation as necessary.)
"Listen to the conversation." (Normal speed)
"Now listen to the conversation again." (Normal speed)
"Now listen to each line of the conversation. You will hear it two times. Then repeat it during the pause."
"Good morning, John. Good morning, John." (Pause)
"Now listen to the whole conversation again." (Normal speed)

*Role-Playing* (This should be preceded by listening and repetition practice.)
• "Are you ready to take part in the conversation? Pretend you are

John. Say what John would say, then listen and compare your sentence with that of the real John. Ready? Begin."

    (Pause) "Good morning, Mrs. Welsh."

    "Good morning, John. How are you?"

    (Pause) "I'm fine, thank you. Is Peter at home?"

"Now, pretend you are Peter," etc.

*Dialogue Variation* (Questions and answers) :

- "Listen to the conversation between X and Y."

    "Listen to the conversation again."

    "Now I'll ask a question. Think of the answer during the pause. Do not say it. Then compare your answer with the answer you hear."

    "Where did John go?" (Pause) "He went to the store."

- "Listen to the conversation between X and Y."

    "Now listen to the conversation again."

    "Now I'll ask a question. I'll ask the question two times. Answer the question. Compare your answer with the one you will hear." (If you wish, you may add, "Repeat the correct answer.")

        "Where did John go? Where did John go?" (Pause) "He went to the store." (Possible pause for student repetition of the confirmation)

*Pronunciation Practice:*

- "Let's practice some important sounds."

    "Listen and repeat."

- "Now you will hear two words. Listen carefully and say whether they are the same or different. Compare your answer with the one you will hear."

    "bag bag" (Pause) "Same."

- "Let's use these sounds in sentences. Listen and repeat."

*Pattern Repetition* (These should be preceded by repetition and substitution drills.) :

- "Listen to these questions and responses. Repeat them."

    "How are you?" (Pause) "I'm fine, thank you." (Pause)

- "When do we use *he* in sentences? When do we use *she*? Listen and repeat."

    "Peter's in the kitchen." (Pause) "He's in the kitchen." (Pause)

*Pattern Practice:*

- "Let's practice making questions."

    "John's in the kitchen. Listen to the question and repeat it.

Where's John?" (Pause)
"Mary's in school. Where's Mary?" (Pause)

• "Now let's practice asking questions. What question would you ask to get the answer you hear?"

"I'm very well." (Pause) "How are you?" (Pause) (Repetition after the confirmation would be desirable in this type of exercise.)

• "Let's practice making sentences negative. First listen to two examples and repeat them."

"I have a pencil." (Pause) "I don't have a pencil." (Pause)
"I need a notebook." (Pause) "I don't need a notebook." (Pause)

• "Are you ready? You will hear a sentence. Make it negative. Listen to the correct answer and repeat it."

"I see John." (Pause) "I don't see John." (Pause)

*Dictation:*

• "Do you remember the story about X? I'm sure you do. I'm going to give you some sentences we read in class. I'll say them two times. Copy them on your paper."


## Audio-Visual Equipment

### Films

*Films* for the language class fall into two categories: 1) those which give insight into various cultural aspects of the foreign country, and 2) those which are designed to teach the language at various learning levels. In this latter type, simple situations often related to the foreign country are portrayed.

All films have the disadvantage of not being able to be turned back easily and quickly to a scene or language exchange that the students may not have grasped. The "culture" films, in addition, are often spoken in language far beyond the ability of the students. In most instances, therefore, they have to be used without the sound track.

When used, films should be carefully previewed; they should be motivated; appropriate follow-up activities should be planned (questions and answers, summaries, or descriptions). Language-oriented teaching films are in preparation and should be available in the near future to supplement the teacher and the simpler instructional materials the teacher would generally use.

*Loop films* which start automatically again without rethreading

183

or rewinding can be used to advantage in teaching. The loop films are generally quite short and provide for immediate reinforcement and overlearning. These, too, are based on either linguistic or cultural themes.

*Films in cartridges* which are merely dropped into a machine, thereby eliminating the need for threading by hand, are appearing more frequently on the market. If they can be produced inexpensively and if their content is linguistically and culturally sound, they will prove a boon to those of us afraid of "equipment."

**Television**

*Television* offers many possibilities as a learning medium. Several courses for teaching foreign languages from the beginning to more advanced levels are available. The television programs which have been designed especially for language learners try to duplicate the classroom situation. Dialogues or dramatic vignettes depicting some cultural situation are utilized; structures are repeated and "manipulated"; some descriptions of word order and forms are given. The camera can come close up to the teacher's mouth to show lip position, mouth movements, or gestures. There are pauses for student repetition. Textbooks are often prepared in conjunction with the programs.

Television programs, however, cannot do the whole job. The majority of programs may be of only twenty minutes' duration. If the programs are used in conjunction with the regular curriculum, they add spice and pleasurable variety to the learning. They provide reinforcement, change of pace, different voices, and wider vistas than the teacher could. It is important, however, that additional explanations and practice be given by a classroom teacher. The television teacher cannot hear students' difficulties and errors; "free" answers are impossible; many oral activities cannot be engaged in.

As with any other tool or technique, it is the teacher's use of television that determines its efficacy as a learning aid.

**Programmed Instruction**

The last several years have seen the wider use of so-called "teaching machines." This is a misnomer because they are not, in fact, machines. A teaching machine may consist of a simple box with an opening on top into which a program is inserted and a knob on the side which a learner can turn. Some machines are much more complicated. They stop, turn back, or turn forward electronically, depending on the student's response, which he indicates by making a mark on the appropriate sheet, or writing a number, a word, or an utterance.

The *program* (the term for the pages of learning material which are inserted in the box) is the important part of the teaching machine. A good program is based on several principles: 1) It is very carefully graded. 2) Each item of learning is broken up into its smallest parts and practiced in as many ways as possible. 3) It permits a student to work at his own speed. 4) It is self-teaching. 5) It gives immediate confirmation of the correctness of one's response. (If the mark on the paper is incorrect, the knob does not turn, a red light appears, or some other signal is given.)

Some publishing houses are doing away with the box or "machine" entirely and are preparing programmed textbooks. The principles of teaching are those described; but in a text, the student is often directed to turn to another page for confirmation of his answer. If the student's answer was not correct, he is directed to another section for study and then back to another "frame" (as it is called) where he is required to select an answer on the same language feature which he will again confirm. Other types of programmed texts supply the answers to the blanks in the frames* or in the passages on the side of the page. With a card, which they slide up or down, students uncover the correct answer after they have tried to insert it on their own.

Because of the fact that language is speech, "programs" for languages are, at this writing, not as successful as they are in other curriculum areas. The perfect synchronization of sound track and teaching machine which would permit the student to work at his own speed has not yet been devised. Since programmed instruction incorporates several basic premises of learning, it is to be hoped that experimentation will permit the production of materials which will promote language learning.

There is no doubt that, thanks to the technological boom all countries are enjoying, we will soon have available machines which synchronize sound and images, both of which are needed for foreign language learning. Already we find cartridges containing films or filmstrips which need only be dropped into a machine; record players combined with screens; and cards which can be placed in a machine and which will reproduce orally the sentence printed on the card.

All of these aids hold great promise as will the many others being devised constantly but all require careful planning if they are to be used to maximum advantage and effectiveness. They should not be used simply because they are either readily available or pleasurable. Devices and techniques should be included in teaching plans only

---

* Teachers can use programmed learning techniques in the preparation of individual or group worksheets which can be duplicated for distribution. Students can use a card to cover the correct response (the confirmation) listed on the side.

when we can answer these questions affirmatively: Do they enhance the pupils' self-image? Do they help develop positive attitudes toward the speakers of the foreign language? Do they engender, increase, or sustain motivation? And, finally, do they bring the students closer to the attainment of the language and cultural objectives of the language program?

## SOME TEACHING TECHNIQUES

All teachers develop a stock of time-honored procedures which help make the learning process more efficient and effective. Some of these are not the province of second language learning nor, indeed, of any special step in the teaching process. A brief listing in no particular order of those we have found particularly pertinent and fruitful follows. A few of these have been touched upon in this book in various sections.

1. *Starting with the Students and Their Environment*

a) Use the students and yourself (your clothing, the things you carry, etc.) to teach appropriate vocabulary before using pictures or other materials.

b) Utilize the known environment of your students before fanning out to the wider foreign-speaking world. Relate your presentations to facets of language or of culture with which you can expect your students to be familiar. For example, if you're going to teach vocabulary related to a beach scene in Spain or France, help the students recall a beach scene (or swimming, boating, or fishing) closer to their homes. Use many questions starting with "Do you" or "Have you."

2. *Making Good Use of Dialogues*

a) Use dialogues wherever feasible. Dialogues duplicate the communication situations in everyday life. Keep building on the same dialogue situation. For example, with classroom objects:

> A — Do you (have) a notebook?
> Yes, I do.
> B — Do you (have) your French notebook?
> (No), I (don't).
> C — 1. Do you want a notebook with lines?
> 2. Yes, please. How much is this one?
> 1. Twenty cents.
> 2. All right, I'll take it.

b) The possibilities for expanding the same dialogue situation

186

are infinite. In addition to expanding the dialogue, you may want to give practice in substituting whole utterances. For example, the "response" in A above could be, "Yes. Do you want it?" or "Do you want to see it?" or "Do you need it?" The response in B could be:

"I'm sorry. I forgot it." or
"Of course. I always carry my French book."

c) Exploit the dialogue judiciously. The moment the students appear uninterested, drop the dialogue and proceed to another activity. Students won't be bored, however, if pairs of them engage in many short dramatizations; if you vary the dialogue utterances; if you ask questions about it; if you personalize it; if they're encouraged to create a similar one; if they're permitted to read it after you sometimes; if they can give a native language equivalent of a difficult or "flavorful" utterance.

3. *Planning Oral Activities*

Plan as many different oral practice activities for each lesson as can be done briskly and with reasonable accuracy. As you write your lesson plan, decide which of the drills outlined above are best suited to the item you are teaching.

4. *Varying the Type of Student Participation*

a) Use chain drills, but break the chain after five or six students have spoken, and start another chain in another part of the room.

b) Call on students in order and then at random.

c) Ask a question. Have *one* student answer. (It is unwise to ask for a choral answer to a question unless it has been thoroughly practiced immediately before.) Ask the question, then call on a student by name.

d) Have a student or a group ask you a question. Answer it.

e) Have a student ask another student a question. (See Directed Practice and Chain Drill Suggestions, pages 98-99.)

f) Have students manipulate the hands of the clock, the sentences in the pocket chart, or the material on the flannel board and say what they are doing or ask questions about what they are doing.

g) Have students "shuffle" the pictures or the flashcards or touch the desired pictures in the picture series charts and ask questions about them. The questions can be asked of you or of fellow students.

h) Divide the class into two or three groups. Have one group ask a question (based on your model); another group answer it; the third group add to it or react to it; e.g.:

① Can you come swimming?

② I can't.

③ Why can't you?

① He's very handsome.

② I think so too.

③ I don't think so at all.
                (What do you see in him?)

i) Encourage students to formulate questions for you or their classmates to answer.

j) Have pairs of students come to the front of the room often to dramatize a dialogue, even if it is only two lines.

k) Provide many opportunities for students to work in pairs during many parts of the lesson. In addition to giving them the structures they will practice, place words on the blackboard for them to refer to for insertion in appropriate slots within the structures.

l) Use games to reinforce language items. These may be team competitions, guessing games of various kinds, and those in which physical movement is associated with language, as, for example, in Gouin Series drills.

5. *Giving and Correcting Homework*

a) Assign homework with care. Plan simple routines for giving and checking it. For example:

— Place or have placed the assignment for the next lesson in a clearly marked corner of the board at the beginning of the hour.

— Have the students copy it *at the beginning of the hour* while you quickly check attendance.

Ask if there are questions. (Your students will have been told and will understand that the homework will be based on the lesson to be done during that class hour.)

b) As you present your lesson or do some practice exercises, draw the students' attention to the fact that some or all of them will be part of the written homework.

c) Avoid giving homework over short holidays, when students are having a test in another subject, or at other times when it may become a hated burden.

d) Give a reasonable amount of homework. Thirty minutes, four times a week (when you have five sessions) is generally enough. Remember, the students are studying four or five additional subjects.

e) If students are expected to attend language laboratory sessions, integrate the homework assignments with them or cut down on the written work.

f) Permit students who have not done their homework to tell you so before you start your lesson.

g) If you wish (but this is not generally necessary when the students realize that you are indeed sincere about permitting their oc-

188

casionally being unprepared), assign the first person in each row to check the performance of homework.

h) Depending on your available board space, have several of your more able students place a designated segment of their completed homework on the board.

- They may be permitted to take their notebooks to the board,

or

- You may prepare (or have prepared) slips of paper on which are written directions to the students.

i) Have the homework exercises placed on the board in the order in which they were done.

j) While the homework is being placed on the board, *engage the rest of the class in related oral activities.* (You should never start a new lesson during this time.)

k) Devise a system for cooperative blackboard correction. After all the homework has been placed on the board, have a "leader" go to the board and ask a question such as "Do you see any mistake ("Are there any errors") on Line 1 or Board 1?" Have class members indicate the errors and say what the correct form should be. Train student leaders to put a line through the incorrect word and to write the correct form over it. (This will serve as a possible reminder to you to "drill out" the error after all the boards have been corrected.)

Change the board "leader" at least once a week.

While the leader and class members are noting errors at the board, you should walk around the room, not only to make sure the students are inserting corrections into their notebooks but also to write something complimentary in student notebooks — a grade, your initials, anything which they can take home and point to with pride.

l) Have the boardwork read after you at beginning levels, only *after* it has been entirely corrected. At the second level and above, have a student other than the one who put the work on the board read it, but always after all corrections have been made.

m) If time permits, ask several students to read their corrected work from their own notebooks. This will encourage them to make the necessary changes from the blackboard.

You will have noticed that this homework correction procedure ensures wide student participation and the active involvement of many class members.

n) Unless you want to spend lots of time "proofreading," it is generally preferable to have your more able students put their homework on the board.

o) With well-trained, highly motivated, and able students, summaries or more creative writing efforts may also be put on the board

189

for class correction. In general, however, such correction takes up a great deal of time which might better be spent on other kinds of oral and written practice.

6. *Preparing Students for "Freer" Composition Writing*

a) Before assigning a composition for students to write at home, it is imperative to help them with the ideas to be included in it. The topic may be based on a current event, a piece of literature you have been reading, an oral discussion you may have had in class, a talk the students have heard, a film, a newspaper item, or anything which interests the students and gives them ideas they want to express.

b) Give students ample time to write the composition — about three days from the time you have discussed the ideas and the language needed to express the ideas.

c) Devise a marking scheme which will be of help to you in reviewing the papers with reasonable speed and which will not discourage your students when the papers are returned.

You may wish to use the following procedure:

— Ask your students to leave a one- or two-inch margin on the left-hand side of their papers.

— Have them divide this margin into four columns. The first could be Sp (Spelling); the second may be P (Punctuation); the third Str (Structure); the fourth V (Vocabulary).

— When you correct the compositions, perhaps once every two or three weeks, merely *underline* the error and *place a check* on the appropriate line in the appropriate column.

| Sp. | P. | Str. | V. | Composition |
|---|---|---|---|---|
| ✓ | | ✓ | | My <u>friend</u> he <u>comed</u> to my house yesterday. |
| | ✓ | ✓ ✓ | ✓ | He said <u>do</u> you <u>need</u> to come <u>to</u> movie. <u>She's</u> a |
| ✓ | | ✓ | ✓ | good <u>picture</u>. We could <u>to</u> go now and be <u>bak</u> in |
| | | | | time to get ............................................. |

— You may wish, on a ten-point scale, to deduct $1/4$ point for each error, or you may deduct $1/2$ point for structures and $1/4$ for vocabulary. In later stages, you may also wish to give one or two points for richness and variety of vocabulary.

d) Have the students rewrite the composition and return *both* the original and corrected copies to you.

e) In cases where students have prepared book reports or reports on cultural topics, give additional credit for the number of appropriate and different ideas expressed.

## 7. *Helping Students Achieve*

a) In drills, always give the model sentence or expression two or three times before asking the class or an individual to give it.

b) Call on your more able students *before* calling on the weaker ones. In this way, the latter group will have more opportunity to practice responses which will be reasonably correct.

c) Utilize incidental happenings in the school or the immediate community to teach or to review language items. Although we believe firmly in lesson planning, *no* plan should be so rigid that it cannot include references to unusual or relevant occurrences (if these are of interest to your students). The use of special events and incidental happenings not only reinforces and extends learning, but also illustrates that the structures or vocabulary practiced within one situation can be used to talk about another one.

d) Give students the feeling and the assurance that the foreign language is a vehicle of communication which serves exactly the same purpose as does their native tongue. What do people all over the world generally talk about? The daily routines of sleeping, eating, dressing, working, and playing; and births, marriages, illnesses, etc. Although it is true that we use different words or expressions, there are equivalent expressions to discuss equivalent events in any culture.

e) Supply the words and expressions which students need to talk about all aspects of holidays and special celebrations in their country, *even though the holiday may not exist* in the foreign country. Students should be enabled to speak to their friends or other native speakers who know the foreign language about events in their immediate environment. "Where, or how, are you going to spend the holidays?" is a normal, authentic, real question and refers to the holiday in the student's country and not to one many miles away.

f) Use *authentic* language at *normal speed* in the classroom. Often, in the desire to simplify language for our students, we give expressions or words which we consider easier simply because they're shorter. Try to remember that sometimes the longer word may be similar to a cognate in your students' language. Also, since everything is different for learners, they may just as well learn the expressions or words that the native speaker of the same age level would use under similar circumstances.

g) Provide opportunities for students to act as listeners and as speakers. Students should be able not only to make statements but also to make comments or responses, to ask questions, and to answer questions.

h) Summarize what has been done at various times during the lesson. Make sure, through questions, charts, diagrams, and, as a last resort, through the native language equivalent that students understand what they are repeating, or what is expected of them.

i) *Teach — Don't Test.* This does not mean that you should not give quizzes, tests, and examinations. (Testing will be the subject of another chapter.) In presenting new material, give numerous examples so that the students perceive the word order or new form. Don't try to elicit an "original" sentence after one or two examples.

j) Practice activities immediately following the presentation of new material — at whichever level — should be confined to repetition after the teacher (class, groups, and individuals) and to simple substitution of *one* item only. The kind of problem-solving exercise where students have to make four or five changes concurrently in a sentence should have no place in the program when material is first presented. Problem-solving ability and increasingly stimulus-free production by the students are developed gradually after much listening and repetitive and manipulative practice.

k) Motivate each step in the lesson. Use transitional (introductory or linking) sentences from one activity to the next. For example, after giving the vocabulary needed for the reading selection, you might say, "Now that we've learned some of the words people use in talking about . . ., let's listen to a conversation (let's read about). . . ."

l) Avoid making a reading selection, particularly a piece of literature, a "hunting through the dictionary" session. While students should be helped to "discover" new word meanings or relationships, they should not have to do it so frequently — and often with poor results — as to mar their enjoyment in reading.

m) Encourage your students to use their imagination in reading and in "free" conversation and composition. "What do you think will happen?"; "What would you do?"; "What would you have done?" should be questions frequently asked. If the language level of your students is not sufficiently advanced to answer such questions in the target language, allow them to answer *briefly* in their native tongue. The important thing is to create an interest in the reading selection and to illustrate the universality of human experience.

n) Spur your students to greater efforts by training them to give longer, more sustained, or multiple responses to a question or statement. The ability to sustain a longer conversation which duplicates real speech will give them a feeling of success and achievement.

o) Help them use connecting words (*and, but*), formulas, short answers, introductory words. Let us consider some brief examples:

• Using a picture series chart on which you or a student indicate or touch the appropriate pictures, notice the possible progression in a beginning level course:

I see milk; I see bread; etc.

I see a bottle of milk, a loaf of bread, etc.

I see a bottle of milk and a loaf of bread.

I see the bottle of milk, but I don't see the loaf of bread.

I don't see the bottle of milk, and I don't see the loaf of bread either.

• Notice the exchanges possible in talking about a movie (depending on the age level of your group and the role-playing exercises you engage the class in, the first word *Golly* might become *Gosh, Whew, My,* etc.) :

1. — (Golly.) That was a great movie.
   — I think so too.
2. — Golly. That was a great movie. I'm glad we came.
   — I am too.
3. — That was a great movie. .................... was wonderful.
   — I agree. It was a good part.
4. — That was a great movie. .................... was wonderful.
       She's my favorite actress.
   — She's mine too.
   — Did you see her in .................... ?
   — I certainly did.
   — Did you like her in that?
   — Yes, very much. I saw the movie three times.

p) Always tell your students *how* you want them to respond (that is, tell them that you want them to make a response and a further comment; or that you want them to respond and ask a question, etc.). When they have learned the appropriate expressions, you may also have them agree, disagree, express surprise, pleasure, anger, sorrow, etc.

q) Encourage your students to prepare materials according to their talents and language ability. Students may be asked to look for pictures, to cut and mount them, to prepare flashcards (with pictures or words), to draw pictures. More able students — even those at beginning levels — may be asked to compose a dialogue with familiar words and structures or to build on a familiar dialogue with newly acquired structure and vocabulary items. At the intermediate or advanced levels, students may be asked to write original conversations and short plays for later dramatization.

r) Above all, never hesitate to return to a preceding step in the language-learning process (see page 79 ff.) if students seem to be having difficulty with the step you are on. For example, if they are encountering difficulty with the step of "conscious" selection, go back to the preceding step — the practice of the separate items. If they cannot do the practice well, go back to giving them some model sentences, reinforcing the generalization, and engaging them in repetition.

## 8. *Bringing the Community into the Classroom*

a) Utilize community resources and bring the people in the community into your program. This is important, not only because it provides additional stimulation for the students but also because it will foster interest in the language learning program within the community.

b) Invite native speakers to come to your classroom to speak about their trips, hobbies, interests, or jobs. The preparation for the visit, social amenities, questions to be asked, listening to the talk, and writing the letter of thanks to the visitor lead naturally to language learning.

c) Start a language club to which community members may be invited. Plan topics and projects for discussion or games, songs, etc. around the interests of the students. Establish a schedule for the entire semester or year, and arrange for the election of a president, vice-president, secretary, and treasurer — all in the foreign language.

Help the students prepare a constitution in the foreign language.

Plan culminating activities — plays, festivals, dramatizations — to which parents and other community members can be invited.

d) Encourage community members who may have visited the target foreign country to give a talk related to their trip. This may be a class or a school-wide activity. If pictures or slides are available, so much the better.

e) Ask the local printer (if possible) to help you print a foreign language or a bilingual newspaper, to which students, parents, and other community members might contribute.

## 9. *Correcting Students' Errors*

a) Allow some errors to go unchallenged or uncorrected unless they impede understanding. This is particularly important during those moments when a student may be expressing an idea or letting his imagination hold sway. When he has completed his thought, *say something complimentary*, and then make one or two corrections in a low voice. Learning when, how, and where to make corrections is the hallmark of a master teacher.

b) In general, immediate corrections should be made during the pronunciation drill phase of your lesson and during the pattern practice activities. It is often not possible or desirable, however, to draw attention to every pronunciation error. A "poor" student who has been absent but who still volunteers may make five errors in six syllables. Concentrate on one or two. Make a mental note of the others and plan to give class-wide or individual practice in them at a later time, as needed.

c) Never say, "No, no, it's not ..............," repeating the student's error. Your repetition of the error may only serve to reinforce it in some students' minds. Merely say, "Listen," and give the correct form.

d) If you have been practicing questions and answers and you hear errors in the students' responses, say to an able student, "Ask me the question." This will give you the opportunity to model the answer and to have it repeated in chorus, if you wish, without unduly embarrassing the students who have made the errors.

e) If a student cannot answer a question or respond in a reasonable length of time, move on to another student and then return, if you wish, to the first student. Any other procedure is time-consuming and basically non-productive.

f) Occasionally — but only if the students have been trained to do so tactfully — a student may be asked to correct a fellow student's error.

g) If in saying a sentence a student mispronounces one or two words, you may isolate the words for correction, but the student should then be asked to say *the entire utterance* again.

## 10. *Creating a Climate for Learning*

a) Simulate a foreign language environment in your classroom. Do this by having pictures, maps, bulletin boards, proverbs, and labels in the foreign language. (Encourage your school head to assign one room to foreign language study.) Use the foreign language as much as possible during the hour, but try to set aside a few minutes toward the end of the hour when students can ask questions or make comments in their native tongue.

b) Use the students' native language judiciously when it would mean saving a great deal of time or ensuring comprehension, or when the safety and welfare of the students are involved.

c) Classroom routines (taking attendance, distributing and collecting materials) and recurring questions ("What does — mean?" or "Who sees (or hears) an error?") should be in the foreign language. Such formulas and expressions can be built up gradually from the very first day of the first level.

d) Simplify and adapt foreign language stories for oral presentation. If you have duplicating facilities, prepare simplified material for reading. The famous novel, "Les Misérables," by Victor Hugo, was adapted and condensed most effectively in a course at the University of Michigan into four double-spaced pages. Of course, it did not have the original "flavor," but the interest in the story line was very high and it afforded excellent practice in language.

## 11. *Enhancing the Student's Self-Image*

a) Arrange many audience situations in which individual students can give book reports, an illustrated talk, etc., to their fellow-students.

b) Display students' work (scrapbooks, drawings) where possible. Try to use everyone's work at one time or another.

c) Send letters of praise home whenever you can.

d) Say something complimentary if and when parents come to visit.

e) Make him feel proud of his parents, his background, his experience, and his language.

Above all, it is important to tailor your course to your students. Their interests, the community in which they live, and their abilities should be kept in mind constantly as you plan every phase of your lesson.

*Vary, adapt, experiment.* Language is dynamic. Teaching can and should be.

## BEYOND THE CLASSROOM

Unless you are teaching in a one-room schoolhouse or doing individual tutoring, it is of crucial importance that you make every effort to become an integral member of the school and community teaching team. In the majority of situations in which we all find ourselves, teaching means much more than going into a classroom daily to present a circumscribed segment of the foreign language. It means working with the administration, with other language teachers, with other school personnel, with other teachers in the community — in short, with anyone in the school or in the community who can help us achieve the broad societal goals of education and not only (important as they may be) the objectives of foreign language teaching.

Textbooks have been written on this subject so that we will again limit ourselves to a few brief comments under several headings. Unfortunately, in the past not enough space has been devoted to this important area of concern in textbooks devoted to foreign language teaching.

*Developing Rapport with:*

a) The Administration.

1. Take attendance each period. (Have a student help you.) Keep a record of attendance. This may often become a matter of great importance to a student or to his parents.

2. Send attendance reports, if required, to the appropriate office promptly.

3. Speak to the students about the proper care of textbooks. If

these are supplied by the school, keep book cards with the students' signatures or other required records. Ask students to write their names and class in each textbook on an appropriate label.

4. Encourage the students to give you any change of address. Notify the office promptly if you are the person asked to do so. About once a month, ask students if they have moved. (This may be important in some communities in which there is high population mobility).

5. Present your lesson plans for the week (or month) to the head of your department or other administrative officer when they are due and in the form in which they are required. Keep a copy of your lesson plans so that you will not be distressed if they are not returned promptly.

6. If there is some comment on a plan that is returned which you do not understand, ask about it at an appropriate time.

7. If you have other school duties (lunchroom, corridor, library, supervision), arrive promptly. (The teacher on duty before you may have a classroom of students waiting or may have another appointment.)

8. If you are asked to prepare an examination for departmental use, do so within the specified time.

9. Get to your examination proctoring assignments on time. Remain there, if an examination is in progress, until you are replaced.

10. Grade departmental examination papers as quickly as possible so that records and report cards can be issued when scheduled.

11. Keep accurate, detailed records of each student's progress or, unfortunately sometimes, of atypical behavior so that you will be prepared with the facts to speak with administrators, guidance counselors, or parents.

12. Find out from the very beginning of the semester what the "ladder of referral" may be for students in your class who present discipline or other problems. Does such a student go from you to the head of your department, to a general guidance counselor, to a dean in charge of discipline, or to the principal? Don't violate protocol either by sending a student to the person not responsible for your particular group or by not giving the first person to whom you have referred the student an opportunity to help you solve the problem before referring him to the next person on the "ladder."

13. Make every effort to solve your own problems (see page 223 ff.), but do not hesitate to seek help if the welfare and safety of your other students are involved, if you have exhausted all channels to no avail, or if you have some questions about the physical or mental health of the "offender."

14. Learn about the written and *unwritten* directives concerning letters to parents and other community members.

15. Show consideration for the administrator who has to program hundreds of students and faculty members. It may not be possible for you to get the program you would like each semester. Other teachers, too, may want to have an earlier lunch hour or not teach three classes in a row. Unfortunately, not everyone can have a "good" program each semester.

16. Volunteer or accept with good grace a request to prepare an assembly program or to supervise a club period or newspaper.

17. Accept "supervisory" visits gracefully. There is no person alive who cannot profit from constructive suggestions made by someone who can see the classroom situation objectively.

18. Invite the supervisor to come into your classroom when students have prepared a special program or when you have a lesson you a) would like to "show off," or b) have doubts about.

19. Make provision for your possible absence by keeping your lesson plans, seating plan, and other pertinent materials in the top drawer of a desk or in another place known to your class president or assistant.

b)  Other Members of Your Department.

1. Share your books and other materials.

2. Never question your students about another teacher's personal or teaching qualities.

3. Never criticize another teacher's grades, preparation, instruction, handling of discipline, etc.

4. Offer to conduct experiments with other teachers or to set up special programs, clubs, assemblies, trips, tutoring.

5. Inform them of materials and other resources you may have found.

6. Be considerate about getting your students in or out of the language laboratory promptly.

7. Leave the classroom clean (blackboards, floor, closets, etc.).

c)  Personnel in Other Departments.

1. Remember that every subject in the curriculum has value. Every teacher feels that his subject will produce the most enlightened citizens.

2. Do not ask students to miss any period in any subject to go on a trip with you or to help you in any way. If absence from another class because of you becomes unavoidable, discuss it with the teacher involved first.

3. Terminate your lesson on time so that your students can arrive at their next class promptly.

4. Try to think of ways in which you can correlate the foreign language with other subject areas. Discuss the possibilities of correla-

tion with the teachers involved. If the project you plan is extensive, discuss it with the head of your department.

## FACING PROBLEMS OF ARTICULATION SQUARELY

Teachers have a major role to play in providing for the smooth, continuous development of foreign language skills in students. While articulation (the term used to talk about the continuous progress of a student from one learning level to another) is generally considered the special domain of administrators, only you, the teacher, can supply the information and offer the cooperation which will make articulation possible.

As teachers, we are concerned with both horizontal and vertical articulation. Horizontal articulation implies that all students at a learning level will be taught the same corpus of material and will be helped to develop fundamental language skills to a similar degree. Vertical articulation is the term used to discuss the progress of students from one learning level to another either in the same school or from one school or community to another.

Poor articulation — either horizontal or vertical — places students at a serious disadvantage. If there are gaps in their knowledge, they will be frustrated, insecure, and liable to failure. If they have "covered" the same material that they are being taught again (we are not talking about normal, desirable review of previous material) by a teacher at the next level, they will also be frustrated and bored and they will no longer feel that they are achieving.

What can you do as a teacher to cooperate in solving this very serious problem? You should:

1. Attend all meetings of your department and listen attentively to colleagues and the department head or principal.

2. Study the departmental or school directives, circulars, or letters concerned with goals for each level, the number of lesson units or pages of reading to be "covered," and other similar matters.

3. Keep accurate records of the lessons you have actually covered, the pages of reading you have actually taught, the skills you feel you have really developed. *You should make these records available to the head of your department.*

4. Prepare detailed comments about the strengths and weaknesses of each of your students in the listening, speaking, reading, and writing skills. Send these to the head of your department, if required. The "absolute" level of a student's mastery of the skills should be indicated along with the number of hours, semesters, etc., which may not be truly indicative of a student's competence and performance.

5. Keep all records, one or two tests, and at least one composition

as samples (where this is pertinent) for each of your students for at least one year.

6. Attend joint meetings with teachers from the next higher level in your school or another school to exchange books, tests, and other materials.

7. Help prepare tests when these are needed.

8. Discuss individual students with appropriate personnel.

9. Visit other teachers at their invitation, and invite other teachers to "observe" you.

### Suggestions

— Prepare a set of word cards. Tell five ways in which you might use them.

— Prepare a set of small picture cards. Indicate when, how, and why you could use them.

— Look through your national magazines. Select advertisements and pictures. Indicate five ways in which each can be used in presenting and practicing language.

— Choose pictures and advertisements from foreign magazines. Indicate five ways in which each can be used in teaching language and giving cultural insight.

— Devise a set of correction symbols you would use consistently in correcting tests, dictations, aural comprehension exercises, homework, and compositions.

— Discuss the reason for changing the weight of certain points (spelling, for example) in assigning grades.

— Write five games useful for teaching pronunciation. Give the exact words of the instructions to students.

— Create three vocabulary games. Give the exact words of the instructions to students.

— Discuss the value of games for secondary school students.

— List several special pronunciation symbols for your language which students might find helpful.

— Indicate, with your reasons, several points during your lesson when the use of the native language would be effective.

— Discuss ten oral reading and writing activities which can be engaged in with any dialogue.

— Discuss the criteria you would establish in displaying student material.

— Construct a table useful in practicing (during the step of conscious selection) the differences between two prepositions (English: *on, in*; Spanish: *por, para*; Italian: *di, da*).

— If you are teaching a highly-inflected language, construct a drill where different prepositions require different case endings. Do this first with nouns of one gender. Next, use nouns of different genders.

— Prepare individual worksheets for students experiencing difficulty with contrasting items (e.g., she or he, present or past). Indicate the sequence of exercises and justify your sequence.

— Discuss the advantages and disadvantages of teaching the speaking skill through the language laboratory.

— Prepare detailed tapescripts for use in practicing or developing: (Indicate introductory remarks, directions, and pauses.)

1. two contrasting sounds
2. word stress
3. a structural item; e.g., a verbal aspect
4. eight vocabulary items
5. the skill of listening
6. reading comprehension

— If time permits, do the above for each learning level.

— Discuss several ways, oral and written, which would permit you to check increased student proficiency as a result of laboratory work.

— Prepare a complimentary letter for parents about their youngster's progress in the language.

— List twenty topics, projects, or activities for a foreign language club program.

— Discuss the problem of articulation. List ten factors about each pupil which you might indicate on an "articulation" card or on a cumulative record card.

### Additional Reading

CARROLL, J. B. "A Primer of Programmed Instruction in Foreign Language Teaching," in *IRAL* 1/2, 1963.

CORDER, S. PIT. *The Visual Element in Language Teaching*. London: Longmans Green, 1966.

DEVEREUX, E. (ed.). *An Introduction to Visual Aids*. London: Mathews, Drew & Shelbourne, 1962.

DORRY, G. *Games for Second-Language Learning*. New York: McGraw-Hill, 1966.

HAYES, A. *Step by Step Procedures for Language Laboratory Planning*. New York: MLA, 1968.

HOCKING, E. *Language Laboratory and Language Teaching*. Washington, D.C.: NEA Monograph 2, 1964.

HUEBENER, T. *Audio-Visual Techniques in Language Teaching*. New York: New York U. Press, 1960.

JOHNSTON, M. and C. SEELEY. *Foreign Language Laboratories in Schools and Colleges*. Bulletin 3. Washington, D.C.: U.S. Government Printing Office, 1959.

LEE, W. *Language Teaching Games and Contests*. London: Oxford U. Press, 1965.

———— and H. COPPEN. *Simple Audio-Visual Aids to Foreign Language Teaching*. London: Oxford U. Press, 1964.

MARTY, F. *Language Laboratory Learning*. Wellesley, Mass.: Audio-Visual Publications, 1960.

STACK, E. *The Language Laboratory and Modern Language Teaching* (rev. ed.). New York: Oxford U. Press, 1966.

WALSH, D. "Articulation in the Teaching of Foreign Languages," in *Foreign Language Teaching*, J. Michel (ed.). New York: Macmillan, 1966.

# VIII
## Testing and Evaluation

Provision for evaluation should be made an integral part of the language curriculum. Indeed, criteria and measures for judging its effectiveness in terms of pupil growth toward the desired terminal behavior, should be built into the program from the very outset. The curriculum, in turn, should be revised and revitalized continuously in light of the findings of a valid, reliable, and comprehensive testing program.

The term "evaluation" in the title is broader than the traditional term, "testing." Evaluation would include 1) assessing the student's progress toward the linguistic objectives of the course; 2) determining his attitude not only toward language learning but also toward foreign speakers; 3) judging the quality of instruction and of the materials in use; and 4) appraising the effectiveness of the total language program in serving the needs of the learners for whom it is intended.

In this chapter we will consider four major questions with relation to testing. We will seek answers in as succinct a fashion as possible to the questions: 1) Why do we test? 2) When do we test? 3) How do we test? 4) What do we test? These are the questions of primary interest to teachers.

### ATTITUDE TESTS

Before proceeding to a discussion of some basic premises underlying each of these questions, we would like to make several comments about two tests which are often mentioned with relation to language study: attitude and aptitude tests. The use of written "attitude" tests to judge interest in the language and in cultural understanding (and here we are using "cultural" in the broad anthropological sense) is still in the experimental stage.

Very promising questionnaires have been prepared based on an analysis of possible factors included in "attitude." As more experimentation is done in sociolinguistics and in anthropology, and as more is learned about the "variables" and "invariables" which constitute attitude, instruments for measuring this essential ingredient for learning will certainly become available. As with any other instrument ready now or available in the future, such tests should be used to measure and analyze attitude, but these, too, must be studied along with numerous other factors, within the large, more comprehensive context of the learning-teaching process.

In the meantime, a way to judge cultural attitude is through observation of a student's reaction to literature and other visual and reading material, to foreign visitors, and to questions about the foreign countries. His interest in the language can be judged through his participation in class. Does he volunteer? Does he give sustained answers? (Of course, lack of response may indicate timidity rather than apathy!) Does he prepare his work? A perceptive teacher is usually the best judge of desirable attitudes.

## APTITUDE TESTS

The other type of test to which we referred is the so-called aptitude or prognostic test. In many school systems, students are tested before being admitted to a language program in order to determine whether or not they have the capacity to learn a language successfully or whether they will need a longer (or shorter) period of time to learn it. In the judgment of the authors themselves and of many teachers, the results of the prognostic tests available at this time should not be considered conclusive. The score on the tests must be studied with additional extensive data about each student before an accurate determination of future success can be made. Experiments have demonstrated clearly that motivation and perseverance on the part of the normal student and good teaching on the part of a competent and sympathetic teacher may be more reliable criteria of success in language learning than a score on a prognostic test. The two batteries of prognostic tests which appear to hold the greatest promise at this time and which are being evaluated in countries outside of the United States will be found in Appendix III.

Carroll and Sapon, and Pimsleur, authors of the two currently used test batteries, emphasize the importance in the prospective learner of the ability to discriminate, identify, and produce sounds; the ability to remember material that has just been heard; the ability to memorize; and the ability to handle grammar using analysis and analogy. But whereas Carroll and Sapon seem to feel at the present time that aptitude, as measured by the test, is a relatively invariant characteristic of the individual and is a reliable indicator of future success, Pimsleur considers motivation, attitude, and achievement in other school subjects of importance in predicting success in foreign language study.

In addition to the attitude and aptitude tests, there are four others generally discussed in connection with foreign language teaching:

- An *achievement test*, which is used to measure how much of the material taught within a textbook or a unit of the text has been learned. If the items are prepared in enough detail, this may become:
- A *diagnostic test*, which enables us to ascertain whether a problem a student is having is due to a poor grasp of some feature of pronunciation, of morphology, etc.
- A *progress test*, which is used in one form at the beginning of a determined period of learning and in another, after that period, to ascertain the learning which has taken place within that period.
- A *proficiency test*, which is used to measure the points at which the student may be on the continua of the four communication skills, without regard to any particular textbook or to formal study.

We will limit the discussion, however, to achievement testing or, to put it in another way, to testing in order to discover the students' problems, weaknesses, or strengths and to ascertain their progress toward the goals of the language program.

We have noted throughout this Guide that language is systematic. There are predictable, systematic patterns of sounds, of structures, of culture, and often of vocabulary which students should learn to use in consonance with their learning level in authentic social and cultural situations. It is obvious, then, that a well-rounded testing program should make provision for doing three major things: 1) judging problems of growth in the phonological aspects as well as in the structural and lexical aspects of the foreign language; 2) evaluating the students' use of the discrete features of language within the listening, speaking, reading, and writing abilities; 3) ascertaining that the students recognize and make use of the overt and "hidden" aspects of culture needed for appreciation, understanding, and communication.

## WHY DO WE TEST?

There are several reasons, some of which have broader implications, as you will see:

1. The obvious reason is that we have to grade students so that we can move them forward to the next higher class or retain them at their present level. In non-graded programs (which are the subject of current experimentation), the movement of students may be to other groups within the same classroom or to other groups on the

same level within the school. If, for example, several of your students are having serious problems in acquiring some skill, they would profit from working with a group (in the class or in the school) in which intensive practice is being given in improving that skill.

What has just been said would be equally true in "graded" programs where groups could spend part of each lesson on simpler or more complex material, according to their ability, within the same classroom. This aspect of group dynamics is discussed further on page 150.

2. Another reason for testing is that, through appropriate instruments, we can set realistic standards of achievement for groups or individuals. By comparing* our test results with results in similar classes or communities teaching under similar conditions, we can judge whether we are setting our standards too high or too low, or whether our curriculum is in need of revision.

3. Tests can also help us assess the effects of experimentation. For example, through a carefully controlled experiment, we may wish to determine whether the use of the students' native language in the classroom or a long strictly aural-oral period retards or increases their progress. Only a reliable and valid testing instrument can provide an answer to knotty, controversial problems such as these.

4. The confidence of the community or nation in a language program may sometimes be based on the results of a testing program. This may be a double-edged sword. Poor results without an examination of all the data (teacher preparation in colleges and universities, school location, monies spent on instructional materials, etc., etc.) may so undermine the confidence of the public in a particular program that they will want to discontinue it. On the other hand, they may decide to strengthen the program through such activities as conferences on school-university coordination, seminars, or the purchase of needed instructional equipment.

5. The three principal reasons for testing as far as classroom teachers are concerned are: a) to diagnose the specific features of language in which individual students or groups are having difficulties; b) to help us gauge our ability as teachers; c) to find out how much our students have learned or achieved.

A few parenthetical remarks particularly with relation to b) above may be pertinent at this point. Failure on the part of a few students does not necessarily mean that we have not planned or taught well. We are all aware that many factors (intellectual, physical, emotional, social) within an individual student may be at the root of the failure.

---

* UNESCO is sponsoring a study at the present time designed to compare the proficiency of language students after similar years of study in fifteen countries.

On the other hand, if the majority of students fail a test, it would be desirable for us to review our presentation and the practice activities critically. It is only to the extent that the classroom teacher translates the results of tests into more effective teaching procedures that students will derive any benefit from a testing program. It goes without saying that poor grades by the majority should signal *reteaching and retesting* of the item or items involved, before proceeding to a new item or topic.

## WHEN DO WE TEST?

In any school system, there are usually mid-term or end-term examinations in which the proficiency of pupils is tested. These proficiency examinations are very often school-wide or community-wide tests which include the language items and skills covered in a prescribed number of units of work, whether or not the same text is used by all classes.

In addition to these tests, you will find it desirable to give a long comprehensive achievement test at the end of each unit of work and, particularly at the beginning levels of language learning, a brief quiz daily or as many times as feasible each week.

This brief quiz is an excellent teaching device and can serve many purposes:

1. If the correct answers are given immediately after the test (as should be done), the knowledge of the correctness or lack of correctness of their responses will reinforce the students' learning of the response or will help extinguish the incorrect response.

2. The students gain a sense of achievement if they have done well. (Below will be indicated some techniques for ensuring success.)

3. It gives you insight into students' difficulties and into segments of a unit of work which may have to be retaught or practiced more intensively.

4. It may be used, where feasible, as the springboard for the new lesson to be presented that day.

5. It gives you and the students a frequent "barometer reading" of progress.

6. An average of the many grades accumulated through this process does away with the unfortunate practice of giving a student a final grade which is based primarily on one or, at most, two examinations. An able student, prevented by illness or some other cause from doing well on one examination, may be saved from mid-term, end-term, or end-year failure by a consideration of the grades on the daily quizzes.

You, the other teachers, and the supervisor should determine the "weight" to be given these daily tests in the final grade. This determination should be announced to your students on the first day of class or within the first week. Students should be asked to keep a record of their grades and even to compute the average of the daily "quizzes." While we realize that every school will have to work out its own system of weights, you may be interested in something the Department one of us chaired found "fair." (When we say "Department," we include students and their parents, teachers, and the principal of the school.)

— Daily quiz (including dictation and listening comprehension exercises) ................................................................................ 30%
— Final examination ................................................................................ 30%
— Classroom participation (e.g., work related to dialogues, pattern practice, reading, writing, cultural study) ............ 20%
— Homework, reports on reading, group projects (e.g., culture, newspapers, assembly program, etc.) ........................ 20%

## HOW DO WE TEST?

Today's generally accepted principles of language teaching make it imperative that we emphasize oral tests as well as written tests. Let us consider written tests* first.

These, as we know, may be of two types: short answer tests and essay tests. Short answer tests may duplicate the practice activities outlined in Chapter III. They may include multiple choice, completion, substitution, or transformation exercises. They have several advantages: They are *objective*; they can be *scored easily* and *quickly*; they permit the testing of a *wide area* of knowledge.

Essay tests should play no part in a beginning language program. They may be useful and desirable at the more advanced levels, however. Only through essay tests can we judge the students' use of varied structures, the richness of their vocabulary, and their ability to express ideas with logic, clarity, and precision. In other words, the longer essay permits us to judge the ability of the students to use language as a tool for written "freer" communication. (See pages 136-37 for further discussion.)

From the teacher's point of view, essay tests are difficult to grade because they require more time than do objective tests. (A scheme such as the one given for grading compositions [see page 190] will be found useful.) From the students' point of view, the subjective ele-

---

* It goes without saying that written tests can be used to test aural understanding and oral production. Examples are given below.

ments in the essay test may cause apprehension. Unless a marking scheme that permits of no scorer's personal judgment is prepared in advance, the test results may be unfair to some of the students.

This is particularly true when teachers other than the classroom teacher grade essays as is often the case in city-wide or nation-wide examinations. To eliminate subjectivity, a score must be assigned for every feature of language or for every idea expressed. In preparing a score sheet, the number of points to be deducted for each error in a sentence, for example, should be indicated with the maximum score to be deducted for that particular sentence. The range of permissible ideas should also be indicated within reason, of course. A brilliant idea that none of the scorers had thought about should be given credit although it did not appear on the score sheet.

When a large number of tests are involved, about twenty-five papers chosen at random should be scored separately by a committee of teachers. A conference should then be held before all the essay papers are marked to change the score sheet (if necessary) or to make it more detailed.

Oral tests are indispensable for judging oral production of sounds, stress, rhythm, and intonation patterns, fluency, and "automatic" responses to oral or written stimuli. Oral tests may be time-consuming, however. Several time-saving techniques you may wish to consider follow:

1. Make a chart of five or six points you want to grade. Each day, for a week or two, call several students to your desk individually while the rest of the class is working on projects or doing some form of silent foreign language work. Ask each to repeat, read, follow directions, etc., as indicated below. Give only as much material as is needed to ascertain their knowledge of the language items you are testing. Grade them only on the key points on which you had decided to grade them. Ignore (although it will be painful for you to do so in many cases) all other incorrect features.

2. If you have one, use a tape recorder on which directions or cues are given. Have the students record their responses on a tape. (Each student will be asked to start at a different number on the counter and to give his name at the end of the test.)

3. Use the tape recorder to give directions and to say the material to be tested. Have the students indicate their responses on an answer sheet. (This would test *aural* comprehension only.)

Combinations of aural and written tests would include those in which students take a dictation (full or spot as explained on pages 133-34) or a comprehension exercise, in which they answer in writing questions (given orally or in writing) on a dialogue or narrative paragraph they have heard.

# WHAT DO WE TEST?

Simply stated, we should test everything we consider important enough in language learning to teach. That means we should test the students' knowledge of the phonemic, structural, and lexical systems, as well as their insight into any of the cultural aspects we helped them acquire.

We should test the students' ability to understand, to speak, and — as soon as feasible — to read and to write. Within the listening and speaking skills, we should judge their ability to understand the formulas of the language, their ability to ask and to answer questions, and their ability to make the normal responses which the situation demands.

At more advanced levels, moreover, we may wish to test the students' understanding of registers and styles, as well as their ability to retain material over a long period of time. For example, they may be asked a question whose answer was given at the beginning of a half hour lecture. With relation to the speaking skill, we may wish, in addition to accuracy of grammar and vocabulary, to consider whether their response is sustained; whether there are many unnecessary pauses in the response; whether the response is given without a long period of silence; whether additional teacher encouragement is needed to elicit a continuous response in describing a scene or in giving a summary, for example.

If literary masterpieces have been studied, the tests may include whatever has been emphasized in class — the author and his time, the relationship of the literary work to some aspect of contemporary culture in your country or in the foreign country, the style, cultural allusions, character study, or whatever you have discussed.

The tests of cultural appreciation should focus on the anthropological and sociological aspects of the society whose language is being studied. For example, do the students have an understanding of the situations in which certain features of language can be used? Do they appreciate the rationale behind the customs and values of people? Do they possess a knowledge of the important historical, geographical, social, and artistic facts? Do they have an attitude of acceptance and appreciation of the people and their language?

There is bound to be overlapping in many tests. For example, a dictation tests listening and writing skills and enables us to judge the students' grasp of the sound, structure, and vocabulary features contained in the passage.

The test stimuli or cues should be varied just as they are in the classroom practice activities. The stimuli might include, therefore: 1) hearing spoken words or utterances (live or on tape); 2) looking

210

at a picture or several pictures; 3) looking at real objects; 4) reading a word, an utterance, or a passage.

Let us consider some simple tests which can be given in the classroom (or in the language laboratory) to test both the receptive and the productive abilities of our students. Whether some of these are given and responded to orally or in writing (or by placing a correct symbol or letter on an answer sheet) will depend not only on the nature of the test but also on the learning level of your students. For these reasons, test suggestions are listed in no particular order.

## Testing the Features of Language

*To test their knowledge of the sound system*

Have students:

1. Indicate whether two sounds — given orally or in writing, isolated or in words — are the same or different.
2. Indicate which pairs of words rhyme (e.g., a. send/lend; b. friend/fiend; c. enough/through).
3. Mark the syllable having the loudest stress (e.g., again/never/turn on/apple tree).
4. Indicate (by a prearranged code) rising or falling intonation (e.g., "Did you go to school? Where did you go?").
5. Indicate from which column of words or pictures you (or a tape) are pronouncing a word or an entire utterance (e.g., think/thing; I saw the ship/I saw the sheep).
6. Imitate sentences of varying lengths (e.g., I want a dress. I want a pretty red dress. I want that pretty red dress.).
7. Indicate stress and juncture in pairs of sentences (e.g., I saw him by the tree/I saw him buy the tree).

*To test their grasp of grammatical items*

Have students:

1. Select the appropriate word from two or three words by underlining, numbering, or filling a blank on an answer sheet (e.g., The [boy/boys] walk to the door.).
2. Perform any of the transformation exercises indicated in Chapter IV (e.g., "Make this a question: 'He went to the door.'" "Say

you have *two*: 'I have a box.'" "Ask a question with 'Who': 'Mr. X is a mailman.'").

3. Use the words "get up" (for example) in these sentences (e.g., It's seven o'clock in the morning. I'm ............................. now. Yesterday I .......................... at seven o'clock too. I usually ....................... at seven every day.).

4. Answer questions in the negative using a full sentence (e.g., Do you have some bread? Did you find someone there?).

5. Ask direct questions based on indirect questions (e.g., Ask X how old he is. Ask someone whether he knows Mr. ...........................).

6. Give the paired sentence (e.g., Mary is going to read later. The boys are going to study later./Mary reads every day. The boys .................................).

7. Make all changes required by a cue (e.g., [These] This boy is tall.).

8. Indicate which pictures you are mentioning (e.g., This is a foot long. This is a long foot. This is a station wagon. This is a wagon station.).

9. Complete sentences:
    I ...................... thirsty. (am/'m/have)
    I'd go if I ...................... time. (have/were/had)

10. Answer questions of various types (cf. Chapters IV and V). Indicate whether you want a Yes or No answer; whether you want a short answer or a long answer; whether you want a combination short and long answer; whether you want them to agree, disagree, express surprise, sympathy, anger, etc.

11. Choose the correct form (e.g., The woman's name is ...................... [Peter/Mrs. Jones/Miss].).

12. Combine sentences (e.g., She's a student. She's very good./That man is my father. He's talking to Mr. Brown.).

13. Match the stimuli and possible responses. Have one less response than the stimuli so that guessing will be minimized, e.g.:

| I | II |
|---|---|
| 1) Thank you. | a) Better. |
| 2) How old is he? | b) He's twelve. |
| 3) When are you leaving? | c) Of course. |
| 4) How are you feeling? | d) You're welcome. |
| 5) May I go out? | e) Tomorrow. |
| 6) Where does he live? | |

14. Rewrite the sentence placing the adjectives in the correct position (e.g., [small/four] I have puppies.).

15. Indicate where a word belongs (e.g., "usually" — He *A* goes *B* to the park *C*.)
16. Select the appropriate coordinating conjunction when two are given (e.g., [and/but] I'd go ..................... I'm tired.).
17. Select the appropriate subordinating conjunction when two are given (e.g., [while/unless] He went to work .......................... she took care of the house.).
18. Select the appropriate connector (e.g., It was freezing. [However/ Otherwise] we went out.).

*To test their knowledge of vocabulary*

Have students:

1. Indicate whether a statement is true or false (e.g., Spring comes before summer.).
2. Complete a sentence (e.g., The cow [barks/moos/shrieks].).
3. Select an unrelated word from a group of words (e.g., meat/ soup/eraser/peas).
4. Give a synonym or choose one from a list (e.g., start [begin]).
5. Give an antonym or choose one from a list (e.g., finish [start]).
6. Give two other words from the same family (e.g., jewel [jewelry, jeweler]).
7. Make nouns from the following verbs (e.g., arrive/deny/permit).
8. Make adjectives from the following nouns (e.g., man/child).
9. Use the prefix meaning "not" in these words (e.g., ability/able/ rational).
10. Use the suffix meaning "pertaining to" in words such as region, nature.
11. Select the appropriate word (e.g., [in/on] The picture is .................. the wall.).
12. Select the appropriate word (e.g., [too/very] I can't drink the tea. It's .................. hot.).
13. Choose the word(s) with the same meaning as the underlined word(s) (e.g., [must/should] I *have* to leave now.).
14. Choose the appropriate word (e.g., [breakfast/lunch/dinner/sup- per] We always have ....................... at seven in the morning.).
15. Paraphrase a sentence (using the same structure but different vocabulary).
16. Write three or more sentences using *different* meanings of a word (e.g., He *got* an A. He *got* the book. He *got* worried.).

# Testing the Communication Abilities

*To test their listening comprehension*

Have students:

1. Carry out a request. Use one utterance with beginners and more than one with more advanced students (e.g., Go to the board. Go to the board and write your name. Go to the board, write your name, and then erase it.).
2. Take a spot dictation.[1] Distribute a sheet with a passage containing some missing words. As you dictate, students will write the missing words on the answer sheet.
3. Take an aural comprehension exercise.[2]
4. Complete the sentence when a choice is given (e.g., It's raining. I'll have to take an ............................ [examination/umbrella/envelope].).
5. Tell whether the items they hear are singular or plural, present or past, present or future.
6. Answer questions according to the cue or direction (e.g., [movies] Where did you go last evening?).
7. Select an appropriate rejoinder (when several choices are given) to a statement or request (e.g., May I smoke? [Not at all./Of course.]).
8. Identify the central theme or the nature of a talk when listening to a news broadcast (e.g., social/political/artistic/educational).
9. Tell which statement (given orally or in writing) embodies the main idea of a passage they hear.
10. Give a summary of a talk they have listened to — live or on tape.
11. Take the role of listener or speaker in a dialogue.
12. Engage in role-playing exercises.

*To test their speaking ability*

Have students:

1. Repeat sentences of varying lengths.
2. Say a passage, poem, or dialogue they have learned.
3. Take one of the roles in a dialogue.
4. Answer questions either when specific instructions are given or without a cue.
5. Make a rejoinder to a statement or request.

---

[1] See pp. 134-35 for the procedure.
[2] See p. 135 for the procedure.

6. Read a passage of familiar material.
7. Read a passage containing new material.
8. Ask direct questions when an indirect statement is given (e.g., Ask me how I got to school this morning.).
9. Transform sentences according to the direction given.
10. Give the equivalent of a short native language utterance.
11. Formulate questions on a passage.
12. Tell what they would say (or do) in a certain situation. They would hear (or read) one or more sentences describing a situation, and they would tell what they would respond (e.g., You know it's a friend's birthday. You meet her(him) on the street. What would you say?/Someone tells you his mother is ill. What would you say?).
13. Describe what they see in a picture.
14. Tell about something they did at some particular time (before coming to school, perhaps), something that happened, or something that is going to happen.
15. Give a summary of something they are asked to read at the examination or that they have read at some time before.

*To test their reading ability**

Have students:
1. Complete sentences based on a passage read when a choice is given.
2. Complete sentences when a choice is not given.
3. Complete a logical inference (e.g., He had worked eighteen hours without stopping. He was [rich/tired/stupid].).
4. Read an unfamiliar passage aloud and answer questions on it.
5. Formulate questions on a passage.
6. Answer several questions on a passage read silently.
7. Give definitions of selected words in a passage. (The ability to use contextual clues would be apparent.)
8. Outline a paragraph.
9. Summarize a passage.
10. Indicate a possible rejoinder or sequence utterance to a statement or a series of statements.
11. Say whether a statement is true or false.

---

* Since the ability to read requires a knowledge of structure and vocabulary, many of the tests already suggested will also serve to judge reading power.

12. Indicate the characters in a story who had expressed a point of view or performed some actions.
13. Read a passage crossing out irrelevant words.
14. Read a passage silently within a limited time and answer questions on it. (This would enable you to test fluency and speed as well as comprehension.)
15. Discuss the cultural allusions in a poem or passage.
16. Give synonyms, antonyms, or paraphrases of certain words or expressions.

*To test their writing ability*

Have students:*

1. Insert punctuation marks and capital letters in a paragraph.
2. Write out in full the words for symbols or abbreviations (e.g., +/%/Mr./Inc., etc.).
3. Reconstruct a sentence from several words (e.g., boys/movies/yesterday).
4. Complete a sentence using the same verb in both spaces (e.g., [eat] He ............... as he had never ............... before.).
5. Expand several sentences into a letter, dialogue, or story.
6. Add details to a topic sentence.
7. Answer questions about themselves or some material they have studied.
8. Answer questions substituting pronouns for all nouns.
9. Take a dictation — spot or regular.
10. Take an aural comprehension exercise.
11. Rewrite a passage or story from their point of view, or in the past or future.
12. Write what they would say or do in a situation.
13. Write what they see in a scene.
14. Summarize a passage.
15. Formulate questions on a passage.
16. Write an essay on one of three topics you indicate (based on their reading, a cultural topic, a news item, etc.). You may wish, at times, to include some of the ideas they are to treat.
17. Rewrite a paragraph using a more casual (or a more formal) style.

---

* Systematic sound-spelling correspondence should be tested, of course. In addition, any of the drills on pp. 89-103 can be written.

18. Give the foreign language equivalent of a passage in the native language or vice versa.

## Testing Cultural Understanding

Objective tests and essay tests may be used to test knowledge of facts and insight into cultural behavior.

Following are some examples:

*Students may be asked to:*

a) Complete a sentence (e.g., In [country], there is no school on ................. and ..................; the .................. is the center of social life.).

b) State which is true or false:
Most (Americans) have lunch at noon.
X was written by Y.

c) Choose (by circling, underlining, or writing on a separate sheet*) the correct answer: Americans belong to unions.
Some/All/None

d) Identify people or places:
All of the following are composers except:
Verdi/Puccini/Tintoretto/Bellini

e) Define or identify by completing a sentence:
Mardi Gras celebrates ..........................................

f) Explain a situation in a brief statement:
The shop will be closed on August 15.

g) Indicate which behavior may be considered typical, A or B:
A — In (              ) people go to the theater at 2 P.M.
B — People go to the theater at 9:30 P.M.

h) Write a brief paragraph when a topic sentence is given:
Children and adults always look forward to Three Kings' Day.

i) Write an essay on any pertinent topic.

## Testing Literary Appreciation

Both objective tests and essays will be useful. The objective tests can be of the types indicated above under Cultural Understanding. Students may be asked to *complete* sentences when a choice is given or when no choice is given, to *identify*, to *match*, to *define*, to *give an explanation*.

---

* The possible choices can be labeled A, B, C.

217

The knowledge tested will depend on the material taught. It may be related, for example, to:

1. Authors and the names of their works.
2. Literary movements: time and milieu. (The Romantic movement flourished in .................... during the .................... part of the .................... Century.)
3. Story line or plot.
4. Works in which certain characters appeared (e.g., Renzo and Lucia are the principal characters in ........................).
5. The main theme of a poem, play, or novel (e.g., ........................... is at the root of the tragedy of *Othello*.).
6. Cultural allusions in a poem, play, or novel.
7. The use and meaning of certain words or expressions in a literary work.
8. The form of a poem (e.g., ........................ is a(n) sonnet/ode.).

Essay tests should be required in certain situations. If we feel that the student has the necessary ability to read a literary work in the original, we must also assume that his writing ability has kept pace. Only through an essay can we judge the students' ability to analyze a literary work; to discuss the differences between the techniques of Corneille and Racine, for example, or the differences or similarities between the philosophical theories of a Hegel and a Vico. In the majority of secondary schools, however, such abilities cannot be assumed even if the foreign language was started in the elementary school. Again, each school will have to decide whether such tests are possible with its particular student population and resources.

## FURTHER COMMENTS ON TESTING

In order to eliminate the fear of testing from the minds of your students and in order to make sure the results have validity, it is desirable to follow several elementary principles of test construction and procedure:

1. Announce your tests in advance.
2. Tell students exactly what you will hold them responsible for. (Students will study for the kind of test they know they will be given.)
3. Test only what you have taught thoroughly.
4. Make sure the directions are clear and familiar to the students. Use their native language if necessary. (You should use the *native* language when feasible when you are giving an unfamiliar type of question or test.)
5. Give an example, if possible, of the response you are seeking.

218

6. Start with the simplest items first.
7. Test their knowledge of the language and not their memory of facts they have met in their reading. A question such as: "Marconi invented the ........................" is *not* a test of English, for example. It is a test of cultural facts.
8. Make aural comprehension questions short and simple so that, again, responses don't become a test of memory. (At more advanced levels, you may require a longer retention span.)
9. Use many cues and devices (pictures, objects, recordings) to stimulate the desired responses.
10. Give an open book test occasionally.
11. Provide a key for immediate checking of responses in short quizzes.
12. Return longer test papers in a reasonable length of time.
13. Permit students to ask questions about their grades. (It is best to have them come to your desk.)
14. *Do not* read grades aloud. Such a procedure may cause embarrassment or unwarranted feelings of superiority or inferiority on the part of some students.

## SOME CONCLUDING REMARKS

As our knowledge about language and the learning process increases, changes in classroom organization, in methods, and in testing are bound to emerge. Two new trends in the field of testing bear further study and examination:

1. Rather than *norm-referenced* tests in which a student's performance is compared with that of other students, some scholars recommend the use of *criterion-referenced* tests which assess and report the student's performance in *absolute* terms; e.g., the student reads well enough to read recombined passages with familiar vocabulary. According to Valette, a true achievement test must by its very definition be a criterion-referenced test.

2. Mastery of clearly specified performance objectives should be promoted for all students and *formative evaluation* tests should be given to judge the degree of mastery attained. Such tests cover a unit of instruction and are graded on a mastery-non-mastery basis. A student is given as many chances as he needs to attain the mastery level. Since these tests are also designed to diagnose a student's weaknesses, the student is then told what he should do to remedy the problems revealed by the testing instrument before he is encouraged to take the test again.

The measurement of students' progress toward the goal of "free" communication is a vitally important facet of the language program. Testing should be a continuous process which will help reinforce our students' interests. Knowledge of one's progress and success, as we all know, acts as a powerful stimulant to learning. The cliché "Nothing succeeds like success" is never truer than in a language classroom.

In addition, test results which point up a serious difficulty in some aspect of the curriculum will enable us to apply remedial measures quickly. Since language is a cumulative subject, it would be unwise to attempt to build a second or third story when the building blocks of our foundation are not well cemented.

In judging achievement, we should use our observation of students' performance as well as scores on more formal instruments of evaluation. For example, the preparation of assignments, participation in classroom activities, and the "carry-over" of language in clubs or after-school experiences also demonstrate interest and growth.

While good testing is essential, good teaching is infinitely more so. As a colleague remarked not long ago, "Let's stop weighing the baby all the time. Let's feed it instead."

### *Suggestions*

— Prepare a two-minute test for each of the following:
1. two contrasting sounds
2. elision
3. word stress
4. intonation
5. an item of grammar
6. two contrasting items of grammar
7. five vocabulary words

— Select an important grammatical feature in your target language (e.g., the use of the partitive [some, any]). Assume you have taught its use in affirmative, negative, and interrogative sentences. Prepare an objective test of about twenty minutes duration to evaluate the students' knowledge of it. Indicate the sequence of the parts, the directions and/or examples for each part, the weight you would assign each.

— Prepare a test on an entire unit from a textbook used in your country.

— Justify the giving of brief, frequent tests.

— Tell three ways in which the students could receive immediate confirmation of the correctness of their responses.

## Additional Reading

BROOKS, N. *Language and Language Learning.* New York: Harcourt, Brace & World, 1964.

CARROLL, J. B. *Notes on the Measurement of Achievement in Foreign Languages.* Cambridge, Mass.: Harvard U. Press, 1954.

HARRIS, D. *Testing English as a Second Language.* New York: McGraw-Hill, 1969.

LADO, R. *Language Testing.* New York: McGraw-Hill, 1964.

MACKEY, W. *Language Teaching Analysis.* London: Longmans Green, 1965.

MLA. *A Handbook on Foreign Language Testing: French, German, Italian, Russian, Spanish.* New York: MLA, 1970.

UPSHUR, J. (ed.). *Language Testing,* Special Issue of *Language Learning.* Ann Arbor, Mich.: U. of Michigan Press, 1969.

VALETTE, R. *Modern Language Testing: A Handbook.* New York: Harcourt, Brace & World, 1967.

# IX

## What If....?
## Some Dos and Don'ts

Although it is our earnest hope that you have found the material in the preceding pages practical and generally applicable to a variety of teaching situations, it would be presumptuous to assume that all questions with relation to language teaching have been answered. Others will arise in the minds of teachers, particularly of new teachers, who find themselves in what they consider unusual teaching situations. Still others will occur to all teachers when findings of research, technological advances, or persuasive "salesmen" make us feel that what we have been doing needs to undergo radical changes lest the school system or the entire social structure collapse!

While we would be among the first to beg you to keep abreast of everything new in the field, to listen to colleagues and others, to experiment with new techniques and new instruments, and to invite constructive criticism by your supervisors, we would also urge you to add a common sense approach to the scientific, but, alas, often pseudoscientific talk or literature. Keep an open mind. Try everything. Give yourself time to make sure that something really does not work before you discard it. But remember that just as each of our students is an individual with strengths and weaknesses, each of us is an individual. Perhaps you can't sing or play an instrument or make a good tape, but there are certainly traits of character — unflagging enthusiasm, a love of people, an intellectual curiosity — and other aspects of your teaching which compensate for the strengths of your next door teaching neighbor.

In addition to recognizing and reinforcing your own teaching strengths, you should also keep the word "judiciously" in mind. If we do not jump high up on a bandwagon built on a weak foundation, the fall will not be so great when we, and others, find that a new vaunted cure-all is not the panacea we thought it would be.

And now, before attempting to deal with situations which some teachers deem unusual, let us state for whatever solace it may offer that teaching situations are surprisingly similar in most corners of the globe. The same questions have recurred wherever we have lectured or worked. The conscientious teachers usually start with, "Yes, but, what if . . .?" We have thought, therefore, that it might be worthwhile to list some of the most frequent questions and to answer them briefly by giving some dos and don'ts where they are pertinent. This procedure will serve in some measure to summarize or recapitulate what has been said in preceding chapters.

For the sake of convenience, the questions will be listed under several categories: the students, teaching colleagues, the school, materials, methods, and the community. Some of these, of course, will not be pertinent to your teaching situation but, who knows, they may be at some future time.

Each of the following statements should be prefaced by "WHAT IF . . .?"

## THE STUDENTS

1. There are over forty students in each class.

a) Devise a set of hand signals and gestures to elicit various types of student participation (chorus, half a class, groups, rows, individuals).

b) Divide the class into four groups for purposes of choral repetition. You may want to give each group a name or a symbol for easy reference.

c) Use choral repetition and group repetition techniques.

d) Train student leaders to help check homework and correct short tests.

e) Establish routines of classroom procedure from the first day (e.g., for taking attendance or distributing and collecting materials).

f) Seat students in alphabetical order or in an order which will be maintained each day.

g) Prepare a seating plan which you will keep before you at all times.

h) Walk to various parts of the room as you model sentences and as you conduct various portions of the lesson so that you can be seen by all students.

i) Change the students' seats in the middle of the semester or more frequently if necessary so that those who had been sitting in the back will be moved forward. (Make a new seating plan.)

j) Engage in many chain drills but break them after six or eight pupils have recited. Start a new chain in another part of the room.

k) Call on individual students from various parts of the room to ensure attention.

l) Train individual students to speak in a loud voice so that they can be heard from all parts of the room.

2. Some students are very able; others are quite "slow."

a) Make use of the abilities of your students. For example, have the more able students go to the blackboard for writing dictations and the answers to aural comprehension drills. Have them recite first after you give the model so that other students will be exposed to reasonably correct answers. If you also provide activities in which the less able students can achieve success (e.g., writing the simpler pattern practice exercises on the board, coming to the front of the room, indicating pictures or objects and calling on classmates, helping to grade papers based on a model), there will be no question of lowered morale on their part.

b) Ask the more able students to help the less able in such activities as preparing assignments or writing compositions.

c) Seat able students next to "weaker" ones so that the latter will be sure to hear more reasonably accurate responses.

d) Gear your lessons to the "average" students. Move forward to another unit of the work as soon as the majority of students have grasped the content of the one you are teaching. Do not slow down for the less able students but make provision for giving them help at their stage of language learning in order that they may catch up to their classmates. Provide for peer teaching, if possible.

Since language learning is cumulative and since the reintroduction of learned material is a basic principle of current teaching practice, the less able students will have many opportunities to learn, with ever-increasing thoroughness, some language item they may not have grasped fully the first time.

e) Differentiate your assignments. The "slower" students could write out many pattern practice exercises, or short summaries or letters, for example. The more able students can answer questions, formulate questions to be asked of their classmates, write longer summaries, prepare dialogues, learn to take notes as you dictate, or write playlets.

f) Do not expect all students to reach the same level of comprehension and of oral production in the same length of time. Some will have to stay at the repetition and pattern practice stages longer than will others.

g) Some people are "slow" starters or "late" bloomers. Many students of normal intelligence (with patience on your part), will finally grasp the organization of the language sub-systems and proceed to learn by leaps and bounds. Others may remain "slow" because of genetic or environmental factors. While these may never become fluent speakers, full of creative ideas, they can still be helped to use the new language effectively for all practical purposes. They can still be enabled to develop attitudes of appreciation and understanding of other peoples.

3. The students appear uninterested.

a) Plan lessons in which there is a great deal of variety. The longest time segment in any lesson should be devoted to the oral practice activities. These in turn should be subdivided into four or five different types to avoid boredom.

b) Ensure wide student participation. Let students formulate questions, prepare pictures or other instructional materials, give cues for oral activities, lead games and songs, dramatize conversations, and help prepare a student publication, an assembly program, or an "Open House" for parents.

c) Keep the pace of the lesson very brisk. Give the students the feeling that they are moving ahead all the time. When a student cannot answer a question, give the correct answer quickly or ask a more able student to give it. (Give a student reasonable time to answer; then move on to someone else and come back to the first student a little later in the lesson.)

d) *Do not correct every mistake that students make.* During the warm-up and motivation segments of the lesson particularly, only those errors which impede understanding should be corrected. Make a mental note of minor errors and give practice in their correction later in the hour or in a future lesson to the entire class or to several individuals, according to need.

e) Do not strive for immediate "mastery." Accept reasonable fluency and reasonable accuracy since you will reintroduce all language items many times during the course.

f) Encourage your students by making it possible for them to enjoy many frequent successes. Do this by announcing tests, differentiating assignments, and creating an audience situation when they have done supplementary outside reading or when they have learned the lines of a poem or a play.

g) Praise them, judiciously of course, but do not wait for them to give a perfect response before you do so. If their response today (although still poor) is better than yesterday's, it is reason enough for praise. The praise need not be oral. A smile or a gesture will often be sufficient for the students to sense your approval.

h) Make it possible for them to talk, as quickly as possible, about the things they would talk about in their native tongue. Demonstrate that the new language permits them to say anything they can say in their language.

i) Utilize the people, places, or happenings in the community to reinforce the students' knowledge of the foreign language while lend-ing interest and variety to your lesson. You should find out about television programs, sports events, and community news items and use them as motivating devices.

j) Plan a little more than you think you can cover in an hour. Plan for the slow and for the gifted.

k) Be flexible in your planning. If something of interest happens in your school or community and if you can use the happening to reinforce or to teach language items or an aspect of the culture, or, just as important, to strengthen your rapport with your students, put aside the lesson you had planned and "discuss" the interesting occurrence.

l) Give the students status in the eyes of their classmates and of their parents. Never expose the students to ridicule in the classroom. Always find something praiseworthy to tell or write parents.

m) Provide balance in the lesson. Rote drill should give way to communication activities as quickly as possible.

n) Plan to have students practice in pairs or in groups of three or four at the most. Communication becomes more natural when only two or three people are involved. Moreover, some students will show less timidity when they know only one other person is listening.

In order to avoid too much movement frequently, the "pair" should consist of two people sitting next to each other. If any human relations problem arises, do not hesitate to change the students' seats.

o) Keep in mind that the students may have different motivations. Some may want to identify with the people and culture of the foreign land ("integrative motivation"); some may want to get better marks in school, enter a college of their choice, find a higher paying job, etc. ("instrumental orientation"). Plan by differentiating assignments, projects, and readings for both types of students.

4. Their native language is completely different from the target language.

a) Give many examples of new structures. Engage in extensive choral repetition and in intensive practice activities.

b) Indicate the contrasts and the essential points in the new items and help the students arrive at workable descriptions of the sounds, forms, position, function, and meaning of language features they are learning.

c) Introduce difficult items early in the program and reintroduce them as often as possible, in different situations, and with other language items.

d) Teach vocabulary items around a center of interest (buying food, clothing, or transportation) so that students can be helped to remember words and concepts through association and so that "real" conversation becomes possible.

e) Teach word families, prefixes, suffixes, roots.

f) Show students how to find the meaning of long words from the smaller words they contain (provided the root meanings are the same).

g) With many examples, teach the grammatical items which must co-occur. Point out and give practice in those items where the language system permits a choice (e.g., "I prefer *to go* by bus" or I prefer *going* by bus." "It started *to rain*" or "It started *raining*.").

h) Grade the material you teach very carefully, building on known language items in the foreign language. For example, teach "What do you eat at noon?" after you have taught "Do you eat at noon?"

i) Teach and, in the initial stages, practice language items or structures with other words which serve as clues. For example, use *now* with the "ing" present; *yesterday* with the simple past.

j) Use many devices (chalkboards, charts, diagrams, pictures) to ensure understanding.

k) Shape the students' performance toward the desired language behavior gradually.

l) Don't expect mastery or complete accuracy too soon. Practice the same material at ever-increasing intervals. Teach something on Monday, for example; review it on Tuesday; practice it again on Wednesday; then on Friday; then on the following Friday. Keep all language items worth knowing "alive" by reintroducing them constantly with newly acquired items in new situational contexts.

5. There's a wide age span in my class.

a) All students will require the same kind of initial presentation. All will need to 1) understand what they are going to repeat; 2) repeat an utterance many times based on your model; 3) practice with a variety of drills; and 4) understand and use language in increasingly longer units of discourse.

b) Divide your class into two groups after the first three steps. Younger students will continue practicing by means of games, puppets, dramatizations. Older students will be given insight into the description of the grammatical phenomena, will read and write, and will engage in more complex drills.

c) Train group leaders for each group. For example, an older student or a community aide can help you with the younger students.

6. Students have different native language backgrounds and I don't know all of them.

a) Prepare a chart of the phonemes and structures you plan to teach.

b) Ask other bilingual teachers or members of the community to indicate which of the phonemes and structures you are teaching exist in the language backgrounds of your pupils. List these on your chart. Plan more repetition drills for those which do not exist in one or more native languages. All students will profit from the additional drills if they are performed briskly and in an interesting manner. Those for whom the drills present no serious conflict will learn to say them more accurately and with more fluency.

c) Give very simple directions in the foreign language which you will illustrate and practice many times. At the beginning you will need only a few: *Listen* (place your hand behind your ear). *Repeat* (indicate — through gestures — that you will say something and they are to say it after you). *Say. Ask. Answer.* You should learn to say these words, particularly *ask* and *answer* (often confused by learners) in one or more of your learners' native tongues.

d) Start teaching those structures and words which you can demonstrate easily.

e) Use numerous pictures and real objects.

f) All students will have to learn the same sounds and structural features of the new language. You will teach these through the techniques indicated above and any other that works for you. You will be able to note, after the very first repetitions, problems caused by conflicts with a particular native language. If you feel that your normal plans for teaching any items to the entire class need to be supplemented for one or more students of a particular native language background, assign some meaningful work to the group that does not need the practice (pattern practice with a student leader, listening to a tape or record, preparing picture cards, etc.), and work intensively on the elimination of the problem(s) with the students experiencing difficulties.

g) It is desirable not to use any native language in the class (even if you are familiar with one), so that all students will have the feeling that they are members of a group and that no one group has special advantages over the other.

7. Some students are "discipline" problems.

a) Attention to some of the points made up to now will minimize discipline problems.

b) Keep the students busy with interesting work in which all participate. Establish routines. Change seats where necessary to separate the problem students. Use choral repetition. Have individuals ask questions or respond in a voice loud enough for all to hear.

c) Make few and very reasonable demands but insist that they be carried out when you do make them. (Don't insist on three notebooks with financially disadvantaged students, for example. "Make do" with one.)

d) Accept reasonable excuses for nonpreparedness of homework or other assignments. As tactfully as possible, find out about home or work responsibilities which may militate against a student's performance or cause his seeming apathy in class.

e) *Excuse them from examinations when they have been absent.*

f) Praise them!

g) Keep your expectations for them within their ability levels. Challenge the brighter ones, for example, by giving them more difficult assignments or by asking them to help their less able friends. Don't expect a "creative" composition from students who would be incapable of writing one in their own language.

h) Make sure they understand exactly what is expected of them. Give directions in their native tongue if necessary. Give several illustrations of the desired response.

i) Do not ask for a choral response to a question unless you are specifically practicing that question and answer. In that way, you will model the answer just prior to their giving it, avoiding the confusion caused by students calling out different responses.

j) Train students, patiently, to keep together in choral repetition.

k) Do not raise your voice or continue to work when students are talking. Just stop and stand quietly. They will soon become quiet.

l) Don't penalize the wrong-doers! *Reward* with praise those who are attentive. Those in the other group will soon be seeking your praise too.

m) Plan on giving them an "unprepared" day — a day when they do not have to bring in any homework. If this day could be planned with other departments in the school, it would decrease the after-school burden of youngsters since each department could set aside a different day.

n) Don't ask them to bring in a long assignment when you know they are having an examination in another subject. (Finding out, tactfully, what is going on in the rest of the school and acting accordingly will give your students the feeling that you are "fair" — the highest praise a teacher can be paid.)

o) Give the "serious" discipline problems some important classroom responsibilities — changing bulletin boards, helping dismiss the class, writing the assignments for the next day on the board, etc.

p) Find out, by talking to the students, consulting records, and talking to other teachers, why a particular student is "hard to reach." Try in your class to remove or minimize the irritant.

q) Learn students' names as quickly as possible.

r) Reward students' good behavior with good grades, commendations, etc.

s) Give every student the feeling that he *can* learn.

8. Older students have varied interests and specializations.

a) All students at the beginning level need to learn the same sounds, the same structures, and much of the common vocabulary which underlies the new language.

b) At intermediate and advanced levels, suggest magazines for them in their specialties. Help them read them. Give them or help them acquire the specialized vocabulary in their field and show them where and how to insert it in the language pattern you are teaching.

c) Have them prepare brief talks about their interests for other class members.

d) Encourage students to ask each other questions about their interests, hobbies, and aspirations.

e) At the advanced level, give individual reading assignments based on their interests and possible specializations.

f) Keep your library corner, where feasible, stocked with books and magazines in various fields. (Ask your colleagues in other departments to lend or give them to you.)

g) Talk to the school librarian and the community librarian. Urge them to make appropriate materials available.

h) Show brief foreign language films in varied areas. Help interested students explain the film content to their fellows.

9. Students are at different learning levels.

a) Find out by giving a proficiency test, listening to them, observing them, studying their records, exactly where they are on the continua of language skills. For example, in listening can they distinguish sounds, hear different intonation patterns, remember what was said at the beginning of an utterance (or passage), etc.?

b) Group the students according to their needs (pronunciation, grammar, vocabulary, sub-skills in listening, speaking, reading, or writing).

c) Prepare *integrative* activities having a common object in which all members of the class participate and *differentiated* activities for groups and for individuals depending on their strengths and weaknesses.

All students in the class will profit from listening to or saying a common core of material — a dialogue, a reading passage, an intonation drill, for example. The integrative activities should always precede the differentiated activities in which small groups or individuals work alone.

d) Plan your schedule so that you can work with a group every second or third lesson. (See page 150 for a suggested schedule.)

e) Assign capable group leaders. Have them keep a record of work done, problems, questions, etc.

f) Supply appropriate material: for example, programmed texts or workbooks; tapes at different learning levels or those containing material with special emphases; instructional cue cards; pictures; reading materials at various levels; individual group worksheets (using programmed techniques).

g) Prepare charts clearly outlining group and individual responsibilities.

h) Keep accurate and detailed records of the progress made by individual students. (The next teacher in your school or in another will appreciate them.)

Where non-graded classes are in operation either because the small number of language learners does not warrant separate classes at one level or separate tracks (for example, for students who had studied a foreign language in the elementary school) or because of the school personnel's conviction that all learners should proceed at their own pace, record-keeping becomes an essential and vitally important part of teaching.

Also important would be well-planned articulation meetings with other teachers and/or schools involved so that continuity of instruction for the pupils would be ensured.


## OUR COLLEAGUES

1. The other teachers haven't used my methods, materials, etc. Students have never ............................... .

a) Spend the first few days training your students to respond to your hand signals or gestures, to engage in chain drills, to ask and answer questions, to dramatize dialogues, to keep together in choral work, etc. Establish types of and standards for student participation.

b) Find out how much your students know by giving a test or preferably asking many questions in the foreign language in the first few days. Do not ask them what they learned in Miss X's class, but elicit the information by asking questions which incorporate the structures and vocabulary you might assume they have learned. Start teaching them from that point.

2. Some teachers are "jealous" and refuse to cooperate.

a) Try to arrange brief, informal meetings (over a cup of coffee, lunch, on the way home).

b) Listen to what they have to say in conferences.

c) Do not brag about your accomplishments.

d) Find something complimentary to say about any of their accomplishments.

e) Offer to work with them in preparing tests, programs, club activities, etc.

## THE SCHOOL

1. We must use the syllabus supplied by the school.

Use it, by all means. Within the items or skills listed in the syllabus, prepare a variety of activities, engage in extensive oral work, follow the six steps in language learning, change the order of presentation of material if the order in the syllabus is not in harmony with some of the principles discussed in this book and with which you agree. You will find it possible to cover the same amount of material prescribed for you but in a manner which may be more interesting to you and to your students.

2. The school (or the Ministry or the Education Department) prepares the examinations.

Everything we have mentioned above can be repeated in answer to this question. One word must be added, however. If the examination also includes translation of unrelated sentences (as may be the case), help your students prepare for such translation. Do so by taking typical sentences from the translations and by giving pattern practice of each type as explained under *Translation* (pages 98-99).

## THE MATERIALS OF INSTRUCTION

1. The textbooks are traditional.

a) Examine each unit carefully. Regroup the structure points for presentation; prepare interesting and varied oral practice drills and activities; practice only the high-frequency and authentic sentences in the text; prepare question-answer drills and dialogues; present and practice everything orally before assigning writing exercises. Grade the sentences within the drill exercises by rearranging them.

b) Do not use the textbook entirely as it is. For example, do not emphasize words and sentences which are not of high frequency. Formulate (or have the students formulate) stimulating questions on the reading material.

c) Choose a limited amount of material for each lesson and build varied activities around that limited material.

d) Prepare or help your able students prepare two or three dialogues using the structural items and vocabulary found in each unit of the textbook. Help the students understand, say, read, and write the dialogues, adapt them, and change them to narrative passages (when they are able to).

2. The school has no money or limited money for equipment.

a) Chalkboards and chalk are found in nearly every school. Things like pictures can be made on any paper, with pencil, pen, or crayon.

b) No one would deny that record players, tape recorders, and projectors of different types could diversify a teaching presentation, but electronic equipment should always be considered *supplementary* equipment. The teacher alone can create a pleasant and productive language class by his enthusiasm, his attitude toward his students, and his careful attention to balance and variety in lesson planning.

## METHODS

1. The students cannot understand a dialogue or a reading passage.

a) Help them to understand through pictures, dramatization, cognates (where logical), and even through giving the native language equivalent if all speak one native language and you are familiar with it.

b) Relate the material to their experiences and their lives in the community in which they are living. Use the students and their lives as the point of departure for your teaching.

2. The students have trouble making the ............ sound even after I have taught it.

a) Reteach it and practice it whenever you can do so. Use diagrams, description of the articulation, phonetic symbols, and reminders of other sounds they know in their native tongue or in the foreign language to help them hear, distinguish, and produce the sound.

b) Reintroduce it whenever possible. Don't expect mastery too soon!

c) Make sure it appears frequently in some of the pattern practice exercises and conversations.

3. The students get bored with (forty) repetitions.

a) No one says that everything should be repeated (forty) times! If ten or fewer repetitions are enough to ensure reasonably good pronunciation and accuracy, go on to the next phase of learning.

b) Strike a happy medium between giving enough repetition to form the correct habit and avoiding boredom. As soon as you note a slackening of interest, proceed to something else but make a note to reintroduce the item which may not have been learned to your complete satisfaction later in the lesson or in a subsequent lesson.

4. Students are afraid to speak in class.

a) Start with choral repetition, followed by group repetition.

b) Call on the more able or less timid students first.

c) Be patient with the really timid persons. In the beginning, have them come to your desk and repeat things after you. (The other students can be busily engaged in another type of language work.)

d) Praise them for any effort, no matter how slight.

e) If they are young, use puppets to give them the feeling they are not seen as they speak.

f) Give them something to speak about: what they saw on the way to school; what they did last night.

g) Prepare a chart of topics of general interest from which students may get ideas.

h) Place them in a position to feel successful. Gear questions to their ability; have them serve as "teachers" first by merely turning pictures, for example, and later by asking their classmates one type of question about each of them.

5. Students want to know why things are said the way they are.

a) Help them answer their own questions about "grammar" by giving numerous examples of a structure.

b) Prove to them that the knowledge of the more traditional type of "rule" will not help them to create sentences or to communicate. Demonstrate the value of a statement which describes what actually happens in saying an utterance.

c) Show them through examples that there may be no reason or logic behind a word or utterance in their language and that many aspects of the language system are arbitrary.

d) Discuss the nature and function of language with them.

6. Students want to keep their books open when I am reading. Our supervisor wants them to keep their books closed.

a) Although some educators consider it desirable for students to keep their books closed during the teacher's oral reading, this need not be a rigid rule. If you have a Language I course, you should be able to train your students from the outset to keep their books closed by clarifying all difficulties previously, giving a short summary, dramatizing, etc. But let us remember (and try to convince your supervisor) that reading always means looking at something in print and very often, the visual symbols could (with teacher guidance) reinforce the acoustic signals.

b) If students have not received training in listening with books closed and if you or the supervisor want them to do so, you may prepare them for closed book reading by using very easy material, by reading very short segments at a time, and by asking simple varied questions on the same piece of reading.

c) Encourage them to try to understand with books closed. Read the same sentence several times, if necessary, until they develop confidence.

d) Vary your procedures. Have "open book" reading sometimes and "closed book" other times.

7. The school wants us to start reading very soon in our program.

a) Introduce reading if your syllabus requires it but make sure your students can say with reasonable fluency the words and sentences they are going to see.

b) Clear all difficulties of pronunciation, structure, vocabulary, and cultural aspects before reading.

c) Read the passage for the students orally several times with books opened or closed depending on the foreign language, the instructional materials available, and other relevant factors.

d) Use the reading as a "jumping off" point for the teaching of pronunciation, grammar, and vocabulary and for the development of related communication skills.

## THE COMMUNITY

1. The community has few or no people or other resources which would be helpful in our program.

a) Get or borrow films from the appropriate agencies in your capital city. Well-chosen films would illustrate places, people, gestures, customs, and situations in the foreign land.

b) Buy or borrow tapes with authentic foreign language voices.

c) Get series of filmstrips and slides depicting one or more aspects of the foreign culture.

d) Invite people who have visited the foreign country to speak to your students, show films or pictures taken on the trip, or play music they had bought there.

e) Borrow or buy recordings or discs (music, speeches, festivals, street scenes, plays). An initial expenditure of money will be repaid a hundred-fold by heightened interest on the part of your students and the community.

f) Invite a foreign cultural officer in your state or your country to visit your community and/or your school. Plan a program around him, a lecture perhaps, followed by questions and answers. Be prepared (and get his permission) to tape these for further study.

g) Start a "pen pal" program with a similar school in the foreign country. The letters and pictures the students will undoubtedly exchange will foster real communication and cultural growth.

h) Visit the foreign country on your own or through a scholarship or grant program and bring back a collection of real objects which will serve you for many years.

i) Subscribe to foreign magazines.

j) Find your own "pen pal" who will be able to send you interesting and pertinent news and materials.

2. Some community members want to tell us how to conduct our program.

a) With the cooperation of your principal and other teachers, it is desirable to encourage the participation of parents and other interested community leaders in your program.

b) Set up a small committee of school and community personnel which will discuss the differing roles of the professional staff and of community members, the objectives of the program, the need for equipment and materials or for additional personnel, the utilization of parent aides for several facets of the program, testing, the value of bilingual informants, etc.

c) Invite parents and community members to serve as bilingual informants or as teacher or school aides. For example, they may help choose or gather audio-visual materials; plan and execute assembly programs, festivals, bazaars or musical evenings; help teachers prepare visual materials or those needed for individualizing instruction; work with individuals or small groups who need special help.

d) Plan to establish a permanent Parent-Teachers Association, with a carefully prepared agenda, scheduled meetings, and regular reports of events, progress, and evolving needs.

e) Build community confidence in your program. Remember that your students are your most important and influential public relations resources. What they tell their parents and what these in turn tell others about the effectiveness of the program will determine to a large extent how they will feel about it.

f) Plan for parents to visit the school on specified days when they can hear and see their children perform in a group project, an assembly program, etc.

g) Send regular reports to parents, not only report cards with final grades, but also letters related to the activities of the program; the kind of homework you will give; the frequent tests; and your hopes for their children.

h) Inform a parent long ahead of time when you think a student will fail the course despite your efforts. Enlist the parent's cooperation tactfully. Does the student have too many home or work responsibilities? Does he need extra tutoring?

i) Make yourself available to parents. Set aside an hour a week when they may come to see you. Let parents know both through their children and through a bulletin or letter that you will be happy to see them at that time.

j) Enlist their help in publishing a bilingual newspaper or in starting an after-school club program.

k) Make available to them the results of city-wide or nation-wide examinations, when feasible.

3. Some community members have heard about early childhood foreign language programs, bilingual programs, programmed learning, team teaching, advanced placement, etc. They want us to try all of them.

a) Great! How wonderful that your community keeps abreast of new movements in the field!

b) Plan meetings with your small committee (see 2b above) in which you explore all aspects of these or any other current theories or practices.

c) Invite experts in the field, not only scientists but experienced teachers who have worked on such programs to discuss the possibilities with you and your committee. Prepare yourself in advance so that you can ask relevant questions — those especially suitable to your school setting.

d) Make professional literature available to the community members as well as pertinent instructional materials.

e) With the cooperation of your principal and the city, state, or national Department of Instruction, offer to start small experimental programs in one or two areas of concern and interest. Make sure, however, that you have (or can get) trained personnel and appropriate materials. Anything else may be doomed to failure.

f) Help them to see the advantages as well as the possible problems which may arise.

g) Evaluate the programs continuously. Inform the community when you feel revisions may be needed. Prepare extensive data to justify your revisions.

## Suggestions

— Assume you have been asked by the principal to prepare a talk for the faculty justifying the introduction of a particular foreign language into your school. Prepare a talk of about twenty minutes documenting it with quotations and ideas from various authors.

— Your chairman has asked you to prepare a five-minute talk to the more traditional members of your department who believe only in grammar, translation, and reading. Indicate the major arguments you would advance for developing the listening and speaking skills and for using currently advocated techniques.

— Some members of the community think that money and time are wasted when foreign languages are taught to "slow learners." Prepare a brief talk justifying their admission into the program.

— The professors of a nearby college which receives your students have complained about their preparation. Indicate ten "cooperative" procedures you could propose which would be effective in articulating both programs.

— A student in class is disruptive. Discuss several procedures you might attempt in order to make him a more cooperative class member.

# X

# In Conclusion

Other questions and problems will undoubtedly arise as you teach various groups of students at different times or as you move from one school or community to another. No two individual students, no two schools, no two communities, no two teachers are exactly alike.

All any book can do or should do is set down the principles and practices which have been found effective by a representative group of teachers in representative communities throughout the world.

A great injustice would have been done if you had been led to believe that there existed only one acceptable method or only one set of materials or techniques. While it is true that our current knowledge of the nature of language and of language learning makes certain principles of teaching more desirable and effective than others adhered to in the past, it is also true that within these principles there is ample opportunity for teacher creativity and for flexibility of procedure and activities. While it is also true that we are teaching a foreign language, we cannot lose sight of the fact that we are teaching it to human beings. As teachers we are, in effect, attempting to graft new habits and new behavior patterns on individuals who come to our classroom with highly diverse backgrounds of ability and of experience.

Moreover, advances in many branches of science may require you to modify or add to your store of knowledge or skills at any time in the future. It is our hope that some of the guidelines indicated will prepare you to adapt your teaching to any situation in which you may find yourselves and to accept new ideas in the context in which you know they will be most helpful to you and to your students.

The suggestions in this book have been so briefly stated, constituting as they do a synthesis of our own teaching experience, observations, interviews, and workshop experiences that a concluding statement becomes exceedingly difficult to write. Nevertheless, it may be desirable to reaffirm several convictions and principles which have been scattered throughout this text:

1. You, the teacher, are more important than any method or material. It is what you do with any method or with any piece of material which will determine its effectiveness in helping your stu-

dents learn. Student growth should be judged not only in terms of the number of language items acquired or increased fluency but also in terms of attitude toward foreign-speaking peoples and toward the continued study of the foreign language you are teaching.

2. Student growth depends to a large extent upon your own professional growth. In a dynamic field such as ours, no teacher can afford to remain at a standstill. We should keep up with new findings, with new materials, and with the reports of teaching and learning experiences of our colleagues. This is possible by subscribing to magazines in the field, attending conferences where possible, becoming members of professional organizations, and doing extensive reading. You should conduct experiments of your own. Many facets of theory and practice are still in need of further research. Your contribution, added to that of others, cannot help but be valuable to many persons engaged in the field.

If the foreign language you are teaching is not your native language, you may want to increase your competency in it (or maintain it if you are not working in the foreign-speaking country) by taking advantage of the numerous seminars which are organized for teachers of language. If possible, you should arrange a visit to the country or countries where the language is spoken.

3. Under professional growth should be included a knowledge of many other areas of learning. The interested and interesting teacher constantly enriches his personality and hence his teaching through the study of aspects of methodology and content culled from other subjects in the school curriculum and from other disciplines.

4. You should learn to blend many ingredients together in order to give students the kind of learning experiences which contribute to the development of correct habits, broad interests and knowledge, basic skills, and desirable attitudes. Every learning experience should be carefully planned. It should have well-defined, carefully circumscribed objectives; it should be made stimulating to the students because it uses them, their interests and abilities, and their environment as a starting point; it should ensure the active participation of all the students; it should utilize varied materials and activities; and it should look back on what has been learned and lead to further language growth. Every segment of newly acquired language should be skillfully woven into the existing fabric of communication.

5. In addition, participation in each class hour should give the students the conviction that what they are learning is valuable and that they are moving forward. That does not mean that they have to learn a new large body of material each time or that they have to start the study of a completely new unit. It may mean that they acquire a little more fluency in saying a familiar sentence, a new

word, a new idea, a new way of doing a drill through a different use of materials or a different type of participation, or a new insight into the foreign culture. Our goal should be continuous and gradual progress rather than immediate "mastery."

6. In the philosophy underlying today's language-learning programs, great emphasis is placed on the ability of the teacher to detect errors in pronunciation (even in choral recitation), to identify and diagnose speech problems of students, and to model new structures. In short, it is considered important that the teacher develop what is generally called a "listening ear." We would like to suggest that a "listening heart" is of equal importance.

The teacher who can give each student the feeling that he is an important part of a group, that he is capable of learning, and that he can achieve success; the teacher who can demonstrate an understanding of conflict, both environmental and linguistic; the teacher who, through his enthusiasm, his art, and his skill, makes language learning a subject to be looked forward to will in the final analysis be the one who will forge ahead of his less perceptive colleague in promoting the desirable attitudes needed for language learning and cultural understanding.

Of primary concern should be the attention given to integration. In this text we have discussed briefly the integration within a language system of all its discrete features; we have spoken of the integration and subsequent reinforcement of the listening, speaking, reading and writing skills in communication. We have mentioned also the integrative class and school activities in which language learners should be engaged before they are assigned group or individual projects.

There is another dimension to the term "integration" which we would now ask you to consider and it is this: Unless the learner is helped to retain pride in his own language and culture; unless he is helped to continue to identify with his own co-nationals as he moves gradually toward acceptance of the foreign language and its speakers, he will not remain or become a well-integrated individual. It is this last dimension of "integration" which should take precedence over all others. It is this which is the key to the success of any language-teaching program.

Teachers who recognize the importance of their responsibilities and who embody the personal and professional characteristics outlined here cannot help but push aside the language barriers which still impede communication among mankind.

# Appendix I

## TEACHER PREPARATION

The importance of the teacher's role in the learning process cannot be overstated. We have seen that the role is a many-faceted one which generally cannot be acquired overnight. It demands systematic, theoretical, and practical preparation, both of which should be given to *prospective* teachers before they face their first teaching experience. Even the most thorough knowledge of the linguistic and cultural content of the target language does not guarantee that the teacher will be able to transmit this knowledge to learners.

We run the risk of turning a promising teacher away from his chosen profession if his early teaching efforts are met with poor results and consequent frustration. We run the further grave risk of stifling the initial enthusiasm of language learners when they feel that they are not achieving because the material of instruction is not selected, graded, and presented effectively and clearly.

Of course in a field such as ours, pre-service training must be followed by in-service courses, seminars, readings, and further study if we are to keep abreast of research findings in the related sciences and of technological advances.

The following "Standards for Teacher Education Programs" form a concise inventory of goals in teacher preparation and of the means of implementing them. These should serve as guidelines for communities and countries which may not have given sufficient emphasis to the pressing problems presented by inadequately prepared teachers.

## Standards for Teacher-Education Programs in Modern Foreign Languages

(Prepared by a conference convened by the Modern Language Association in December 1963, this statement is addressed to state departments responsible for the certification of teachers and to institutions that prepare elementary and secondary school teachers of modern foreign languages. Its purpose is to identify and clarify acceptable standards of preparation.)

1. Only selected students should be admitted to a teacher-preparation program, and those selected should have qualities of intellect, character, and personality that will make them effective teachers.

2. The training of the future teacher[1] must make him a well-educated person with a sound knowledge of (United States)[2] culture, the foreign culture and literature, and the differences between the two cultures. It must also enable him to:

   a) Understand the foreign language spoken at normal tempo.
   b) Speak the language intelligibly and with an adequate command of vocabulary and syntax.
   c) Read the language with immediate comprehension and without translation.
   d) Write the language with clarity and reasonable correctness.
   e) Understand the nature of language and of language learning.
   f) Understand the learner and the psychology of learning.
   g) Understand the evolving objectives of education in the (United States) and the place of foreign language learning in this context.

3. In addition to possessing the requisite knowledge and skills, the language teacher must be able to:

   a) Develop in his students a progressive control of the four skills (listening, speaking, reading, writing).
   b) Present the language as an essential element of the foreign culture and show how this culture differs from that of the (United States).
   c) Present the foreign literature effectively as a vehicle for great ideas.
   d) Make judicious selection and use of methods, techniques, aids, and equipment for language teaching.
   e) Correlate his teaching with that of other subjects.
   f) Evaluate the progress and diagnose the deficiencies of student performance.

4. An approvable program to prepare such a teacher must include:

   a) Intelligent evaluation and utilization of his pre-college language training through course placement according to results of proficiency tests.
   b) An offering of language and literature courses advanced enough to enable him to teach the gifted student.
   c) Courses and directed reading that give him a first-hand acquaintance with major works of literature, to be tested by a comprehensive examination.
   d) Use of the foreign language as the language of instruction in all language and literature courses.
   e) Extensive and regular exposure to several varieties of native speech, through teachers, lecturers, discs, tapes.
   f) Instruction in the foreign geography, history, and contemporary culture.
   g) Instruction in stylistics, phonetics, and linguistics.

---

[1] These specifications apply to the specialist in modern foreign languages at all levels.

[2] Substitute your country for "United States."

h) Instruction in the psychology of language learning and the philosophy of education.

i) Instruction and practice in the use of the language laboratory and audio-visual aids.

j) Systematic observation of the foreign language being expertly taught, followed by the experience of teaching under expert direction.

k) Evaluation of the teacher candidate through (1) proficiency and other appropriate tests, (2) appraisal of his teaching skill by experts.

5. An approvable program should also make provision for:
   a) Native speakers as teachers or informants.
   b) Study abroad for at least one summer.
   c) Organized extra-curricular foreign-language activities.
   d) Training in evaluating and diagnosing pupil progress.

6. The institution must be able to demonstrate that its modern foreign language staff is of sufficient size and competence to give the desired instruction. There should be at least two well-qualified teachers of each language and at least one teacher of each language should hold the Ph.D.*

7. A candidate's readiness to teach (as attested by his foreign language department, the education department, the academic dean, the principal of the school in which he does his apprentice teaching) must be certified not only by the departments directly concerned but in the name of the whole institution.

8. Teacher-preparing institutions should regularly evaluate the effectiveness of their programs by arranging for visits to their graduates on the job and by inviting evaluations from administrators of the schools in which their graduates teach. It is the responsibility of institutions that prepare teachers of foreign languages — together with the state departments of education that certify them — to scrutinize constantly the effect of their programs upon foreign language learning in the schools that employ their graduates.

## A TEACHER'S GUIDE TO SELF-EVALUATION

Class:
Date:
Major teaching emphasis (e.g., structure, dialogue, composition):
Teaching level:
Materials used (include purpose):

### Me

A) Was my manner friendly, warm, understanding?

B) Was I patient in eliciting information, engaging in repetition and other drills, in correcting possible errors?

C) Did I praise students at every opportunity?

---

* Or a comparable degree. (Authors' note)

D) Was I sensitive to their problems and questions?

E) Was my voice clear and audible in all parts of the room?

F) Was my appearance pleasing? (Was I well-groomed, for example?)

G) Was I well prepared? For example:
   — Was I able to answer questions related to culture?
   — Was the material I needed readily available?
   — Was my presentation orderly and sequential?
   — Had I "memorized" the steps of my lesson?
   — Did my lesson have balance and variety?

H) Did I use gestures carefully to elicit different types of participation?

I) Did I let the students do most of the talking?

J) How was my questioning ability? Did I, for example:
   — Ask appropriate, logical questions?
   — Ask questions of all students, then call one by name?
   — Avoid choral response to questions?
   — Call on volunteers?
   — Call on non-volunteers?
   — Provide opportunities for students to question me and to question each other?
   — Repeat answers unnecessarily?
   — Vary types of questions (yes/no, alternative, full answer, short answer, inferential, personal)?

K) Did I help students maintain pride in their native language and background?

L) Did I ascertain their aspirations and needs and those of the community?

M) Did I make every attempt to involve parents and community members in the program?

## My Lesson in General

A) Was the method appropriate? Was it suitable to the age and ability levels of the students? Was it in accordance with accepted principles (i.e., listening and speaking before reading and writing)?

B) Was the content too much; too little; geared to the students' level; geared to their language level?

C) Was the aim clear to students? How did I make it clear (stated by me, written on blackboard)? Was it logical, important? Was it adhered to during the entire lesson? Was it achieved?

D) Was the lesson development smooth, sequential, logical? For example, did I introduce each new step or activity with a transitional or introductory statement or comment?

E) Was there a variety of drills (repetitive, pattern practice, question-answer, "freer" communication)?

F) Was there a summary? Given by whom? Had material for easy reference been left on the board?

G) How did I evaluate whether my goals had been achieved?

H) How was the tempo of the lesson (too slow, too brisk, hurried, sustained)?

I) Did I use the native language judiciously (where necessary — when, why, how)?

J) Was there sufficient time given to the maintenance and/or development of listening and speaking skills?

K) Did I adhere slavishly to the textbook?

L) Did I individualize instruction?

M) Did the lesson look back on material covered and ahead to the next lesson?

N) Did I use audio-visual aids efficiently and effectively?

## Lessons with Special Emphasis

A) Pronunciation
1. Did I help students hear and distinguish sounds and contrasts before asking them to produce them orally?
2. What aids were used (diagram of speech organs, explanation of points of articulation, arrows or dots for intonation, etc.)?
3. Were all new sounds and other pronunciation features used in context with appropriate intonation after they were taught?
4. Was I satisfied with reasonable progress?

B) Dialogue Presentation
1. Was the dialogue situation made clear to the students? How?
2. Were students made aware of the speaker for each utterance? How?
3. Did I model the individual utterances several times before expecting the students to repeat them?
4. Did I move to various parts of the room so that all students could hear me and see me?
5. Did I have the two groups facing each other as they recited a dialogue role?
6. Did I "break down" long sentences into manageable segments?
7. Did I offer help to individuals who took roles in the dialogue?
8. Did I stop practicing the dialogue before boredom and a "plateau" set in?
9. Did I personalize the dialogue, vary utterances in it, ask questions about it?
10. Did I help students combine dialogues?

C) Grammar Items
1. Was there an obvious relationship to known material (familiar target language or native language structure)?
2. How was the meaning clarified? What "situations" did I use?
3. Were examples modeled by me? How many did I give? How many times was each example given? What was their quality? Was the language used in them authentic?
4. Was repetition done chorally first, then by sub-groups, then by individuals?
5. How was the recurring feature clarified, emphasized, and described (diagrammed on board, elicited)?

6. Pattern-practice activities:

a — Were the most appropriate chosen?

b — Was the type of activity varied (e.g., substitution, replacement, question-answer, transformation)?

c — Was the type of pupil participation varied (did I "cue" pupils; did pupils "cue" me or other pupils; did we vary the type of chain drills)?

d — How was the new structure used in authentic communication (dialogue, directed dialogue, dramatization, listening, reading, action series, writing)?

D) Reading and Word Study

1. How was motivation developed (related to students' lives, to longer story)?
2. How were difficulties clarified (cognates, pictures, objects, paraphrases, dramatization, native language equivalent, other)?
3. How was my oral reading (tempo, phrasing, rhythm)?
4. Which techniques did I use to ensure comprehension (questioning to elicit the main thought and to note cause-and-effect relationships, completion exercises, true-false questions)?
5. Was a summary given? How did I elicit it?
6. Did I include time for word study (antonyms, synonyms, words of same family, derivations)?
7. Was any oral reading done by students? Were able students called on first? How much class time was spent on it?
8. Was the homework assignment based on what had been done in class (answers to questions, outline, note-taking, summary)?

E) Cultural Appreciation

1. How did I provide motivation for the particular aspect of culture?
2. Did I relate the culture of the foreign land to our culture?
3. Do I feel that the presentation helped to reduce prejudice and to develop appropriate attitudes?
4. What mode of presentation was used (lecture, demonstration, other)?
5. What visual materials were available?
6. Were any follow-up activities assigned to students (group projects, book reports, composition writing)?

F) Composition Writing

1. How did I motivate the topic?
2. How did I elicit ideas related to the topic?
3. What questions or techniques were used to place ideas in logical sequence?
4. Were students given enough help with structures and vocabulary needed to expand each idea?
5. Did I allow students enough time in class to write an introductory paragraph?
6. Did I give them enough time to prepare the composition at home?

# EVALUATING STUDENTS' PERFORMANCE

## Testing Oral Ability

Following is an oral ability rating scale which you may find useful in measuring your students' receptive and production abilities.

BOARD OF EDUCATION OF THE CITY OF NEW YORK
Bureau of Foreign Languages—Bureau of Curriculum Research

*ORAL ABILITY RATING SCALE*
City-Wide Foreign Language Examinations, Level II

*PART I: ORAL ABILITY,* to be determined by the teacher's estimate of a pupil's total oral performance for the entire term. 10 credits.

------------------------------------------------

Encircle the language to which this rating refers: FR....... ITAL.......
    SPAN........
Pupil's Name.................................... Date..............
Teacher's Name ............................ Language Class........
Junior H.S. No. & Boro................. Senior H.S..................

------------------------------------------------

*DEFINITIONS:* 1. *Quality* pertains to pronunciation, intonation, pitch, stress, phrasing, juncture, and fluency.

2. *Aptness* pertains to promptness, correctness, and appropriateness of responses and rejoinders in the light of directions given, questions asked, statements made, and situations indicated.

3. *Echo Ability* pertains to the quality of the pupil's oral reproduction or mimicry of words, phrases, and sentences spoken by the teacher or by a recorded voice.

4. *Recitation* pertains to the quality of the pupil's oral production in oral reading, recitation of memorized dialogues, and of memory selections.

5. *Drill* pertains to quality of oral production in pattern drills (repetition, substitution, expansion, etc.).

6. *Drill Responses* pertains to quality and aptness of responses in transformation drills.

7. *Directed Responses* pertains to quality and aptness of "choice," "yes/no," "cued," and directed dialogue responses.

------------------------------------------------

*RATING SCALE:* Unintelligible, inaudible, or no response ........... 0
    Partially intelligible ........................... ½
    Intelligible but labored ........................ 1
    Readily intelligible but not perfect ............... 1½
    Intelligible and with native intonation ........... 2

------------------------------------------------

*DIRECTIONS:* Check one box after A and enter its numerical value in the last column on the right. Repeat this procedure for B, C, D, E. Enter the total of all five ratings at the bottom of the last column.

| QUALITY | 0 | ½ | 1 | 1½ | 2 | Ratings |
|---|---|---|---|---|---|---|
| A. Echo Ability | | | | | | |
| B. Recitation | | | | | | |
| C. Drills | | | | | | |
| APTNESS | | | | | | |
| D. Drill Responses | | | | | | |
| E. Directed Responses | | | | | | |
| Total..... | | | | | | |

## NATIONAL FRENCH CONTEST

(Taken from the *French Review*, 1966, pp. 453-56. Director of the contest was James Glennon, Wisconsin State University, United States.)

### French I

For students in their first year of French, above Grade 7; Grades 7 and 8 together are considered equivalent to first-year high school French. The test consists of two parts and takes approximately one hour. The first part counts 60 points, and the second part counts 40 points.

PART A: Listening has 5 sections.

I. Aural Comprehension (20 points). Twelve questions are asked about a sketch. The student selects the correct answer from a multiple choice of 4.

II. Rejoinders (20 points). In this section there are questions or commands to which the student responds by selecting the logical response from among 4 choices.

III. Factual Questions (10 points). This group comprises 10 questions on France and French culture to which the student responds by selecting the proper answer from among 4 choices.

IV. Narrative (10 points). The student hears a short narrative on which 5 questions are based. He has a multiple choice of 4 answers.

PART B: Reading and Grammar (40 points).

I. Reading Comprehension (20 points). In this section, the student reads two paragraphs. His comprehension is then tested by a series of 10 questions on each passage, a total of 20 questions. For each question there are 4 possible answers.

II. Grammar (20 points). This section consists of 20 questions on structure. Generally, the questions cover word order, agreement, and verb tenses.

## French II

PART A: Listening is recorded on tape and accounts for 50 points.

 I. Sound Discrimination (10 points). Two sentences are printed for each number. One sentence is heard twice on the tape. The student circles the letter that corresponds to the sentence heard. There are 10 questions in this section.

 II. Rejoinders (10 points). The student hears four possible rejoinders to each question or statement printed on his answer sheet. He selects the most suitable. There are 10 such questions in this section.

 III. Dictation (20 points).

 IV. Aural Comprehension (10 points). The student hears a sentence on the tape. If it is in agreement with the statement printed on his answer sheet, he circles OUI; if not, he circles NON. There are 5 such questions in this section.

PART B: Reading and Grammar (50 points).

 I. Reading Comprehension (30 points). There are ten true-or-false questions about a passage by Victor Hugo.

 II. Grammar (20 points). This section comprises 20 questions requiring the student to give the correct French response to an English cue. This section covers numbers, demonstrative pronouns, interrogative adjectives, agreement of adjectives, and pronouns.

## French III

 The test consists of two parts and requires 30 minutes for each part.

PART A: Listening is recorded on tape and has a value of 50 points.

 I. Aural Comprehension (20 points). A passage from De Maupassant is broken into 10 segments of varying lengths. A question is based on each segment.

 II. Dictation (20 points).

 III. Rejoinders (10 points). In reply to a printed statement, the student selects the most plausible from three replies he will hear on the tape. There are 5 rejoinder questions.

PART B: Reading, Civilization, Grammar (50 points).

 I. Reading Comprehension (20 points). Two passages are offered; each is followed by 5 questions.

 II. Civilization (10 points). The questions are of a general nature based on contemporary culture and area study. There are 10 questions.

 III. Grammar (20 points). Generally, the questions cover the proper use of prepositions, tense, mode, and pronouns. There are 20 questions.

## French IV

 The test consists of two parts and takes approximately 30 minutes for each part.

PART A: Listening is recorded on tape and has a value of 40 points.

I. Aural Comprehension (20 points). A situation is related to the student who then selects one of 4 possible answers to a question based upon it. There are 10 such questions in this section.

II. Dictation (20 points).

PART B: Reading, Vocabulary, Grammar, Civilization: (60 points)

I. Reading Comprehension (16 points). Eight questions are based on a passage from *Madame Bovary*.

II. Vocabulary (10 points). The 10 vocabulary questions are based on a reading selection. Four choices are given for each vocabulary item.

III. Grammar (20 points). Ten questions are presented with 4 accompanying answers. The student selects the most suitable. Generally, the questions involve inversions, reflexive verbs, agreement of the past participle with direct objects, word order, and relative pronouns.

IV. Civilization (14 points). There are 7 questions; each has 4 answers. The student chooses the most appropriate. This section involves the identification of authors, works, and an understanding of the movements in French literary history.

## French V

This test is designed for those students who are pursuing a fifth year of French in an accredited secondary school. These students, most probably, are enjoying a fifth year thanks to advanced placement upon entering high school as a result of previous study in the elementary grades.

PART A: Listening is recorded on tape and takes 30 minutes. (50 points)

1. Aural Comprehension (30 points).

The student hears a dialogue and arranges five statements summarizing the dialogue in their order of appropriateness.

2. Dictation (20 points).

PART B: Reading, Grammar, and Culture (50 points).

1. Reading Comprehension (20 points). The student reads five statements and selects an adjective which most appropriately describes the mood of the author. Seven adjectives are given for the five statements.

2. Grammar (15 points). In this section, the student is asked to recognize and correct errors committed by French authors. There are 5 questions in this section.

3. Culture (15 points). The student has a choice of 3 answers for each of 15 questions. The emphasis in this section is primarily on French literature.

## EVALUATING THE FOREIGN LANGUAGE PROGRAM

The following statements are not intended to serve as a blueprint for an ideal program. Some of the items listed will not apply to you because, for example, the number of students involved in your program might not warrant the formation of more than one "track" or the offering of more than one or two languages.

It is always desirable, however, to familiarize ourselves with various possibilities and practices, not only as stimuli for our own professional growth but also as guidelines for discussion, further reading, and implementation as needed at some future time.

As with everything else we have said throughout this book, you are urged to accept (and adapt) only what is pertinent to you in the situation in which you find yourself now. Only a few representative items are indicated under each category. Repeating all of the guidelines in all of the chapters would have meant printing a book twice this size.

## Pupils

1. All are programmed for foreign language instruction.
2. Where feasible, they are permitted to choose from among the languages offered in the school.
3. If they have studied a foreign language in a lower school and if you offer that language, they are programmed for it.
4. They are not dropped from foreign language study without extensive study of all records, talks with parents and other teachers, remedial help, change of teacher, and any other measure your school can take.
5. They are given remedial help when needed.
6. They are encouraged to continue the study of the foreign language (preferably the one started in the lower school) for the maximum time available.
7. They are urged (especially the more able ones) to begin the study of a second foreign language after one year of study of the first foreign language in a secondary school.

## Teachers

1. They are selected because they have been licensed to teach a foreign language, and because they possess the qualifications and attributes for teaching it.
2. They are encouraged to continue their in-service training through such activities as attendance at seminars, courses at a university, reading, attendance at meetings, research studies, experimentation, committee membership, and related travel.
3. Native speakers with the required background, except for training in the teaching of a foreign language, are given intensive training and insight into linguistic, psychological, and educational principles needed for effective teaching.

# The Program

1. *Offerings*
   - The languages offered are selected on the basis of community interest and national need, the language offered in the lower schools within the community, and the availability of trained and licensed teachers.

2. *Organization of Classes*
   - If possible, there are two tracks: one for beginners in the language; the other for those who have studied language in the lower schools.
   - In the absence of two tracks, teachers are helped to group students within the class and to prepare appropriate materials for the groups.
   - Non-graded classes are established where feasible as teachers become familiar with practices of group dynamics and as more self-pacing materials become available.
   - Language courses are offered each semester. There are no gaps in the program.
   - Courses are taught daily for a minimum of forty minutes.
   - The same foreign language is offered for a minimum of four years.
   - Where possible, special college preparatory courses are established for the more gifted pupils beyond the minimum four years, or concurrently with the last semester or year.

## Objectives

1. Terminal objectives are in harmony with current thinking and research in foreign language learning and teaching.
2. They are realistic in terms of the community, the school, the pupil population, the length of the program, and all other pertinent factors.
3. They are clearly and specifically set down for each level in terms of the communication skills to be acquired, the language items to be taught, and the cultural insights to be provided.

## The Curriculum

1. The material to be taught at each level is selected and graded with attention to linguistic and psychological principles of learning, but priority is always based on students' needs.
2. A "spiral" approach is used in the presentation of all linguistic and cultural material.
3. Provision is made for continuous review and reentry of previously taught material in subsequent units and at successive learning levels.
4. Provision is made for the continuous integration of familiar and newly acquired material in authentic communication activities.
5. Continuity of instruction is ensured through careful selection of materials and through the maintenance of detailed records.
6. Cultural insight is provided both incidentally, through the study of language in use, and systematically, in specially prepared talks, projects, and activities.

253

7. The curriculum is revised as teacher observation, tests, research studies, student and parent feedback, etc., point up the need for such revision.

## Methodology

1. There is recognition that student attitude and motivation are key factors in learning.

2. Listening precedes speaking. Listening and speaking precede reading.

3. Listening and speaking skills continue to be developed and reinforced throughout the entire program.

4. Reading is introduced as quickly as feasible after consideration of all pertinent pupil and program factors.

5. Writing is also introduced after a flexible period of possible deferment depending on such factors as writing system and "fit."

6. The introduction to language material stems from many sources. Common everyday situations within the environment and experience of the learners are used by teachers to clarify the meaning and function of all items.

7. Pupils are engaged in a variety of practice activities. Rote repetition and strictly controlled manipulative activities quickly give way to "freer" communication activities relevant to the actual situations in which pupils are learning.

8. Dialogues, reading passages, songs, poems, and other materials are "exploited" to the fullest.

9. Discrete features of language, communication skills, and socio-cultural situations are continuously integrated.

10. Audio-visual materials are used when feasible to lend variety to teaching, to reinforce and consolidate material acquired, and to clarify linguistic and cultural concepts.

11. Team teaching procedures are attempted in order to utilize the strengths of staff members.

## Materials of Instruction

1. These are carefully selected by a committee of teachers on the basis of criteria which have been established (e.g., Can they make a contribution to the program objectives?).

2. Language laboratory materials — commercial or teacher-prepared — are integrated with classroom teaching materials.

3. Individualization of instruction is provided for through teacher-prepared materials or commercial materials which have been adapted for the particular situation.

4. Self-checking devices are prepared to permit self-instruction or some degree of self-instruction and self-pacing.

5. Teachers are trained in the use of newer types of equipment (e.g., the overhead projector).

6. Needed materials are available in a central, easily accessible place.

7. Student service squads are formed to aid in the distribution and care of equipment and materials.

8. Materials are evaluated periodically.

9. Community members are encouraged to assist in the gathering of appropriate material, its care, and its distribution.

10. Community members and other aides are trained to use the material effectively in working with students.

## The Testing Program

1. If aptitude tests are given, their results are studied with all other pertinent records of pupils. No one is barred from the program on the basis of an aptitude test alone.

2. Provision is made for several long tests each semester and for as many daily tests as possible.

3. All tests reflect the program objectives and the instructional program.

4. The tests reflect city-wide, state-wide, or nation-wide goals.

5. The school cooperates in city, state, national, or agency testing programs.

6. The tests are used not only to check students' achievement but also to signal the need for curriculum revision, in-service training of teachers, the establishment of tutoring programs, changes in instructional materials, and all other program components.

## The School

1. Monies are allocated to make necessary material and equipment available.

2. Student, parent, and community aides are encouraged to assist in various aspects of program implementation.

3. The library includes a large collection of appropriate books, magazines, and pictures.

4. In the absence of a language laboratory, one or more tape recorders are provided.

5. A detailed schedule for the use of all equipment is made available to teachers and other interested personnel at the beginning of each school year.

6. A rich co-curricular program is offered (clubs, newspapers, assembly programs, films, etc.).

7. Correlation with appropriate subject areas is explored and encouraged.

8. Guidance services are provided for pupils.

9. A tutoring or remedial program is established for students in need of help.

10. Honor societies, contest participation, and other activities which enhance the pupils' self-concept are encouraged, but only where appropriate.

11. Classroom experimentation, research projects, and various patterns of teaching arrangements are promoted (e.g., team teaching, flexible grouping, inter-class transfer, continuous progress, non-graded classes).

255

12. Continuity of instruction for pupils is ensured through attention to problems of articulation. Exchange of records, tests, and instructional materials, frequent meetings, and intervisitation between the secondary school and the lower and higher school are routine procedures.

13. Pupil placement is flexible. Pupils are permitted to transfer to another section of a level or to a lower or higher one depending on need and ability.

14. Pleasant, cooperative relationships are established with community members and related agencies.

## Program Supervision

1. In-service training is a continuing process. Regular meetings are scheduled, and an agenda is planned for each meeting by members of the staff in cooperation with supervisory personnel.

2. Teachers are encouraged to attend meetings in other schools or cities.

3. A supervisory bulletin is issued regularly. This may contain titles and reviews of pertinent books, research findings, test results, forthcoming events, etc.

4. Demonstration classes are given by the supervisor or by a teacher to which other teachers and interested persons are invited.

5. Curriculum bulletins are prepared as needed (e.g., when new books are introduced).

## The Community

1. The resources — people and places — are continuously tapped (e.g., bilingual informants, speakers, printing facilities, teacher and school aides).

2. Field trips into the community are encouraged when feasible and pertinent.

3. The reporting to parents and to interested community members of student achievement, program objectives, and evolving needs is systematic.

4. A committee of community members and teachers of foreign languages is formed and meets on a regular basis and as needed.

5. Wherever possible, the interests, needs, and concerns of the community are given serious consideration in program planning and implementation.

## EVALUATING MATERIALS OF INSTRUCTION

### *A Brief Checklist*

### I. The Basic Textbook

A. Approach and Method.
*Does it:*
1. Suit the age level of the students for whom it is intended?

2. Make provision for introducing the four skills in the currently favored sequence — listening, speaking, reading, writing?
3. Provide for activities in which the four skills are integrated?
4. Present grammatical material in incremental steps?
5. Grade all items and structures logically and sequentially?
6. Plan for the systematic reentry of all previously taught material and for its integration in dialogues and other authentic communication activities?
7. Contain dialogues and other listening-speaking activities? Are the situations of the dialogues summarized or made explicit before they are studied and dramatized?
8. Provide for various ability levels in the classroom in terms of differentiated activities or homework assignments?
9. Suggest "freer" conversation activities even at the beginning levels?
10. Introduce reading and writing activities in accordance with the philosophy of your school or school system?

B. Treatment of Pronunciation
1. In what order and sequence are the sounds taught (e.g., those needed immediately in the dialogue utterances or in high-frequency words)?
2. What provision is made (pictures, other devices) for students to be made aware that the sounds are phonemic?
3. Are the words used in the pronunciation drills of high frequency?
4. Is attention paid to stress, intonation, pause, rhythm?
5. Are sounds taught in isolation or inserted into authentic utterances for immediate practice?
6. Are pairs of contrasting sounds taught together?

C. Treatment of Grammar
1. Is the presentation of the grammar in harmony with current research? (Is it presented through situations, in dialogues, in reading passages, in model utterances?)
2. Is there provision for repetition of model sentences?
3. Are generalizations given? Are these descriptive or prescriptive? How are they elicited? How are students led to discover them?
4. Is there a variety of practice activities for each grammatical item?
5. Are there a minimum of six to eight utterances under each drill?
6. Are the drills suggested the most appropriate for the particular structure?
7. Are the drill items grouped together logically for ease in student perception and performance?
8. Are the changes required in the drills minimal when a structure is first introduced?
9. Are the drill utterances authentic?
10. Are question forms introduced early so that "conversation" will be possible?
11. Are grammar items reintroduced in subsequent communication activities?

12. Is there provision for "freer" conversation with the grammar items which have been presented and practiced in controlled drills?

D. Vocabulary
1. Is the vocabulary grouped around centers of interest?
2. Is it in harmony with the probable experiences and interests of the students?
3. Is the vocabulary load too great? Insufficient?
4. What provision is made for the explicit awareness of cultural items embedded in the vocabulary?
5. Are the vocabulary items of high frequency?
6. Are there pictures for clarifying important items or concepts?
7. Is there provision for systematic reintroduction of the vocabulary?
8. Is there a summary of the vocabulary at the end of the text? Does the summary contain an indication of the unit or lesson in which the vocabulary item was introduced?
9. Are word study activities included (synonyms, antonyms, definitions, words of the same family)?

E. Reading Passages
1. Are they interesting (e.g., in consonance with the age and probable interests of the students)?
2. Do they recombine the vocabulary and grammar items taught in the text?
3. Do they present an up-to-date picture of the culture of the target language speakers?
4. How is comprehension ensured (questions and answers, true-or-false statements, multiple-choice, matching items, other)?
5. Is the vocabulary load too heavy?

F. Writing Activities
1. Do they provide for the sequential introduction of skills leading to "free" composition?
2. Do they reinforce the listening, speaking, and reading activities?
3. Could the writing assignments be differentiated (for slower or more able learners)?
4. Are the utterances in the writing assignments grouped logically with relation to structure and vocabulary?
5. In cases where the native language and the target language writing systems differ, is there provision for studying written models and for copying them?

G. Other Language Learning Activities
1. Is there provision for games, puzzles, songs, proverbs, contests, poems, speeches?
2. What provision is made for paired practice? For choral group, subgroup, and individual practice?

H. Format and Other Considerations
1. Is the print legible?

258

2. Are the pictures clear?
3. Is the binding satisfactory?
4. Is there an adequate index?
5. Is it expensive?
6. Is it heavy?
7. Is it part of a series which can be used at the lower or higher level?
8. Is it accompanied by tapes and other appropriate materials?
9. Is a clear, detailed Guide provided for your use in presenting each facet of the text?

## II. Other Materials

A. Tapes: high-quality sound; integrated with the basic text or reinforcing some language activity or grammar item; different voices; provision for student repetition; provision for confirmation and for appropriate concurrent activity.
B. Visual and Audio-Visual Materials: simple, clear, uncluttered; up to date; making possible the immediate association of concept and image; useful at many levels of learning and in a variety of teaching steps; ease of manipulation.
C. Cultural Readers: up to date; fair (no stereotypes); anthropological point of view; achievements credited; discussion of government, politics, economy.
D. Reference Grammars:
   1. Is the material well-organized?
   2. Are the explanations brief, clear, descriptive?
   3. Are sufficient examples given?
   4. Is the index clear?
   5. Are cross-references included?
E. Dictionaries:
   1. Is there a preface and explanation for efficient use of the dictionary? Are symbols used? How are they clarified?
   2. Are all words of high frequency included?
   3. Is the most common range of meaning for words included with illustrative sentences?
   4. Are the definitions accurate and clear?
   5. Are pronunciation and syllabification indicated?
   6. Is it up to date?

## BRIEF GUIDELINES FOR COMPARING THE TARGET LANGUAGE AND YOUR STUDENTS' NATIVE LANGUAGE*

It will be helpful for you to develop an awareness of the broad similarities and differences between the target language and your stu-

---

* Titles of contrastive studies in several languages will be found in Appendix III.

dents' native language. A comparative analysis serves many useful purposes. It can:

1. Give you a sympathetic understanding of the difficulties your students face as they struggle to learn a new language feature which is either in complete contrast to a familiar one or which may bear a partial similarity to it.

2. Guide you in grading material for presentation.

3. Be of inestimable use to you in gathering and preparing effective instructional materials.

4. Suggest the items which will have to be reintroduced frequently so that their use will gradually be internalized.

In presenting the broadest, most general overview of the features and operations to look for or to ask a native speaker about, we will list them under the same sub-systems used throughout this text.

## I. The Sound System of the Native Language

A. Vowels and Consonants
    1. Which phonemes in the target language do not exist?
    2. Which phonemes exist but in different positions?
    3. Which phonemes bear some points of similarity in articulation?
    4. Which consonants cluster? In which positions?
    5. Which vowels cluster? In which positions?
    6. Are vowels ever reduced to /ə/, for example?
    7. Are there any diphthongs?
    8. What morphophonemic changes take place?
    9. Is there liaison between two words in juxtaposition?
    10. What sounds are omitted or elided entirely? In what circumstances?

B. Intonation
    1. What are the major intonation patterns in statements, questions, requests?
    2. How does intonation change in emphatic or emotional speech?
    3. Are intonation changes within words phonemic?

C. Stress, Pause, Rhythm
    1. Is word stress phonemic?
    2. Which words, if any, are given more stress in an utterance?
    3. Is pause phonemic?
    4. Is rhythm stress-timed or syllable-timed?

## II. The Grammar System of the Native Language

A. What are the meaningful signals: word order, inflection, function words, other?

B. Does the phenomenon of derivation exist? Does it bring with it a functional shift?

C. What are the word order arrangements for modifiers, complements, etc.?

D. Which word classes are inflected (nouns, verbs, adjectives, adverbs, articles)? In which functions and operations?
   1. How many "genders" are there?
   2. Which classes of words must agree with which other classes?
   3. Are verbs inflected for tense? Which tenses exist?
E. How are verb phrases formed?
F. Which are the major sentence patterns?
G. How are kernel sentences transformed (combination, deletion, addition, integration, embedding, other)?

## III. The Vocabulary System

A. Is there a marked division between content words and function words?
   1. Which classes of words are considered content words?
   2. Which classes are considered function words?
B. Is derivation a phenomenon (prefixing, suffixing, infixing)?
C. Do words have a wide range of meaning depending on the context?
D. Are many words borrowed from other languages?
E. Which formulas are used? In what situations?

## IV. The Culture System (as reflected in language)

A. How many forms of address are there?
B. Do verb forms change depending on whether you are talking to people or about people? Does the sex or family relationship of the person talked about require a change?
C. What gestures are used? When? How?
D. What distances are maintained?
E. What other unarticulated sounds are used?
F. How are addresses, phone numbers, dates, etc., said?

## V. The Writing System

A. What kind of writing system is used?
B. Is the fit between sound and spelling good?
C. How is a page read (left to right, right to left, etc.)?
D. How are numbers, dates, addresses, etc., written?
E. What contractions are generally permitted?
F. Which punctuation marks are used? What do they represent?

## INTEGRATING SITUATION AND STRUCTURE

### Some Examples

In order to help students associate the sounds they hear with the concepts they represent, it is important to use language items within authentic situations which not only clarify their function and meaning but also illustrate the dimensions of experience with which the items can be used.

261

We know, of course, that the same language item can be used in numerous situations. It is a question, therefore, of your selecting the situation for the *initial* presentation of an item with regard to such factors as the age of your students, their level of second language learning, and the facilities easily available to you in the school and in the community. In general, it is desirable to start with the classroom situation and then to "fan out" to the wider community. This "fanning out" in many cases can only be accomplished by means of visual aids. The community — native or foreign — must be brought into the classroom. While it is true that the experiences of the students will be vicarious rather than real, they can be made most effective and productive nonetheless.

The situation you choose or "design" will depend also on the particular function or meaning of an item you are planning to teach. For example, in teaching *at*, you could start with expressions of *time* or *position*, or with *addresses*. Any of these starting points would be feasible and "right."

Following are some practicable situations you might wish to use in presenting selected structural items. Only the most common situations, those generally possible wherever language is being taught, will be indicated. You should not hesitate, however, to use the "Let's pretend" technique. "Let's pretend," with a clear picture or drawing which simulates reality, permits you and the class to leave the confines of the classroom.

The language items will be listed under several sections: *word order, function words, inflections,* and *verb phrases.* The examples are in English. They have been roughly sub-divided under *beginning, intermediate,* and *advanced* levels but as has been indicated throughout this book, the placement of an item or of a given function or meaning of an item at any particular level depends on numerous factors.

| FEATURE OR ITEM | SITUATION | |
|---|---|---|
| | *Possible Presentation*[1] | Material, People, or Activity |
| | BEGINNING LEVEL | |
| *Word Order* | | |
| **Be—Present**[2] | This is (country). We live in (country). *I'm* a (an) (nationality). You're a (an) too. | Map; you and students |
| **Have—Present** | I *have* a (pen). | Items in your pocketbook, pocket, or on desk |
| Regular verbs— Present | I *get up* at (seven). | Clock; pictures |
| Noun complements | I'm a (an) (*nationality*), or I have a (*book*). | Map; school items; you and the students |

---

[1] Precede each utterance simply with the words, "Look, Listen" or "Listen."

[2] It is assumed that all pronouns, negative and interrogative forms, and plurals will also be presented in logical sequence.

| | | |
|---|---|---|
| Adjective comple-<br>ments | The (book)'s (*red*). | School items |
| Adjective modifiers | I have a (*red*) (book). | School items |
| **Wh** questions | *Where*'s the (notebook)? | Desk or other surface;<br>school items |
| | John's a student. *What's*<br>John? He's a student. | You and the students |
| *Function Words* | | |
| Prepositions | The (book)'s (*in*) the desk. | Classroom items |
| | The (English) class starts *at*<br>(9). | Clock; school schedule |
| | Stand *near* the (desk). | You and students |
| | I always write *with* (chalk). | School items; blackboard |
| Determiners | You're *a* student (pointing to<br>them one at a time). I'm *the*<br>teacher. | You and the student;<br>school items; parts of<br>the room |
| | or | |
| | That's *a* desk. That's *a* desk.<br>That's *the* door.<br>*This* (book) is (red).<br>*That* (book) is (green). | |
| Conjunctions | X *and* Y are students.<br>I have a pen *and* a pencil.<br>I have a pen, *but* I don't have<br>a pencil. | Students and you; school<br>items |
| Pronouns | *He*'s a student.<br>This is *his* notebook. | School items; students |
| *Inflections* | There are five *boys* in this<br>row. | Students |
| | *These* are *boys*. *These* are<br>*girls*. | Pictures or students |
| *Verbs and Verb<br>Phrases* | I *come* to school every day.<br>I'*m* writ*ing* now. | Pictures; clock; calendar<br>Dramatization with items<br>or by going to various<br>parts of room |
| | I'm *going to eat* later.<br>*Go* to the (door). *Come* to the<br>(desk). *Open* the (book). | Clock; pictures<br>Students; dramatization |
| *Miscellaneous* | | |
| Unstressed **There** | *There*'s a book on my desk.<br>*There are* five girls in this<br>row. | School items; students |
| Numbers | Let's count the books. *One*, etc. | School items |
| Days | Today is (*Tuesday*). | Calendar |
| Seasons | It's (*snowing*). It's (*winter*). | Pictures; thermometer |
| Greetings and leave-<br>takings | It's ( ) o'clock. What would<br>you say in meeting some-<br>one? | Clock; pictures; students |
| Time | It's (*half past eight*). | Clock with movable hands |

263

*Word Order*

| | | |
|---|---|---|
| Prepositional phrases | | |
| of *time* | We study (history) *in the afternoon.* | Clock; pictures; school schedule |
| of *place* | I'm going *to the library.* | Pictures of places in the school and community |
| of *place and time* | We come *to school in the morning.* | Clock; pictures of places; calendar |
| Frequency words | I get up at (seven) on Monday, etc. I *always* get up at (seven). | Clock; calendar |
| Comparisons with **more** and **most** | May I have a *more expensive* pen? This is *the most expensive* pen I have. | Pictures of shops; school and other items |
| Two complements | (Give) *him the pen.* (Give) *it to him.* | Students; items |
| Noun-noun combinations | This is a comb. I usually keep it in my pocket. It's a *pocket comb.* | Appropriate items; pictures; students |

*Function Words*

| | | |
|---|---|---|
| Modals | He *can* (swim). He learned how to (swim) last year. X *can* touch the (desk). He *can't* touch the ceiling. | Pictures; dramatization |
| Intensifiers | X can't touch the ceiling. It's *too* high. It's *very* hot today. Let's go (swimming). | Pictures; students; parts of room / Pictures; thermometer |
| Determiners | May I have *some* (ink)? (I'm sorry) I don't have *any* (ink). | Pictures of mass noun and count noun items |
| Exclamations | X liked the (dress). She said, "*What a* pretty (dress)." | Pictures of shopping scenes |

*Inflections*

| | | |
|---|---|---|
| Object pronouns | I'm talking to John and Mary. I'm talking to *them.* This is Mary. I'm giving *her* a pen. | You; students; items |
| Possessives | This book is *mine.* It's not *yours.* | You; students; items |
| **Whose** | *Whose* book is this? *Whose* is it? | You; students; items |
| Possession with nouns | This is *John's* notebook. This is *the leg of the table.* | Students; objects |

264

| | | |
|---|---|---|
| Comparisons | This line is *longer than* this line.<br>This line is *the longest.* | Lines drawn on the black-board |
| Adverbs | Look, I'm walking *slowly.*<br>Now, I'm walking *quickly.* | Dramatization of actions |

*Verbs and Verb Phrases*

| | | |
|---|---|---|
| **Let's** | *Let's* open our books. | Dramatization |
| Past tense | What's today? Yes, it's (Wednesday). Yesterday *was* Tuesday. | Calendar; clock |
| Two-word verbs | I'm *taking off* my (jacket). | Dramatization |

## ADVANCED LEVEL

*Word Order*

| | | |
|---|---|---|
| Position of multiple modifiers | I'd like *two white linen* (handkerchiefs). | Pictures of shopping scenes |
| Prepositional phrases | I like the girl *with the long brown hair.* | Pictures of young people |
| Included clauses | Let's read *while he writes the homework on the board.* | Dramatization; pictures |
| **How long?** | *How long have you lived* on ―― Street? | Addresses of students |
| Reported speech (indirect questions and statements) | What did X say? Listen. *He said* (that) *he would go* to the game tonight. | Dramatization (Prompt students to repeat questions or statements after you.) |
| | What did X ask you? He *asked me if I could go to the game tonight.* | e.g., "I'm going to the game. Can you come with me?" |
| Adverbials | I come to school *by bus.* | Pictures of means of transportation |
| Intensifiers with adverbs | You speak *too quickly.* We can't understand you. | Dramatization |

*Function Words*

| | | |
|---|---|---|
| Modals | I *might go* to the (movies) later but I'm really not sure. | Pictures of places of recreation |
| Substitute words | I think it's going to rain.<br>I think *so* too. | Pictures of weather; dialogues |
| Indefinites | Is *anyone* absent today?<br>*Everyone* is here today. | The students; taking attendance |

265

*Verbs and Verb*
    *Phrases*

| | | |
|---|---|---|
| Present perfect | *I've gone* to X *many times.*<br>*I've known* John *for* a year.<br>*I've known* him *since* ——. | Calendar; map; people |
| If clauses | I won't go out *if it rains.*<br>*If I had* money, *I'd buy* some<br>    fruit.<br>*If I had had* money, *I'd have<br>    bought* some fruit. | Pictures of weather, of<br>    food; clock; real money |
| Verbals | I *like to* swim. I *enjoy<br>    swimming.*<br>I'm interested in *swimming.* | Pictures of sports |
| Passive | This (house) *was built* in<br>    (1900). | Pictures of well-known<br>    buildings |

## VOCABULARY AREAS OR SITUATIONAL TOPICS

The centers of interest listed below will be useful to you in planning numerous types of language activities. They may suggest 1) possible themes for a dialogue, a dictation, a listening comprehension exercise, a reading passage, some directed dialogue, a discussion, a written composition; 2) topics for cross-cultural research; or 3) "situations" around which to present and practice language items.

Addresses
Addressing people
Age
Appointments, making
Art
Banking services
Barber shop, using a
Beauty shop, using a
Cardinal numbers
Clothing (See also Shopping):
    altering
    buying
    cleaning
    describing
    making
    taking care of
    wearing
Dancing
Dates
Days of the week
Dentist, seeing a
Directions:
    asking for
    giving

266

food
household supplies
medicines
toilet articles
Sizes (See also Clothing, Shopping)
Sports (See also Recreational activities)
Telephoning:
    leaving messages
    long distance
    getting information
    public booths
    saying phone numbers
Television
Telling time
Theater
Time, expressions of
Transportation:
    buying tickets
    means of
    schedules
    terminals
    timetables
    using a car
Visiting people and places
Weather
Work:
    aspiring to certain kinds of
    hours of
    laws related to
    looking for
    preparing for
    payment received for
Worshiping

## EXAMPLES OF DIALOGUES

DIALOGUE I: Two persons meet. One of them asks the other where he comes from.
    A — Where are you from, Mr. Girard?
    B — I'm from France.
    A — I was in France last year. What city are you from?
    B — From Avignon.
    A — Oh! I was in Avignon. It's a beautiful city.
    B — Thank you. I was born there and of course I love it very much.

DIALOGUE II: Someone is asking a girl if she has any sisters.
    A — Do you have any sisters?
    B — No, I don't. I'm the only daughter, but I have two brothers.

DIALOGUE III: Someone asks a young lady what she wants to do after graduation.

    A — What would you like to do after you graduate from high school?
    B — Frankly, I'd like to get married.

DIALOGUE IV: Two friends who work together decide to go out for a coffee break.

    A — What time is it?
    B — It's four o'clock.
    A — How about some coffee?
    B — That's a good idea. Let's take a ten-minute break.
    A — Fine. Let's go to the coffee shop next door.

DIALOGUE V: Two boys are talking about playing baseball.

    A — What are you going to do today after school?
    B — Nothing. Why?
    A — Let's play a game of baseball.
    B — Great. Let's get some other boys together.

DIALOGUE VI: In the post office, a young man has a letter weighed to find out the correct amount of postage.

    A — I'd like to send this letter air mail.
    B — I'll weigh it for you. That will be forty cents.
    A — Thank you. May I have the stamps?
    B — Here they are.
    A — Where can I mail it?
    B — There are slots outside. Put it in the slot marked "air mail."

DIALOGUE VII: Two girls are waiting for the bus. They are afraid of being late for school.

    A — What time is it?
    B — It's eight-forty-five.
    A — We'll be late. We must be in school by nine.
    B — Let's walk.
    A — We can't. It's too far.
    B — Oh! Here's the bus. We may still get there on time.
    A — I hope so. I've been late twice this semester.

DIALOGUE VIII: A child is asking his mother about the weather.

    Child — How's the weather, Mom?
    Mother — It's miserable. It's raining and it's quite cold.
    Child — Oh, no! Not again. It's been raining for three days.
    Mother — It's going to rain for a few days more. That's what the weatherman said.

DIALOGUE IX: John and his friend George meet Jane on the street. The two boys are going to the movies. They ask Jane to go with them, but she has an appointment with another girl.

    John — Hello, Jane.
    Jane — Oh! Hello, John. How nice to see you again!

John — May I introduce my friend, George?

Jane — I'm very pleased to meet you, George. John has often spoken about you.

George — I'm happy to meet you, Jane.

John — George and I were going to the movies. Would you like to come?

Jane — Thank you, but I'm afraid I can't. I have an appointment with Mary.

John — Let's ask Mary to come to the movies, too.

DIALOGUE X: One person is asking another who the head of the government is in his country.

A — Who is the head of your country?

B — We have a premier. What about you?

A — We have a president.

DIALOGUE XI: Two persons are talking about holiday festivities.

A — How do you celebrate Carnival?

B — There are parades with beautiful floats. We eat a lot of special foods, too.

A — That sounds nice.

A — Do you celebrate Christmas or Three Kings' Day?

B — Both.

A — The children must like that.

A — We're going to have a long school holiday.

B — I know. What are you going to do?

A — I'm going to work in my father's store.

A SPIRAL DIALOGUE: A boy is going to school.

A — Where are you going?

B — I'm going to school.

A — What school do you go to?

B — The "Kay Day School."

A — Where are you going?

B — I'm going to school.

A — You seem to be in a hurry.

B — I have to be there at 8:30 and if I'm late, I have to stay in after school.

A — What school do you go to?

B — The "Kay Day School."

A — Where are you going in such a hurry?

B — I'm going to school and I have to be there at 8:30. If I'm late, I'll have to stay in after school for an hour.

A — What school do you go to?

B — The "Kay Day School."

271

# SUGGESTED ITEMS FOR A PICTURE FILE*

## I) Living in an Urban Community

A) The School
   — Personnel: principal, nurse, custodian, librarian, faculty members (e.g., math teacher, science teacher)
   — Places: gymnasium, auditorium, cafeteria, shops, nurse's office, principal's office, general office, classrooms
   — Instructional materials: bulletin boards, books, charts, pencils, pens, notebooks, maps
   — Rules: fire drills, safety on stairs, getting to school on time

B) The Home
   — The exterior: sidewalk, entrance, mailbox
   — Rooms: bedroom, bathroom, kitchen, living room, dining room, hall
   — Furniture: dresser, closet, tables, chairs, lamps, rugs, stoves, refrigerators, iceboxes, bookcases, beds (mattresses, sheets, blankets), pillows
   — Utensils and tools: knives, forks, spoons, plates, cups, saucers, broiler, pots, pans, hammer, scissors
   — Home activities: cooking, eating, sweeping, washing, sewing, dressing, reading, studying, brushing teeth, combing hair
   — Meals: setting the table, serving; types of food for breakfast, lunch, dinner, snacks, parties
   — Recreation: radio, television, cards, word games, checkers, parties, books, phonograph, crossword puzzles, knitting, sewing, cooking, dancing, singing, playing musical instruments

C) The Community
   1. The neighborhood of the school and home
      — Mail and fire alarm boxes
      — Post office: various departments (stamps, air mail, parcel post, inquiry window, money orders, forms), mailboxes
      — Police station: receiving desk, radio room, radio cars, uniforms, equipment, different types of police jobs
      — Firehouse: equipment, uniforms, people performing various duties
      — Business establishments: grocery, meat store, candy store, repair shops, vegetable market, beauty parlor, pet shops, chain stores, drugstores, supermarkets, gift shops
      — Sanitation: street cleaners, exterminators, garbage cans
      — Health: doctors, nurses, ambulances, clinics, hospitals
      — Occupations: mechanics, sales clerks, manual labor jobs, armed services, professional, industrial, etc.

---

* You should keep two picture files: one in which the schools, houses, rooms, etc., are of the foreign nation; the other, of your native country. The latter pictures should be chosen with care to conform, as far as possible, to *your students'* lives and experiences.

272

— Places of worship
2. Transportation
    — Signs such as: stop, go, right, left, uptown, downtown, one way, detour, this way out, exit, entrance
    — Types of transportation in neighborhood: bus, train, car, bicycle, scooter, wagon, carriage, truck
    — Traffic lights
    — Terms outside of the neighborhood: boat, airplane, bus, train, terminals, stations, bus stops, shipping dock, coin box, turnstile, taxi, railroad, trolley, transfer
3. Recreation
    — In the neighborhood: playgrounds, schoolroom, gym, street, parks, afternoon centers, community centers, settlement houses, sports equipment (such as gloves, bat, ball)
    — Out of the neighborhood: skating rinks, movies, libraries, museums, beaches, swimming pools, ball parks, bowling alleys, zoo, organizational activities such as the Boy Scouts
4. Pictures related to an understanding of history and cultural values
    — Historic landmarks: buildings, statues
    — Holidays: religious, political, special days of national groups
    — Heroes
    — Documents
5. Miscellaneous
    — Weather, seasons
    — Pets: dogs, cats, turtles, fish, pigeons, rabbits, canaries, monkeys, etc.
    — Care of pets: bathing, feeding, training, responsibilities
    — Leisure-time activities: stamps, coins, scrapbooks, photography, sewing, knitting, painting, baking, science, reading, musical instruments, concert or playgoing, fishing

## II) Living in a Rural Community

A) The General Scene
    — Farmhouses (various types)
    — Barn
    — Silo
    — Chicken houses
    — Well (pump, buckets)
    — Fields
    — Crops
    — Orchards
    — Pastures
    — Brooks
    — Woods
    — Farm implements: tractor, truck, threshing machine, automobile, hoe, spade, fork

273

— Animals: cows, horses, pigs, sheep, chickens, ducks, geese, dogs, cats
— Wild animals: deer, bears, etc.
— Fish and wild birds

B) Customs and Resources
— Recreational: country dances, hay ride, skating, sleighing, swimming, horseback riding, county fairs, carnivals, picnics
— Religious (places of worship)
— Educational: schools, library

C) The Home
— Farm kitchen
— Rooms
— Wood or coal stove
— Electric washer
— Bathrooms
— Washstands
— Sleeping facilities
— Utensils
— Lamps and other lighting

D) Transportation and Communication
— School bus, automobiles, station wagons, trains, bus
— Telephone, mailman, mailboxes, letters, mail-order catalogues, magazines, newspapers

E) Miscellaneous
— Drugstores
— General store
— Volunteer fire company
— Roads: dirt, concrete, asphalt, highways
— Bridges: country bridges, large bridges
— Depot

# Appendix II

## DEFINITIONS OF USEFUL TERMS

On the pages which follow, you will find, alphabetically listed, brief, simple definitions of terms as they have been used in the context of this book and of other words you may come across in further study.

ACCENT: 1) A synonym for *stress* (see STRESS). 2) Marks indicating the four-word, phrase, or sentence stresses ╱ (primary); ∧ (secondary); ╲ (tertiary); ∪ (weak). 3) A written mark over certain vowels of a word to differentiate it from another word spelled in the same way — Italian: e (and); è (is). 4) A written mark indicating syllabic stress

— Spanish: está (he is); ésta (this one). 5) A written mark indicating vowel quality — French: père (father); allé (gone). 6) A "foreign" accent — a pronunciation deviation in the target language which identifies or marks the speaker as non-native. 7) Regional or dialectal accents.

ACHIEVEMENT TEST: One which measures how much of a body of language material taught has actually been learned by the student.

ACTION SERIES: also called the Gouin Series from the name of its originator: Utterances which verbalize a series of sequential actions being performed; e.g., I'm getting up; I'm going to the board; I'm writing my name; etc.

ACTIVATED HEADPHONES: Those which amplify a speaker's voice and permit him to hear himself as he speaks.

ACTIVE VOCABULARY: The content and function words of a language which are learned so thoroughly that they can be used in the performance of any communication act; the vocabulary which can be easily recalled for production. PASSIVE VOCABULARY refers to words understood when heard or read, but not used in speaking or writing.

ALLOPHONE: One of the variant sounds of a phoneme. For example, the different *p* sounds in *pill, spill, cup* are all variants, or *allophones*, of the phoneme /p/. Allophones do not differentiate meaning.

ANALOGY: The ability to form a word or pattern on the basis of knowledge of similar words or patterns. For example, if your students know the forms *boy/boys, girl/girls, ruler/rulers*, they should by *analogy* be able to give the form *pencils* when you give the stimulus word *pencil*.

ANOMIE: A traumatic feeling experienced by learners who no longer identify with the native language community but who are not yet ready to "belong" to the foreign language community.

ANTHROPOLOGY: One of the social sciences which studies all the features of the culture (including language) of a society.

ARTICULATION: 1) The smooth, continuous development from one level of language learning to the next. 2) The production of distinct sounds by the vocal organs — e.g., tongue between the teeth or tip of tongue against the tooth ridge.

AUDIO-LINGUAL: 1) A term used currently to indicate an approach to language learning — first by hearing, then by repeating. 2) Listening and speaking. (Another term for audio-lingual is aural-oral.)

BACKWARD BUILD-UP: The teaching technique whereby long sentences are divided and reconstructed from the end into small meaningful segments for ease in repetition. (See page 81.)

BEHAVIOR: A way of doing something habitually as a result of the assimilated acquisition of a skill or a body of information or knowledge.

BILINGUALISM: The state of being able to use two languages with almost equal facility.

CHAIN: The type of pupil activity in a classroom in which a student makes a statement, asks a question, or responds; then the student next to him or behind him makes a statement, responds, or asks a question. (See page 187.)

275

CHORAL REPETITION: The imitation of spoken material by an entire class or by a group speaking together.

CLUSTER: 1) The sequence or bunching together of consonants; e.g., wo*rks,* *spr*ing. 2) The sequence or bunching together of other language elements (vowels, nouns, verbs, etc.).

CODE: The total shared language system of a community. (See PAROLE)

COGNATE: A word in one language which looks similar to and has a meaning equivalent to a word in another language; e.g., (Spanish/English) *nacional/national.* Beware of false cognates, that is, words which look the same but have different meanings; e.g., (Italian) *attualmente* = at the present time; (English) *actually* = really.

COGNITIVE CODE THEORY: The learner perceives (or is guided to discover) the "rule" or generalization underlying a feature of language from several examples of it. This understanding should precede practice activities. Language is rule-governed behavior.

COMPETENCE: 1) In a psycholinguistic sense, the achieved ability of the speaker or listener to understand and produce language utterances. 2) In transformational theory, the ability to recognize well-formed sentences. (See PERFORMANCE)

COMPOUND SYSTEM: One in which the foreign language is learned and used in relation to the native language. (See COORDINATE SYSTEM)

CONFIRMATION: Knowledge given a learner — orally or through some other technique — that his response is correct.

CONFLICT: Interference or problem in learning a second or foreign language caused by the ingrained habit of saying something in a certain way in one's native tongue.

CONNOTATIVE: The personal meaning a word may have for individuals depending on their experiences with the word or its referent.

CONSCIOUS SELECTION: The step in the learning process in which students choose between two language items which are in contrast. (See page 73.)

CONSOLE: The teacher's control center in a language laboratory.

CONSTITUENT: Any one of the smaller structural units linked together in a larger construction. For example in *The boys bought balls, the boys* (the NP or Noun Phrase) and *bought balls* (the VP or Verb Phrase) are the *immediate constituents* of the sentence. The *ultimate constituents* would be boy/s and ball/s which cannot be divided further.

CONTENT WORDS: Vocabulary items that refer to *things, actions,* or *qualities.*

CONTEXT: The forms or words within any connected stretch of speech which surround other words and thus help to give them their particular meaning. (Often *context* and *situation* are used interchangeably but they should not be.) *Context* is *intralingual* whereas *situation* is *extralingual.* (See SITUATION)

CONTINUANT: A sound which can be prolonged indefinitely like *m* or *f.*

CONTINUUM: An uninterrupted sequence of steps or phases in a process. In foreign language learning, we speak of the stages in acquiring full listening comprehension, for example, as points or steps on a "continuum."

CONTRASTIVE ANALYSIS: A comparison of all the features of the native language of a learner which differ from those of the target language.

CO-OCCURRENCE: 1) The normal, permitted combination of words in an utterance; e.g., we can say, *I watched a film,* but not *I watched a book.* (The British term for this is "collocation.") 2) The environment (the surrounding words) of a word or structure; e.g., the Queen *of* (England).

COORDINATE SYSTEM: One in which the target language is learned as a parallel, completely independent system, without relation to the native language. (See COMPOUND SYSTEM)

CORRELATION: 1) The act of bringing together learnings from more than one subject area for their mutual enrichment. 2) A positive or negative relationship between two tests or two abilities or factors; e.g., There is not necessarily a high (or positive) correlation between intelligence and the ability to learn the elementary mechanisms of foreign language.

COUNT NOUN: One that can be modified by a numeral; e.g., four *apples.* *Ink* on the other hand is called a *mass noun* since it cannot easily be modified by a numeral.

CUE: A stimulus which is given to elicit a response. The cue may be a gesture, a picture, a word, a sentence, etc., which is used to call forth a desired response.

CULTURAL ISLAND: The total immersion of the foreign language learners into the foreign culture through the continuous use of the foreign language in class, the display of its authentic materials, listening to its speakers, etc.

CULTURE: The language, customs, values, beliefs, art forms, and achievements of a society.

CURRICULUM: The knowledge, information, skills, abilities, activities, materials, etc., which are included in the teaching of any subject.

DECODE: The process by which a hearer derives the total meaning (linguistic and cultural) of a verbal message. (See ENCODE)

DEDUCTIVE PROCESS: One in which a rule is formulated first and then followed by examples which conform to it. (See INDUCTIVE PROCESS)

DENOTATIVE: The dictionary meaning of a word. (See CONNOTATIVE)

DERIVED: An utterance, word, or expression produced by the application of a transformation rule to a basic word or utterance; e.g., *kindness* is derived from *kind; Hamlet was written by Shakespeare* is derived from *Shakespeare wrote Hamlet.*

DETERMINER: A word such as an article, a possessive adjective, or a partitive which marks a noun; e.g., *the, a, some, each, any.*

DIAGNOSTIC TEST: One which permits the examiner to judge the student's strengths or weaknesses, problems or difficulties.

DIALECT: A variety of the national language used by members of a speech community living in a given geographical area.

DIPHTHONG: A sound which combines two vowel sounds; e.g., /ɔɪ/, /aʊ/.

DISTRACTOR: An incorrect item given purposely by the examiner in a test.

ENCODE: The process through which a speaker conveys his thought by means of a verbal message; to put thought into linguistic form. (See DECODE)

ENVIRONMENT: The surrounding sounds, syllables, or words of any element of language.

EQUIVALENT: A word, expression, utterance, or sentence in one language which is not a word for word translation of a word, etc., in another language but which conveys the same meaning.

EVALUATION: Tests (oral, written, short answer, essay, etc.) and other measures such as observation and/or questionnaires to ascertain results being achieved and progress being made toward objectives of language learning.

FADE: 1) In teaching, the gradual withdrawal of cues so that the student is required to produce utterances on his own. 2) In speech, the lowered volume at the end of an utterance.

FEEDBACK: The control of one's performance derived from the awareness of its effects; e.g., the speaker controls his flow of speech by hearing his own words.

FIT: The relationship between the sounds of the oral language and the writing systems which represent it.

FLES: The widely used abbreviation for Foreign Languages in the Elementary Schools.

FORMAL: Pertaining to the arrangement of sounds, letters, or words in an utterance.

FORMULA: A fixed expression of greeting, thanks, agreement, etc., such as *Thank you* and *How do you do*, which native speakers use habitually in communication.

FORMULATE: Verbalize; put into words.

FRAME: 1) In programmed instruction, a minimal unit of instruction. 2) A syntactic pattern, each slot of which would always contain words of the same class (determiner, noun, verb, etc.).

FUNCTION: The grammatical role of an item or structure; e.g., subject, object.

FUNCTION WORDS: Words which have no meaning by themselves but which are used in utterances to signal grammatical relationships (e.g., auxiliaries and prepositions). With *content words*, they constitute the vocabulary or lexicon of a language.

GENERALIZATION: The verbalized "rule" or description of a language item which results from the learner's perception of its recurring, consistent sound, form, position, function, and meaning.

GENERATE: 1) In generative-transformational grammar, to list the rules which account for the existence of all the acceptable (well-formed) sentences in the language. 2) To create or produce.

HABIT: A permanent ability to act in a particular manner.

IDIOLECT: The way the individual uses the language of the community; his "parole."

IDIOM: An expression whose total meaning cannot be derived from the meaning of each individual word within it; e.g., *I can't do without you.*

IMMEDIATE CONSTITUENTS: Two or more units on one level of structure which form a single unit on the next higher level; e.g., The subject

278

and predicate are IC's of the sentence; the verb phrase and complement are IC's of the predicate.

INCREMENTAL LEARNING: Learning in small steps.

INDUCTIVE PROCESS: One in which a series of examples or model sentences are given in order to enable the learner to formulate a generalization, description, or "rule." (See DEDUCTIVE PROCESS)

INFLECTION: A change in the form of a word to indicate plurality, possession, etc.

INFORMANT: A native speaker or one with near-native ability who may be used as an authentic resource person with relation to his language or culture.

INTEGRATION: 1) The process of combining related material or elements which belong together. 2) The fusion of different elements into a coherent whole. 3) In discussing individuals, one speaks of a well-adjusted, or well-integrated, personality.

INTERACTION: The give-and-take of communication.

INTERCHANGE: A conversation of two or more utterances.

INTERFERENCE: A difficulty or problem in the learning of one habit because of the existence in the learner of a conflicting one; e.g., the difficulty of learning to produce a sound in the target language because it does not exist or exists in another position in the learner's native tongue.

INTERNALIZE: To understand and learn material so thoroughly that it can be produced at will.

INTERVOCALIC: Between two vowels.

JACK: A box or other piece of equipment for a tape recorder to which additional headphones can be attached.

JUNCTURE: A change in the quality of sounds and in the meaning of an utterance produced by pauses in speech; e.g., nitrate/night rate; I scream/ ice cream.

KERNEL SENTENCE: A basic sentence in a language — usually simple, active, and without modifiers — which can undergo many transformations based on a series of rules. A kernel sentence has two parts or two constituents: a noun phrase (NP) and a verb phrase (VP).

KINESICS: The study of the non-verbal motions used in communication; e.g., gestures, facial expressions.

LANGUAGE FEELING: (Sprachgefühl) The intuitive awareness, resulting from intensive practice in the foreign language, enabling the learner to recognize and to control his production of well-formed sentences.

LANGUE: The total language system — the code — of the community as compared to an individual's expression (his "parole"). Both terms, "langue" and "parole," originated with Ferdinand De Saussure, a Swiss linguist.

LEARNING: The process which leads to the acquisition of any form of behavior.

LEVEL: 1) The height to which the voice rises or falls in speaking. In English, for example, we distinguish four pitch levels. 2) The stage of learning — beginning, intermediate, advanced. 3) The degree of achievement toward a goal.

279

LEXICAL COMBINATION: Words which co-occur; e.g., part of.

LEXICON: The words or vocabulary of the language.

LINGUISTICS: A science which systematically analyzes and describes a language as it is used by its native speakers. There are several branches of linguistic science; e.g., historical, comparative, contrastive.

MACHINE TRANSLATION: The equivalent of a text in one language rendered in another language by means of a computer.

MARKER: A word or morpheme that helps identify the function of another word; e.g., 's added to a singular noun indicates possession; the before a word identifies it as a nominal.

MASTER: 1) (verb) to learn thoroughly. 2) (noun) an original recording from which copies can be made.

METALINGUISTICS: The scientific study of linguistics and its relation to other cultural factors in a society. Paralinguistics, kinesics, proxemics, for example, are included in metalinguistics.

MIM-MEM: Mimicry-memorization. A teaching technique in which students imitate a model and then repeat it to the point of memorization.

MINIMAL PAIR: Two words that sound alike except for one phonemic difference; e.g., bag/back; ship/sheep; bit/pit.

MODEL: 1) The perfect or near-perfect production of a sound, word, or utterance given by the teacher or a recording for imitation by the learners. 2) A tentative or hypothetical design or explanation for any phenomenon.

MONITOR: To listen to students through any inter-communication device as they record.

MONOSTRUCTURAL APPROACH: A teaching method in which individual structures are presented one at a time through several examples and not in a dialogue or reading passage.

MORPHEME: The smallest meaningful unit of language. It may be "free" (a word such as girl which can stand alone) or "bound" (the s of girls which indicates plurality but which cannot stand alone).

MORPHOLOGY: The study of the changes in forms of words produced by inflection or derivation.

MORPHOPHONEMICS: The study of the relationships and changes in phonemes because of their environment or position within a word (a morpheme) or before another word; e.g., in English, the plural morpheme changes its sound depending on the final letter of the word (/z/ in boys but /s/ in books and /ɪz/ in boxes).

MULTIPLE-CHOICE TEST: One in which the student is asked to select an answer to a question or problem from among several choices given.

OPERANT CONDITIONING: The shaping (reinforcing or extinguishing) of the learner's responses through the forging of a bond between stimulus and response and confirmation of the correct response (termed "reward").

PARADIGM: A complete systematic set of the forms of a word or of a verb conjugation; e.g., English: I, me, my, mine; Spanish: present of the verb hablar (to speak): hablo, hablas, habla, etc.

PARALINGUISTICS: The study of tone of voice, tempo of voice, groans,

280

sighs, and other non-articulated sounds which convey meaning to a listener.

PAROLE: The individual speaker's use of language to convey messages.

PATTERN: An arrangement of sounds or words which recurs systematically and is meaningful.

PATTERN PRACTICE: Drills and activities in which the patterns of a language are learned to the point where students can repeat, alter, or respond to them habitually and fluently.

PAUSE: Another word for JUNCTURE.

PEER TEACHING: Two or more students helping each other to learn by practicing and engaging in communication activities with each other.

PERFORMANCE OBJECTIVE: The degree of learning of an item or a skill which a student is expected to achieve under certain well-defined, clearly specified conditions.

PERSONALIZATION: Relating dialogues, readings, etc., to the learners' lives and experiential background through questions.

PHONEMICS: The systematic study of the meaningful sounds of language.

PHONETICS: The study of the sounds of speech — the phonemes and the allophones — and the way they are produced, transmitted, and received by the listener.

PHONOTACTICS: The arrangement of sounds in a language.

PHRASE STRUCTURE RULE: One which governs the construction of the two basic parts of utterances: the noun phrase (NP) and the verb phrase (VP) of kernel sentences.

PITCH: A voice tone which distinguishes meaning.

PROFICIENCY TEST: One which permits the measurement of a person's knowledge and ability in a foreign language without regard to formal study or text used.

PROGNOSTIC TEST: One which permits the making of hypotheses about a person's possible success in language study. Synonym = APTITUDE TEST.

PROGRAMMED LEARNING: The systematic grading and sequencing of language material and its presentation in the smallest possible segments, generally in frames. The material to be learned (the program) is generally placed in a "teaching machine" or in a text. Since this is often used without an instructor, the device or text directs the student to proceed to the next step when his response has been correct; to go back to a previous step or engage in related drills if the response has been incorrect. It is generally self-pacing; that is, a student can work at his own speed.

PROMPT: To whisper a word or expression to the learner in order to help him produce an utterance.

PROP: A real object (a flag, a flower, a piece of bread) or any device used in teaching to simulate reality and to elicit student response.

PROXEMICS: The study of distances maintained by speakers of different languages as they speak to each other or to others.

PSYCHOLINGUISTICS: The scientific study of the relationships between linguistic data and psychological processes.

RECOMBINE: To bring together familiar sentences, dialogues, or reading passages in order to create new dialogues, etc., in which all the elements are familiar to the learners.

REDUNDANCY: The multiple clues in language, some of which could be eliminated without loss of essential information; e.g., in *The boys are wearing their coats*, the /z/ sound, the verb *are*, the possessive *their*, and the /s/ sound in *coats* all indicate plurality.

REENTRY: The systematic reuse or reintroduction of words and structures which have been learned with newly acquired language items (in dialogues, readings, etc.) in order to 1) keep them alive in the learners' minds, and 2) demonstrate that a word or pattern can be used in many different situations.

REFERENT: The actual object or situation in the real world to which a word is related or to which it refers.

REGISTER: The variation in language (in pronunciation, grammar, or vocabulary) as used by persons in different *jobs* or *professions*, in different *situations (formal* or *informal)*, and in different *modes (speaking* or *writing)*.

REINFORCEMENT: 1) The consolidation or further learning of material. 2) The confirmation or reward which increases the likelihood of a student's giving a correct response again at another time.

REJOINDER: An emphatic response given to a statement or question. The rejoinder may be a formula, another question, or another statement which reiterates or emphasizes the initial utterance.

RELIABILITY: The degree to which a test is consistent in measuring what it is supposed to measure.

RHYTHM: The regularity of speech sequences.

RULE: 1) The description of the form, function, and position of a recurring systematic feature of language. 2) In transformation theory, the instructions or directions which account for the existence of kernel sentences (Phrase Structure Rules) and derived sentences (Transformation Rules).

SANDHI: Changes in the sounds of words because of their placement or co-occurrence with other words; e.g., French: dix /di/ cahiers but dix /diz/ hommes; Italian: *l'amica* from *la* and *amica*.

SEGMENT: A syllable of a word or a group of words in an utterance.

SEGMENTAL PHONEMES: The vowels and consonants.

SEMANTICS: The study of word meanings and their effect on communication, interaction, and interpersonal relationships.

SEMIOTICS: The study of the exchange of any messages whatsoever and of the signs which underlie them.

SHAPE: To lead the learner gradually to a closer approximation of the desired terminal behavior through successive listening and speaking experiences.

SIGN: The general term which designates anything which stands for or represents something else.

SITUATION: The relationship between the elements, events, or things present in the environment and the language used in talking about them; e.g., buying groceries in a market, going to a doctor's office, watching a television program.

SLOT: The position of a word or phrase in a sentence which can be occupied by other words or expressions of the same class; e.g., in "I went to the store," the slot *I* can be occupied by *He, Mary, The boys,* etc.

SPEECH: The oral expression of verbal behavior.

SPIRAL APPROACH: A method of presentation of material in which the same language item or cultural topic is taught in increasingly greater depth at each succeeding level of learning.

STIMULUS: Any signal (manual, oral, visual) to which a person responds or reacts. Also called a "cue."

STOP: A consonant which is made with a momentary stoppage of breath; e.g., /p/, /t/.

STRESS: The prominence of syllables or words in speech.

STRING: A sequence of language items. In transformational theory, the terminal string, for example, is the final sequence of words in an utterance that may have undergone one or more transformations.

STRUCTURE: 1) The recurring patterns of language elements as they occur in forms of words and in arrangements of words in utterances. 2) The grammar of the language. 3) A grammatical item that contains more than one word; e.g., *may have gone.* 4) Any organized, systematic item of language.

STRUCTURE DRILL: An exercise or oral activity in which patterns or structures are practiced.

STRUCTURE WORD: A synonym for FUNCTION WORD.

STYLISTICS: The study of the use of the most appropriate expression available, both connotatively and denotatively, to convey any idea.

SUPRASEGMENTAL PHONEMES: Pronunciation features of pitch, stress, and juncture which co-occur with or are superimposed on the vowels and consonants.

SYMBOL: A meaningful sign which is consciously produced; e.g., a word or a phonetic symbol.

SYNTAX: The arrangement of words in utterances and sentences.

SYSTEM: Sets of recurring combinations and sequences of sounds and words in patterns which signal meaning.

TAGMEME: 1) The slot and its filler. 2) A significant unit of syntax.

TARGET LANGUAGE: The foreign language that is being learned.

TAXONOMIC: Pertaining to the description and classification of structures of language.

TEACHING MACHINE: A mechanical device used in some forms of programmed instruction. (See page 184.)

TENSE: The *formal* categories of verb inflections; e.g., in English, we speak of the simple present and past tenses only: walk*s*; walk*ed.*

TERMINAL BEHAVIOR: The desired outcome that a learner should achieve in terms of the acquisition of some habit, skill, knowledge, or attitude.

TERMINAL CONTOUR: The intonation patterns at the end of an utterance. In English, for example, there are three: rising, falling, and sustained.

TRACK: 1) A pattern of subject or course organization in a school or school system. For example, in the first year of the secondary school, there may be two foreign language tracks, one for students who had studied the foreign language in the elementary school and one for beginners. 2) A stretch or path along a tape on which a recording can be made.

TRANSFER: The ability to use knowledge about a feature of one's native language or of the target language in learning another related feature. (Negative transfer implies the making of false analogies. See page 85.)

TRANSFORMATION THEORY: A theory of language analysis which assumes 1) that all utterances (the surface structure of the language) are derived from basic kernel sentences (the deep structure of the language) by a series of rules; 2) that all native speakers have competence in recognizing well-formed sentences but cannot necessarily produce them; 3) that language is creative and stimulus free. (See page 12 and Appendix III, pages 285-88 and 292, for further study.)

UNCONSCIOUS SELECTION: The habitual, fluent use of the correct sound, word form, or word arrangement in "free" communication.

USAGE: The selection by a speaker of a certain language variety or register.

UTTERANCE: A word, a fixed expression, or a sentence said by a speaker which has meaning, and before which and after which there is silence on his part.

VALIDITY: The degree to which a test measures what it is supposed to measure.

VARIATION: 1) A change of some kind. 2) In audio-lingual methodology, the asking of questions on the dialogue itself.

VERBAL BEHAVIOR: 1) Language. 2) Any manifestation of self-expression and/or communication.

VOICED SOUND: A sound made with the vocal cords vibrating; e.g., /b/, vowels.

VOICELESS SOUND: A sound made while the vocal cords are not vibrating; e.g., /p/.

# Appendix III

## *TEXTS AND RESOURCES*

The first two listings below include the titles recommended within the text for additional reading and other well-known texts. They represent some of the books which we have examined carefully and which we feel make a further contribution to the topic of developing foreign language skills. It is obvious that there are many additional, excellent materials not included here which could be read with profit. For example, few journal articles have been noted. You will find them listed under **Bibliographies** below, in the Mackey text, *Language Teaching Analysis*, and in the end bibliographies of other texts listed under **Books** (pages 286-98).

# Bibliographies

AARONS, A. C. "TESOL Bibliography," in *Florida Foreign Language Reporter*, Jan. 1965.

ALDEN, D. W. (ed.). *Materials List for Use by Teachers of Modern Foreign Languages*. New York: MLA, 1959.

ALLEN, V. F. and S. FORMAN. *English as a Second Language*. New York: Teachers College Press, 1967.

BAKER, HUGH S. *A Checklist of Books and Articles for Teachers of English as a Foreign Language*. NAFSA. New York: 1959.

BIRKMAIER, E. and D. LANGE. "A Selective Bibliography on the Teaching of Foreign Languages 1920-1966," in *Foreign Language Annals I*. New York: MLA, May, 1968.

BROZ, J. and A. HAYES. *Linguistics and Reading*. Washington, D. C.: CAL, 1966.

CHAMBERLAIN, J. S. *Source Materials for Teachers of Foreign Languages*. Washington, D. C.: National Education Association (NEA), 1968.

DINGWALL, W. O. *Transformational Generative Grammar*. Washington, D. C.: CAL, 1965.

EATON, E., M. HAYES, and H. O'LEARY. *Source Materials for Secondary School Teachers of Foreign Languages*. Washington, D. C.: USOE, 1966.

FRANK, M. *Annotated Bibliography of Materials for English as a Second Language*. New York: NAFSA, 1962.

HAMMER, J. and F. RICE. *A Bibliography of Contrastive Linguistics*. Washington, D. C.: CAL, 1965.

JOHNSTON, M. and A. JEWETT. *Resources for Teaching English. References for Teachers of English as a Foreign Language*. Washington, D. C.: USOE, 1956.

KEESEE, E. *References of Foreign Languages in the Elementary Schools*. Washington, D. C.: USOE, 1963.

LADO, R. *Annotated Bibliography for Teachers of English as a Foreign Language*. Washington, D. C.: U.S. Government Printing Office, 1955.

*Language Teaching Bibliography*. London: Center for Information on Language Teaching, 1968.

NOSTRAND, H. L. (ed.). *Research on Language Teaching. An Annotated International Bibliography*. Seattle, Wash.: U. of Washington Press, 1965.

O'HANESSIAN, S. *Interim Bibliography on the Teaching of English to Speakers of Other Languages*. Washington, D. C.: CAL, 1963.

————. *30 Books for Teachers of English as a Foreign Language*. Washington, D. C.: CAL, 1967.

OLLMAN, M. J. *MLA Selective List of Materials for Use by Teachers of Modern Foreign Languages in Elementary and Secondary Schools*. New York: MLA, 1965.

PEDTKE, D. et al. *Reference List of Materials for English as a Second Language*. Washington, D. C.: CAL, 1969.

RICE, F. and A. GUSS. *Information Sources in Linguistics*. Washington, D. C.: CAL, 1965.

ROBINSON, J. (comp). *An Annotated Bibliography of Modern Language Teaching (1946-67)*. London: Oxford U. Press, 1969.

RUTHERFORD, P. *A Bibliography of American Doctoral Dissertations in Linguistics*. Washington, D. C.: CAL, 1968.

SHEN, YAO and R. CRYMES. *Teaching English as a Second Language*. Honolulu: East-West Center Press, 1965.

STEHLIK, V. *An International Bibliography of Foreign Language Teaching Methods for 1967*. Prague: Academy of Sciences, 1969.

SVOBODNY, D., *Research and Studies about the Use of Television and Films in Foreign Language Instruction: A Bibliography with Abstracts*. New York: MLA, 1969.

UNESCO. *A Bibliography on the Teaching of Foreign Languages*. Paris, 1955.

WALTERS, T. *The Georgetown Bibliography of Studies Contributing to the Psycho-Linguistics of Language Learning*. Washington, D. C.: Georgetown U. Press, 1965.

WYLIE, L. et al. *Six Cultures. Selected and Annotated Bibliographies*. New York: MLA, 1961.

## Books

ABERCROMBIE, D. *Problems and Principles: Studies in the Teaching of English as a Second Language*. London: Longmans Green, 1964.

AGARD, F. B. and R. DI PIETRO. *The Grammatical Structures of English and Italian*. Chicago: U. of Chicago Press, 1963.

———. *The Sounds of English and Italian*. Chicago: U. of Chicago Press, 1963.

AGARD, F. B. and H. DUNKEL. *An Investigation of Second Language Teaching*. Boston: Ginn, 1948.

ALATIS, J. (ed.). *Bilingualism and Language Contact: Anthropological, Linguistic, Psychological, and Sociological Aspects*. Washington, D. C.: Georgetown U. Press, 1969.

ALLEN, H. (ed.). *Teaching English as a Second Language: A Book of Readings*. New York: McGraw-Hill, 1965.

ANDERSON, W. and N. STAGEBERG. *Introductory Readings on Language*. New York: Holt, Rinehart and Winston, 1966.

ANDERSON, T. "The Teacher of Modern Foreign Languages," in *Education in the Secondary School*, Ernest Stabler (ed.). Middleton, Conn.: Wesleyan U. Press, 1962.

———. *The Teaching of Foreign Languages in the Elementary School*. Boston: D. C. Heath, 1953.

BACH, E. *An Introduction to Transformational Grammar*. New York: Holt, Rinehart & Winston, 1963.

BAGSTER-COLLINS, E. *Studies in Modern Language Teaching*. New York: Macmillan, 1930.

BARRUTI, A. *Linguistic Theory of Language Learning as Related to Machine Teaching*. Heidelberg: Verlag, 1969.

BELASCO, S. *Anthology for Use with a Guide for Teachers in NDEA Language Institutes*. Boston: D. C. Heath, 1961.

BELYAVEV, B. V. *The Psychology of Teaching Foreign Languages.* New York: Macmillan, 1964.

BENEDICT, R. *Patterns of Culture.* Boston: Houghton Mifflin, 1934.

BENNETT, W. A. *Aspects of Language and Language Teaching.* Cambridge, England: Cambridge U. Press, 1968.

BILLOWS, F. L. *The Techniques of Language Teaching.* London: Longmans Green, 1961.

BIRKMAIER, E. "Modern Languages," in *Encyclopedia of Educational Research.* New York: Macmillan, 1960.

———— (ed.). *The Britannica Review of Foreign Language Education.* Chicago: Encyclopedia Britannica, Inc., 1968.

BLOCK, B. and G. TRAGER. *Outline of Linguistic Analysis.* Baltimore: Linguistic Society of America, 1942.

BLOOMFIELD, L. *Language.* New York: Henry Holt, 1933.

————. *Outline Guide for the Practical Study of Foreign Languages.* Baltimore: Linguistic Society of America, 1942.

———— and C. BARNHART. *Let's Read: A Linguistic Approach.* Detroit: Wayne State U. Press, 1961.

BLOOMFIELD, M. and L. NEWMARK. *A Linguistic Introduction to the History of English.* New York: Alfred Knopf, 1963.

BOAS, FRANZ. *Race, Language, and Culture.* New York: Macmillan, 1940.

BOLINGER, D. *Aspects of Language.* New York: Harcourt, Brace & World, 1969.

BROOKS, N. *Language and Language Learning.* New York: Harcourt, Brace & World, 1964.

————. "Teaching Culture in the Foreign Language Classroom," in *Foreign Language Annals, I.* New York: MLA, March, 1968.

BRUNER, J. *The Process of Education.* Cambridge, Mass.: Harvard U. Press, 1961.

————, R. OLIVER and M. GREENFIELD. *Studies in Cognitive Growth.* New York: John Wiley & Sons, 1966.

BUCHANAN, C. *A Programmed Introduction to Linguistics.* Boston: D. C. Heath, 1963.

CADOUX, R. *French for Secondary Schools.* Albany, N. Y.: New York State Department of Education, 1962.

CARDENAS, D. *Applied Linguistics: Spanish. A Guide for Teachers.* Boston: D. C. Heath, 1961.

CARROLL, J. B. *Language and Thought.* Englewood Cliffs, N. J.: Prentice-Hall, 1965.

————. "A Primer of Programmed Instruction in Foreign Language Teaching," in *IRAL* 1/2, 1963.

————. *Research on Teaching Foreign Languages.* Cambridge, Mass.: Harvard U. Press, 1960.

————. *The Study of Language.* Cambridge, Mass.: Harvard U. Press, 1953.

CASSIRER, E. *Language and Myth.* New York: Dover Publications, 1964.

CATFORD, J. *A Linguistic Theory of Translation.* London: Oxford U. Press, 1965.

CHERRY, C. *On Human Communication.* New York: John Wiley & Sons, 1961.

CHOMSKY, N. *Aspects of the Theory of Syntax.* Cambridge, Mass.: The M.I.T. Press, 1965.

————. *Language and Mind.* New York: Harcourt, Brace & World, 1968.

————. *Syntactic Structures.* The Hague: Mouton & Co., 1957.

———— and HALLE. *The Sound Patterns of English.* New York: Harper & Row, 1968.

COLE, R. and J. B. THARP. *Modern Foreign Languages and Their Teaching.* New York: Appleton-Century-Crofts, 1937.

COLEMAN, A. *The Teaching of Modern Foreign Languages in the United States.* New York: Macmillan, 1929.

CORDER, S. PIT. *The Visual Element in Language Teaching.* London: Longmans Green, 1966.

CORNELIUS, E. *Language Teaching: A Guide for Teachers of Foreign Languages.* New York: Thomas Crowell, 1953.

CORNFIELD, R. *Foreign Language Instruction: Dimensions and Horizons.* New York: Appleton-Century-Crofts, 1966.

*Curricular Changes in the Foreign Languages.* Princeton, N. J.: College Entrance Examination Board, 1963.

DACANAY, F. R. *Techniques and Procedures in Second Language Teaching.* Quezon City: Phoenix, 1963.

DAVIES, A. *Language Testing Symposium.* London: Oxford U. Press. 1968.

DE CECCO, J. (ed.). *The Psychology of Language, Thought and Action.* New York: Holt, Rinehart & Winston, 1967.

DE SAUSSURE, F. *A Course in General Linguistics.* New York: Philosophical Library, 1959.

DETERLINE , W. *An Introduction to Programmed Instruction.* Englewood Cliffs, N. J.: Prentice-Hall, 1962.

DEVEREUX, E. (ed.). *An Introduction to Visual Aids.* London: Mathews, Drew & Shelbourne, 1962.

DINEEN, F. *An Introduction to General Linguistics.* New York: Holt, Rinehart & Winston, 1966.

DIPIETRO, R. *Language Structure in Contrast.* Rowley, Mass.: Newbury House, 1971.

DIXSON, R. *Practical Guide to the Teaching of English as a Foreign Language.* New York: Regents, 1960.

DODSON, C. *Language Teaching and the Bilingual Method.* London: Pitman & Sons, 1967.

DONOGHUE, M. (ed.). *Foreign Languages and the Schools: A Book of Readings.* Dubuque, Iowa: Wm. C. Brown Co., 1967.

————. *Foreign Languages and the Elementary School Child.* Dubuque, Iowa: Wm. C. Brown Co., 1969.

DORRY, G. *Games for Second Language Learning.* New York: McGraw-Hill, 1966.

DUNKEL, H. *Second Language Learning.* Boston: Ginn, 1948.

———— and R. PILLET. *French in the Elementary School: Five Years' Experience.* Chicago: U. of Chicago Press, 1962.

DUTTON, B. *Guide to Modern Language Teaching Methods.* London: Cassell & Co., 1965.

EATON, E. *Foreign Languages in Public Secondary Schools*. Washington, D. C.: USOE, 1963.

EMIG, J. et al. *Language and Learning*. New York: Harcourt, Brace & World, 1966.

ERIKSON, M. et al. *Foreign Language in the Elementary School*. Englewood Cliffs, N. J.: Prentice-Hall, 1964.

FERGUSON, C. A. (ed.). *Contrastive Structure Series*. Chicago: U. of Chicago Press, 1960.

———— and W. STEWART. *Linguistic Reading Lists for Teachers of Modern Languages*. Washington, D. C.: CAL, 1963.

FIFE, R. H. (ed.). *A Summary of Reports on the Modern Foreign Languages*. New York: Macmillan, 1931.

FINOCCHIARO, M. *English as a Second Language: From Theory to Practice*. New York: Regents, 1964.

————. *Teaching Children Foreign Languages*. New York: McGraw-Hill, 1964.

————. *Teaching English as a Second Language* (rev. ed.). New York: Harper & Row, 1969.

FIRTH, J. *The Tongues of Men and Speech*. London: Oxford U. Press, 1964.

FISHMAN, J. (ed.). *Language Loyalty in the United States*. The Hague: Mouton, 1966.

———— (ed.). *Readings in the Sociology of Language*. The Hague: Mouton, 1968.

FODOR, J. and J. KATZ (eds.). *The Structure of Language: Readings in the Philosophy of Language*. Englewood Cliffs, N. J.: Prentice-Hall, 1964.

FOTITCH, T. (ed.). *Teaching Foreign Languages in the Modern World*. Washington, D. C.: Catholic U. of America Press, 1961.

FRANCIS, N. *The Structure of American English*. New York: Ronald Press, 1958.

FRENCH, F. *Teaching English as a Foreign or Second Language*. London: Oxford U. Press, 1963.

FRIES, C. *Linguistics and Reading*. New York: Holt, Rinehart & Winston, 1963.

————. *The Structure of English*. New York: Harcourt, Brace, 1952.

————. *Teaching and Learning English as a Foreign Language*. Ann Arbor, Mich.: U. of Michigan Press, 1948.

———— and A. FRIES. *Foundations of English Teaching*. Tokyo, Japan: Kenynsha Language Exploratory Committee, 1961.

———— and R. LADO. *English Pronunciation*. Ann Arbor, Mich.: U. of Michigan Press, 1954.

————. *English Sentence Patterns*. Ann Arbor, Mich.: U. of Michigan Press, 1954.

————. *Lessons in Vocabulary*. Ann Arbor, Mich.: U. of Michigan Press, 1956.

FUCILLA, J. *The Teaching of Italian in the United States: A Documentary History*. New Brunswick, N. J.: Rutgers U. Press, 1967.

GAARDER, A. "Conserving our Linguistic Resources" in *PMLA*, Vol. LXXX, May, 1965.

GAGE, H. L. (ed.). *Handbook of Research on Teaching*. New York: Rand McNally, 1963.

GARDNER, R. and W. LAMBERT. "Motivational Variables in Second Language Acquisition," in *Canadian Journal of Psychology*, 1959.

GATENBY, E. V. *English as a Foreign Language*. London: Longmans Green, 1944.

GAUNTLETT, J. *Teaching English as a Foreign Language*. London: Macmillan, 1957.

GLEASON, H. *An Introduction to Descriptive Linguistics*. New York: Holt, Rinehart, 1961.

―――. *Linguistics and English Grammar*. New York: Holt, Rinehart & Winston, 1965.

GOUIN, F. *The Art of Teaching and Studying Language*. London: G. Phillips & Son, 1912.

GRAZIA, A. DE and D. SOHN (eds.). *Programs, Teachers and Machines*. New York: Bantam Books, 1964.

GREENBERG, J. *Anthropological Linguistics: An Introduction*. New York: Random House, 1968.

―――. (ed.). *Universals of Language*. Cambridge, Mass.: The M.I.T. Press, 1963.

GRITTNER, F. *Foreign Language Teaching in America's Schools*. New York: Harper & Row, 1969.

GURREY, P. *Teaching English as a Foreign Language*. London: Longmans Green, 1955.

―――. *Teaching English Grammar*. London: Longmans Green, 1964.

HAGBOLDT, P. *Language Learning*. Chicago: U. of Chicago Press, 1935.

HALL, E. T. *The Hidden Dimension*. Garden City, N. Y.: Doubleday, 1966.

―――. *The Silent Language*. Garden City, N. Y.: Doubleday, 1959.

HALL, R. *Introduction to Linguistics*. Philadelphia: Chilton, 1965.

―――. *Applied Linguistics: Italian. A Guide for Teachers*. Boston: D. C. Heath, 1961.

―――. *Linguistics and Your Language*. Garden City, N. Y.: Doubleday, 1960.

―――. *New Ways to Learn a Foreign Language*. New York: Bantam Books, 1966.

HALLIDAY, M., A. MCINTOSH, and P. STREVENS. *The Linguistic Sciences and Language Teaching*. London: Longmans Green, 1964.

HANDSCHIN, C. *Methods of Teaching Modern Languages*. Yonkers, N. Y.: World, 1940.

HARRIS, D. *Testing English as a Second Language*. New York: McGraw-Hill, 1969.

HARRIS, Z. *Methods in Structural Linguistics*. Chicago: U. of Chicago Press, 1951.

―――. *Symbol, Status and Personality*. New York: Harcourt, Brace & World, 1958.

HAYAKAWA, S. *Language in Thought and Action*. New York: Harcourt, Brace & World, 1964.

HAYES, A. *Language Laboratory Facilities*. Washington, D. C.: USOE, 1963.

HILL, A. *Introduction to Linguistic Structures.* New York: Harcourt, Brace & World, 1958.

HJELMSLEV, L. *Prolegomena to a Theory of Language.* Madison: U. of Wisconsin Press, 1961.

HOCKETT, C. *A Course in Modern Linguistics.* New York: Macmillan, 1958.

HOCKING, E. *Language Laboratory and Language Learning.* Washington, D. C.: NEA, Monograph 2, 1964.

HOIJER, H. (ed.). *Language in Culture.* Chicago: U. of Chicago Press, 1954.

HOLTON, J. (ed.). *Sound Language Teaching.* New York: University Publishers, 1962.

HORNBY, A. *A Guide to Patterns and Usage in English.* London: Oxford U. Press, 1954.

————. *The Teaching of Structural Words and Phrases.* London: Oxford U. Press, 1961.

HUEBENER, T. *Audio-Visual Techniques in Teaching Foreign Languages* (rev. ed.). New York: New York U. Press, 1965.

————. *How to Teach Foreign Languages Effectively.* New York: New York U. Press, 1959.

————. *Foreign Language Careers.* New York: Universal, 1964.

————. *Why Johnny Should Learn Foreign Languages.* Philadelphia: Chilton, 1961.

HUGHES, J. *The Science of Language.* New York: Random House, 1962.

————. *Linguistics and Language Teaching.* New York: Random House, 1968.

HUTCHISON, J. *Modern Foreign Languages. The Language Laboratory.* Washington, D. C.: U.S. Government Printing Office, 1961.

HYMES, D. (ed.). *Language in Culture and Society: A Reader in Linguistics and Anthropology.* New York: Harper & Row, 1964.

IODICE, D. *Guidelines to Language Teaching in Classroom and Laboratory.* Washington, D. C.: Electronic Teaching Laboratory, 1962.

JAKOBOVITS, L. *Foreign Language Learning: A Psycholinguistic Analysis of the Issues.* Rowley, Mass.: Newbury House, 1970.

————. (ed.). *Readings in the Psychology of Language.* Englewood Cliffs, N. J.: Prentice-Hall, 1968.

JAKOBSON, R. and M. HALLE. *Fundamentals of Language.* The Hague: Mouton, 1956.

JERMAN, J., D. VAN ABBE, and B. DUTTON. *A Guide to Modern Language Teaching Methods.* London: Cassell & Co., 1965.

JESPERSON, O. *Essentials of English Grammar.* New York: Henry Holt, 1933.

————. *How to Teach a Foreign Language.* London: Allen & Unwin, 1961.

————. *Language: Its Nature, Development and Origin.* London: Allen & Unwin, 1922.

JOHNSTON, M., J. REMER, and F. SIEVERS. *Modern Foreign Languages: A Counselor's Guide.* Washington, D. C.: USOE, 1960.

———— and C. SEELEY. *Foreign Language Laboratories in Schools and Colleges.* Washington, D. C.: U.S. Government Printing Office, 1959.

JONES, L. and J. WEPMAN. *A Spoken Word Count.* Chicago: Language Research Associates, 1966.

JONES, D. *An Outline of English Phonetics*. Cambridge, England: Heffer, 1960.

JOOS, M. *The Five Clocks*. Bloomington, Ind.: Indiana U. Press, 1962.

KANSLER, D. (ed.). *Reading in Verbal Learning*. New York: John Wiley & Sons, 1966.

KARP, T., P. O'CONNOR, and B. ROBINETT. *Principles and Methods of Teaching a Second Language: A Motion Picture Series*. Washington: CAL, 1963.

KATZ, J. & P. POSTAL. *An Integrated Theory of Linguistics*. Cambridge, Mass.: The MIT Press, 1964.

KAULFERS, W. *Modern Foreign Languages for Modern Schools*. New York: McGraw-Hill, 1942.

KEATING, R. *A Study of the Effectiveness of Language Laboratories*. New York: Teachers College Press, 1963.

KEESEE, E. *Modern Foreign Languages in the Elementary Schools*. Washington, D. C.: U.S. Department of H.E.W., Bulletin 29, 1960.

KINGDON, R. *The Groundwork of English Intonation*. London: Longmans Green, 1958.

KLUCKHOHN, C. *Culture and Behavior*. New York: The Free Press, 1962.

——. *Mirror for Man*. New York: McGraw-Hill, 1949 .

KREIDLER, C. and M. SUTHERLAND. *Flash Pictures*. Ann Arbor, Mich.: Edwards Bros., 1963.

KRENSLER, A. *The Teaching of Modern Foreign Language in the Soviet Union*. Leiden, The Netherlands: Brill, 1963.

KROEBER, A. (ed.). *Anthropology Today*. Chicago: U. of Chicago Press, 1953.

KUFNER, H. *The Grammatical Structures of English and German*. Chicago: U. of Chicago Press, 1963.

LABOV, W. *The Social Stratification of English in New York City*. Washington, D. C.: CAL, 1969.

LADO, R. *Language Teaching: A Scientific Approach*. New York: McGraw-Hill, 1964.

——. *Language Testing*. New York: McGraw-Hill, 1964.

——. *Linguistics Across Cultures*. Ann Arbor, Mich.: U. of Michigan Press, 1957.

LAMBERT, W. and O. KLINEBERG. *Children's Views of Foreign Peoples*. New York: Appleton-Century-Crofts, 1967.

——. "Psychological Approaches to the Study of Language," in *Modern Language Journal*, March 1963 (pp. 51-62 and 114-21).

LANDAR, H. *Language and Culture*. New York: Oxford U. Press, 1965.

*Latin in the Curriculum* (three essays). New York: MLA, 1968.

LEE, W. *Language Teaching: Games and Contests*. London: Oxford U. Press, 1965.

—— and H. COPPEN. *Simple Audio-Visual Aids to Foreign Language Teaching*. London: Oxford U. Press, 1964.

LEFEVRE, C. *Linguistics and the Teaching of Reading*. New York: McGraw-Hill, 1964.

LENNEBERG, E. *The Biological Foundations of Language*. New York: Wiley & Sons, 1967.

LEOPOLD, W. *Speech Development of a Bilingual Child.* Evanston, Ill.: Northwestern U. Press, 1949.

LEVENSON, S. and W. KENDRICK (eds.). *Readings in Foreign Languages for the Elementary School.* Waltham, Mass.: Blaisdell, 1967.

LIBBISH, B. (ed.). *Advances in the Teaching of Modern Languages.* New York: Macmillan, 1964.

LIN, SAN-SU. *Pattern Practice in the Teaching of Standard English to Students with a Non-Standard Dialect.* New York: Teachers College Press, 1965.

LONG, R. *The Sentence and Its Parts.* Chicago: U. of Chicago Press, 1961.

LUMSDAINE, A. and R. GLASER. *Teaching Machines and Programmed Learning.* Washington, D. C.: NEA, 1960.

MACKEY, W. *Language Teaching Analysis.* London: Longmans Green, 1965.

MCRAE, M. *Teaching Spanish in the Grades.* Boston: Houghton Mifflin, 1957.

MAGNER, T. *Applied Linguistics: Russian. A Guide for Teachers.* Boston: D. C. Heath, 1960.

MALINOWSKI, B. *A Scientific Theory of Culture and Other Essays.* New York: Oxford U. Press, 1960.

MALLINSON, V. *Teaching a Modern Language.* London: Heinemann, 1953.

MALSTROM, J. *Language in Society.* New York: Hayden, 1965.

MARCKWARDT, A. *Linguistics and the Teaching of English.* Bloomington, Ind.: U. of Indiana Press, 1966.

————. *Studies in Language and Linguistics in Honor of Charles Fries.* Ann Arbor, Mich.: U. of Michigan Press, 1964.

———— and R. QUIRK. *A Common Language.* New York: MLA, 1964.

MARTINET, A. *Elements of General Linguistics.* London: Faber, 1964.

————. *A Functional View of Language.* Oxford, England: Clarendon Press, 1962.

MARTY, F. *Active French: Dialogues.* Roanoke, Va.: Audio-Visual Publications, 1966.

————. *Language Laboratory Learning.* Wellesley, Mass.: Audio-Visual Publications, 1960.

————. *Programming a Basic Foreign Language Course.* Virginia: Hollins College Press, 1962.

MATHIEU, G. (ed.). *Advances in the Teaching of Modern Language.* London: Pergamon Press, 1962.

MCINTOSH, A. and M. HALLIDAY. *Patterns of Language: Papers in General, Descriptive, and Applied Linguistics.* London: Longmans Green, 1966.

MEAD, M. *Continuity in Cultural Evolution.* New Haven, Conn.: Yale U. Press, 1964.

*The Meaning and Role of Culture in Foreign Language Teaching.* Washington, D. C.: Georgetown U. Institute of Language and Linguistics, 1961.

MERAS, E. *A Language Teacher's Guide.* New York: Harper & Row, 1962.

MICHEL, J. (ed.). *Foreign Language Teaching: An Anthology.* New York: Macmillan, 1966.

MILLER, B. *Sources of Free and Inexpensive Teaching Aids.* Riverside, Calif.: Bruce Miller, 1962.

————. *Sources of Free Pictures.* Riverside, Calif.: Bruce Miller, 1963.

MILLER, G. *Language and Communication.* New York: McGraw-Hill, 1963.

MLA. *A Handbook on Foreign Language Classroom Testing: French, German, Italian, Russian, Spanish.* New York: MLA, 1970.

*Modern Foreign Languages in the Comprehensive High School.* Washington, D. C.: NEA, 1959.

*Modern Languages: Teaching and Testing.* (filmstrips) Princeton, N. J.: Educational Testing Service, 1968.

MONTAGU, A. *The Cultured Man.* New York: World, 1958.

MORRIS, I. *The Art of Teaching English as a Living Language.* London: Macmillan, 1954.

MOULTON, W. *A Linguistic Guide to Language Learning.* New York: MLA, 1966.

————. *The Sounds of English and German.* Chicago: U. of Chicago Press, 1963.

NAJAM, E. (ed.). *Language Learning: The Individual and the Process.* Bloomington, Ind.: Indiana U. Press, 1966.

NEWMARK, M. (ed.). *Twentieth Century Modern Language Teaching: Sources and Readings.* New York: The Philosophical Library, 1948.

NIDA, E. *Learning a Foreign Language.* New York: Free Press, 1960.

————. *Toward a Science of Translating.* Leiden, The Netherlands: Brill, 1964.

O'Connor, P. *Modern Foreign Languages in High School: Pre-Reading Instruction.* Washington, D. C.: USOE, 1960.

OINAS, F. *Language Teaching Today.* Bloomington, Ind.: U. of Indiana Press, 1960.

*Oral English: Planning and Conducting Conversation Classes and Discussion Groups.* Washington, D. C.: USIS Information Center.

ORNSTEIN, J. and W. GAGE. *The ABC's of Language and Linguistics.* Philadelphia: Chilton, 1964.

OSGOOD, C. and T. SEBEOK. *Psycholinguistics: A Survey of Theory and Research Problems.* Bloomington, Ind.: Indiana U. Press, 1965.

PALMER, H. *The Teaching of Oral English.* London: Longmans Green, 1940.

————. *Principles of Language Study.* London: Oxford U. Press, 1964.

PAQUETTE, A. (ed.). *Guidelines for Teacher Education Programs in Modern Foreign Languages: An Exposition.* New York: MLA, 1966.

PARKER, W. *The National Interest and Foreign Languages.* Washington, D. C.: U.S. Department of State, 1962.

PEAL, E. and W. LAMBERT. "The Relationship of Bilingualism to Intelligence," in *Foreign Language Teaching,* J. Michel (ed.). New York: Macmillan, 1967.

PEI, M. *Glossary of Linguistic Terminology.* New York: Doubleday, 1966.

————. *An Invitation to Linguistics.* New York: Doubleday, 1965.

————. *Language for Everybody.* New York: Devin-Adair, 1957.

————. *Voices of Man.* New York: Harper & Row, 1962.

PEPE, T. *Free and Inexpensive Educational Aids.* New York: Dover, 1960.

PIAGET, J. *The Language and Thought of the Child* (trans. by M. Gabain). New York: Humanities Press, 1959.

PIERCE, J. *A Linguistic Method of Teaching a Second Language*. New York: Pageant, 1968.

PIKE, K. *The Intonation of American English*. Ann Arbor, Mich.: U. of Michigan Press, 1953.

―――. *Phonemics*. Ann Arbor, Mich.: U. of Michigan Press, 1947.

PIMSLEUR, P. "Testing Foreign Language Learning," in *Trends in Language Teaching*, A. Valdman (ed.). New York: McGraw-Hill, 1966.

―――― et al. *Under-achievement in Foreign Language Learning*. New York: MLA, 1966.

POLITZER, R. *Foreign Language Learning: A Linguistic Introduction*. Englewood Cliffs, N. J.: Prentice-Hall, 1965.

―――. *Teaching French: An Introduction to Applied Linguistics*. Waltham, Mass.: Blaisdell, 1965.

―――. *Teaching German: A Linguistic Orientation*. Waltham, Mass.: Blaisdell, 1968.

―――― and C. STAUBACH. *Teaching Spanish: A Linguistic Orientation*. Boston: Ginn, 1961.

―――― and D. BARTLEY. *Practice-Centered Teacher Training: Spanish*. Stanford, Calif.: Stanford Center for Research in Teaching, 1968.

POSTMAN, N. and C. WEINGARTNER. *Linguistics: A Revolution in Teaching*. New York: Dell, 1967.

POTTER, S. *Modern Linguistics*. New York: Norton, 1964.

PRATOR, C. *A Manual of American English Pronunciation*. New York: Holt, 1960.

REMER, I. *A Handbook for Guiding Students in Modern Foreign Languages*. Washington, D. C.: U.S. Government Printing Office, Bulletin OE 27018, 1963.

*Reports of Surveys and Studies in the Teaching of Modern Foreign Languages*. New York: MLA, 1962.

RICE, W. (ed.). *Planning the Modern Language Lesson*. Syracuse, N. Y.: Syracuse U. Press, 1964.

RICHARDS, J. and M. POLIQUIN. *English through Songs*. Rowley, Mass.: Newbury House, 1973.

RIVERS, W. *The Psychologist and the Foreign Language Teacher*. Chicago: U. of Chicago Press, 1964.

―――. *Teaching Foreign Language Skills*. Chicago: U. of Chicago Press, 1968.

ROBERTS, P. *English Sentences*. New York: Harcourt, Brace & World, 1962.

―――. *English Syntax*. New York: Harcourt, Brace & World, 1964.

ROBINS, R. *General Linguistics: An Introductory Survey*. London: Longmans Green, 1964.

ROSENBERG, S. (ed.). *Directions in Psycholinguistics*. New York: Macmillan, 1965.

―――― and J. KOPLIN. *Developments in Applied Psycholinguistic Research*. New York: Macmillan, 1968.

ROUCEK, J. (ed.). *The Study of Foreign Languages*. New York: Philosophical Library, 1968.

SAPIR, E. *Culture, Language, and Personality.* Berkeley, Calif.: U. of California Press, 1956.

———. *Language: An Introduction to the Study of Speech.* New York: Harcourt Brace, 1921.

SAPORTA, S. and J. BASTIAN (eds.). *Psycholinguistics: A Book of Readings.* New York: Holt, Rinehart & Winston, 1961.

SCHERER, G. and M. WERTHEIMER. *A Psycholinguistic Experiment in Foreign Language Teaching.* New York: McGraw-Hill, 1964.

SEBEOK, T. (ed.). *Current Trends in Linguistics.* The Hague: Mouton, 1968.

———. *Portraits of Linguists 1746-1963.* Bloomington, Ind.: Indiana U. Press, 1966.

SEELYE, N. "Analysis and Teaching of the Cross-Cultural Content," in *The Britannica Review of Foreign Language Education.* Chicago: Encyclopedia Britannica, Inc., 1968.

SHEN, YAO. *Articulation Diagrams of English Vowels and English Consonants.* Ann Arbor, Mich.: Braun & Bruenfield, 1965.

———. *The Pronunciation of American English for Teachers of English as a Foreign Language.* Ann Arbor, Mich.: U. of Michigan Press, 1964.

SHERIF, J. *Handbook of Foreign Language Occupations.* New York: Regents, 1966.

SHUY, R., W. WOLFRAM and W. RILEY. *Field Techniques in an Urban Language Study.* Washington, D. C.: CAL, 1968.

SKINNER, B. *Verbal Behavior.* New York: Appleton, 1957.

SLEDD, J. *A Short Introduction to English Grammar.* New York: Scott, Foresman, 1959.

SMITH, W. and J. MOORE. *Programmed Learning: Theory and Research.* Princeton, N. J.: D. Van Nostrand Co., 1962.

STACK, E. *The Language Laboratory and Modern Language Teaching* (rev. ed.). New York: Oxford U. Press, 1966.

STAGEBERG, N. *An Introductory English Grammar.* New York: Holt, Rinehart & Winston, 1965.

STARR, W. et al. *Modern Foreign Languages and the Academically Talented Student.* Washington, D. C.: NEA, 1960.

STERN, H. *Foreign Languages in Primary Education.* UNESCO, 1963.

———. *Languages and the Young Child.* London: Oxford U. Press, 1969.

STEVICK, E. *Helping People Learn English.* Nashville, Tenn.: Abingdon Press, 1957.

———. *A Workbook in Language Teaching.* Nashville, Tenn.: Abingdon Press, 1964.

STOCKWELL, R. and D. BOWEN. *The Sounds of English and Spanish.* Chicago: U. of Chicago Press, 1965.

——— and J. MARTIN. *The Grammatical Structures of English and Spanish.* Chicago: U. of Chicago Press, 1965.

STREVENS, P. *Aural Aids in Language Teaching.* London: Longmans Green, 1958.

———. *Modern Languages in Great Britain and England.* London: Longmans Green, 1967.

————. *Papers in Language and Language Teaching*. London: Oxford U. Press, 1965.

STURTEVANT, E. *An Introduction to Linguistic Science*. New Haven, Conn.: Yale U. Press, 1947.

SWEET, H. *The Practical Study of Languages*. London: Oxford U. Press, 1964.

TAYLOR, A. *Equipping the Classroom*. London: Nelson, 1953.

THOMAS, O. *Transformational Grammar and the Teacher of English as a Second Language*. New York: Holt, Rinehart & Winston, 1965 .

———— (ed.). *The Structure of Language*. Indianapolis, Ind.: Bobbs-Merrill, 1967.

THOMPSON, E. and R. HAMALAINEN. *Foreign Language Teaching in Elementary Schools*. Washington, D. C.: NEA, 1958.

THORNDIKE, E. and I. LORGE. *The Teacher's Wordbook of 30,000 Words*. New York: Teachers College Press, 1944.

TITONE, R. *Studies in the Psycholinguistics of Language Learning*. Zurich, Switzerland: PAS, 1964.

————. *Teaching Foreign Languages: An Historical Sketch*. Washington, D. C.: Georgetown U. Press, 1968.

TRAGER, G. and H. SMITH. *An Outline of English Structure*. Washington, D. C.: American Council of Learned Societies, 1957.

TROUBETZKOY, N. *Introduction to the Principles of Phonological Description*. The Hague: Maritmus Nojhoff, 1968.

TWADELL, F. *Foreign Language Instruction at the Second Level*. New York: Holt, Rinehart & Winston, 1963.

ULLMANN, S. *Semantics: An Introduction to the Science of Meaning*. Oxford, England: Blackwell, 1962.

*The Use of Vernacular Languages in Education*. UNESCO Monograph on Fundamental Education #8, 1953.

UNESCO. *Second Language Teaching in Primary and Secondary Schools*. Vol. 13, #3, 1961.

————. *The Teaching of Modern Languages*. Paris, 1955.

UPSHUR, J. and J. FATA (eds.). *Problems in Foreign Language Testing*. Ann Arbor, Mich.: U. of Michigan Press, 1969.

VALDMAN, A. (ed.). *Trends in Language Teaching*. New York: McGraw-Hill, 1966.

VALETTE, R. *Modern Language Testing*. New York: Harcourt, Brace & World, 1967.

*Visual Aids to English as a Second Language*. Washington, D. C.: CAL, 1964.

VYGOTSKY, L. *Thought and Language*. New York: John Wiley & Sons, 1961.

WALLACE, B. *The Pronunciation of American English for Teachers of English as a Second Language*. Ann Arbor, Mich.: George Wahr, 1957.

WALSH, D. *What's What: A List of Useful Terms for the Teacher of Modern Languages*. New York: MLA, 1964.

WEINREICH, U. *Languages in Contact*. New York: Linguistic Circle of New York, 1953.

WEST, M. *A General Service List of English Words*. London: Longmans Green, 1953.

297

————. *Learning to Read a Foreign Language*. London: Longmans Green, 1941.

————. *Teaching English in Difficult Circumstances: Teaching English as a Foreign Language*. London: Longmans Green, 1960.

———— and J. ENDICOTT. *The New Method Dictionary*. London: Longmans Green, 1968.

WHORF, B. *Language, Thought and Reality*. Cambridge, Mass.: The M.I.T. Press, 1956.

WISHON, G. and T. O'HARE (eds.). *Teaching English: A Collection of Readings*. New York: American Book Co., 1968.

ZANDVOORT, R. *A Handbook of English Grammar*. Englewood Cliffs, N. J.: Prentice-Hall, 1966.

## Tests

*American University Language Center Tests*. Washington, D. C.: Educational Services, 1961.

BURNETT, R. *Basic Reading Inventory*. Bensenville, Ill.: Scholastic Testing Service, 1966.

*Carroll-Sapon Modern Language Aptitude Test*. New York: The Psychological Corp., 1959.

*College Board Achievement Tests*. Princeton, N. J.: Educational Testing Service (revised annually).

HARRIS, D. *Listening Test*. Washington, D. C.: American Language Institute, 1961.

———— and PALMER. *Listening Test, Form B*. ....................., 1962.

————. *English Vocabulary Test*. ................................., 1963.

————. *Vocabulary and Reading Test*. ..........................., 1961.

LADO, R. *English Language Test for Foreign Students*. Ann Arbor, Mich.: U. of Michigan Press, 1962.

*MLA Foreign Language Proficiency Tests for Teachers and Advanced Students*. Princeton, N. J.: Educational Testing Service, 1962.

*MLA Cooperative Foreign Language Tests*. Princeton, N. J.: Educational Testing Service, 1964.

*Pimsleur Language Aptitude Battery*. New York: Harcourt, Brace & World, 1966.

*Pimsleur Modern Foreign Language Proficiency Tests*. New York: Harcourt, Brace & World, 1967.

TOEFL. Princeton, N. J.: Educational Testing Service. (revised annually)

## SOME ADDITIONAL RESOURCES

### Agencies and Associations

*American Council of Teachers of Foreign Languages* (ACTFL). 60 Fifth Avenue, New York.

*Association of Teachers of English to Speakers of Other Languages* (TESOL). Georgetown University, Washington, D. C.

*Binational Centers.* Many countries — schools jointly sponsored by the United States and Ministries of Education in the host country.

*British Council.* State House, London.

*Center for Applied Linguistics* (CAL). 1717 Massachusetts Avenue N.W., Washington, D. C.

*Education Section* of Ministries of Education, of Migration Offices, and of private educational and social agencies.

*English Teaching Division.* United States Information Service. Washington, D. C.

*Modern Language Association* (MLA). 60 Fifth Avenue, New York.

*National Association of Foreign Student Advisers.* 809 United Nations Plaza, New York.

*National Council of Teachers of English.* Champaign, Ill.

*Nuffield Foundation.* Leeds, England.

*UNESCO.* United Nations Plaza, New York. (also Belgium)

*U.S. Dept. of Health, Education and Welfare* (HEW). Washington, D. C.

*U.S. Office of Education* (USOE). Washington, D. C.

## Periodic Collections, Monographs, and Reports

*Annual Bibliography on Teaching Foreign Languages.* New York: MLA.

*Britannica Review of Foreign Language Education.* Chicago: Encyclopedia Britannica. (published yearly)

*ERIC Clearinghouse on Linguistics.* Washington, D. C.: CAL.

*ERIC Focus Reports on Foreign Language Teaching.* New York: ACTFL.

*Language Research in Progress.* Washington, D. C.: CAL.

*Georgetown Round Table Monographs.* Washington, D. C.: Georgetown University.

*Northeast Conference Reports.* New York: MLA. (Reports available from 1954.)

*Research in Education.* U.S. Government Printing Office. Washington, D. C.

## Periodicals and Journals

*Anthropological Linguistics.* Bloomington, Ind.: University of Indiana.

*Archiv für das Studium der Neuren Sprachen und Literaturen.* Braunschweig, Germany.

*Audio-Visual Aids and Teaching of Languages.* Antwerp, Belgium.

*Audio-Visual Language Journal.* Hertfordshire, England.

*Babel.* Journal of the Australian Federation of Modern Language Teachers Association, Melbourne, Australia.

*Cahiers Ferdinand de Saussure: Revue de Linguistique Générale.* Geneva, Switzerland.

*Canadian Journal of Linguistics.* Toronto, Canada.

*Canadian Modern Language Review.* (Ontario Modern Language Teachers Association). Toronto, Canada.

*Classical Journal.* Columbus, Ohio: Ohio State University.

*Contact.* (Fédération Internationale des Professeurs de Langues Vivantes). Berne, Switzerland.

*English — A New Language.* Sydney, Australia: Commonwealth Office of Education.

*The English Journal.* Champaign, Ill.: National Council of Teachers of English.

*English Language Teaching.* London: British Council.

*English Teaching Abstracts.* London: British Council.

*English Teaching Forum.* USIA. Washington, D. C.

*English Teaching News.* London: British Council.

*Foreign Languages in School.* Moscow, U.S.S.R.

*Foundations of Language.* Dordrecht, Netherlands: Reidel.

*Français dans le Monde.* Paris, France.

*French Review.* (American Association of Teachers of French). Baltimore, Md.

*German Quarterly.* (American Association of Teachers of German). Cincinnati, Ohio.

*Glottodidactica.* Poznan, Poland.

*The Grade Teacher.* Darien, Conn.

*Hispania.* (American Association of Teachers of Spanish and Portuguese). Washington, D. C.

*The Instructor.* Dansville Park, N. Y.: Owen Publishing Company.

*International Journal of American Linguistics.* Bloomington, Ind.: University of Indiana.

*International Journal of Applied Linguistics in Language Teaching* (IRAL). Heidelberg, Germany.

*Italica.* (American Association of Teachers of Italian). Evanston, Ill.

*Journal of English as a Second Language.* New York: American Language Institute, New York University.

*Language.* Austin, Texas: Linguistic Society of America, University of Texas.

*Language and Language Behavior Abstracts* (LLBA). Ann Arbor, Mich.: University of Michigan.

*Language Learning: A Journal of Applied Linguistics.* 1522 Rackham Building, Ann Arbor, Mich.

*Linguistic Reporter.* Center for Applied Linguistics, 1717 Massachusetts Avenue N.W., Washington, D. C.

*Modern Language Journal.* Curtis Reed Plaza, Menasha, Wisc.

*Modern Language: Journal of the Modern Language Association of the United Kingdom.* London.

*NAFSA Newsletter.* NAFSA (National Association of Foreign Student Advisers), United Nations Plaza, New York City.

*Publications of the Modern Language Association of America* (PMLA). Modern Language Association, 60 Fifth Avenue, New York City.

*Programmed Learning and Educational Technology.* London: Journal of the Association for Programmed Learning.

*Rassegna italiana di linguistica applicata.* Mario Bulzoni (ed.). Rome, Italy.

*Revista de Educación.* Madrid, Spain.

*Russian Review.* The Hoover Institution, Stanford, Calif.

*School and Society.* 1860 Broadway, New York City.

*Scuola e Lingue Moderne.* (Official Bulletin of the National Association of Language Teachers). Rome, Italy.

*TESOL Newsletter.* TESOL, Georgetown University, Washington, D. C.

*TESOL Quarterly.* TESOL, Georgetown University, Washington, D. C.

*Word.* Linguistic Circle of New York, St. Peter's College, Jersey City, N. J.

## Useful Addresses (in addition to those listed above)

*American Council of Learned Societies* — 345 East 46 Street, New York City.

*American Association for the Advancement of Slavic Studies* — 1207 W. Oregon, Urbana, Ill.

*American Association of Teachers of Arabic* — Harvard University, Cambridge, Mass.

*American Association of Teachers of Chinese Language and Culture* — 125 E. 65 Street, New York City.

*American Association of Slavic and East European Languages* — Northwestern University, Evanston, Ill.

*Association of Teachers of Japanese* — Yale University, New Haven, Conn.

*Australian Federation of Modern Language Teachers Associations* — Carlton, N 3, Victoria, Australia.

*College Entrance Examination Board* — 475 Riverside Drive, New York City.

*Conference Board of Associated Research Councils* — 2101 Constitution Avenue, Washington, D. C.

*Educational Testing Service* — Princeton, N. J.

*Institute of International Education* — 809 United Nations Plaza, New York City.

*National Education Association* (NEA) — 1201 16 Street, N.W., Washington, D. C.

*Pen Pals*

International Friendship League — 40 Mt. Vernon Street, Boston, Mass.

Letters Abroad — 18 East 60 Street, New York City.

World Pen Pals — University of Minnesota, Minneapolis, Minn.

*UNESCO Publications Center* — 317 East 34 Street, New York City.

# INDEX

word order, importance of, 4, 52
word study exercises, 121, 123, 127
writing, developing skills in, 6,
129, 130
  compositions, procedures for
    assigning, 134-37
    correction of, 190-91
    "creative," 135-37

dictations, 133-34
  "freer," 135-37
  guided, 129, 130, 131-33
  mechanics of, 130
  secondary system, as, 6
  teaching of, 129ff.
  testing of, 216-17
writing the lesson plan, 150-52